Bibliotherapy

Also by Nancy Peske and Beverly West

Cinematherapy: The Girl's Guide to Movies for Every Mood

Frankly Scarlett, I *Do* Give a Damn!: Classic Romances Retold

And under the pseudonym Lee Ward Shore:

How to Satisfy a Woman Every Time on Five Dollars a Day

Meditations for Men Who Do Next to Nothing
(and Would Like to Do Even Less)

Bibliotherapy

The Girl's Guide to Books for Every Phase of Our Lives

NANCY PESKE AND BEVERLY WEST

A DELL TRADE PAPERBACK

A Dell Trade Paperback

Published by Dell Publishing
a division of Random House, Inc.
1540 Broadway
New York, New York 10036

Dell books may be purchased for business or promotional use or for special sales.
For information please write to: Special Markets Department, Random House, Inc.,
1540 Broadway, New York, N.Y. 10036.

DTP and the colophon are trademarks of Random House, Inc.

Library of Congress Cataloging-in-Publication Data
Peske, Nancy K., 1962-
Bibliotherapy : the girl's guide to books for every phase of our lives / Nancy Peske and Beverly West.
p. cm.
ISBN 0-440-50897-5 (pbk.)
1. Women—Books and reading.   2. Women—Psychology.   3. Best books.   4. Women in literature.
5. Psychology and literature.   I. West, Beverly, 1961-   II. Title.
Z1039.W65 P47 2001
028'.9'082—dc21
00-060246

Printed in the United States of America

Published simultaneously in Canada

Original art by Daniel Lynch

March 2001

10   9   8   7   6   5   4   3   2   1

FFG

This book is dedicated to the many teachers,
young and old, who help us learn to read
between the lines.

Thanks to our editor, Kathleen Jayes, for her keen editorial eye and good girl-sense; our copy editor, Janet Biehl; our jacket artist, Beth Adams; and special thanks to our agent, Neeti Madan, for her patient ear, her ready smile, and her wicked sense of humor.

Bev wishes to thank the following people:

Thanks to my mom for reading me Make Way for Ducklings; to my dad for reading me "The Tell-Tale Heart"; to my brother, Tod, for letting me read him Lyle the Crocodile; and to my dear friends Pam, John, Mark, Richie, and Kim for knowing how to read me like a book. A very special shout out to Sean Daniel, for teaching me how to say things like "shout out," and lots more besides. And, last but not least, many thanks to my identical cuz, Nancy, who is the very best friend and writing partner that a girl ever had.

Nancy wishes to thank:

My dad, G. Richard Peske, who instilled in me a love of reading; my mom, Sally Powell, who is responsible for my having Milwaukee Public Library card no. J68–34143B burned into my mind; and my brother Richard for nabbing all those great Daphne du Maurier first editions for me.

My husband, George, for his patient responses to my deadline freakouts, and for having a wonderfully eclectic personal library that I raid regularly.

My son Dante, who gives me such joy as I watch him discover the magic of books.

My writing partner, identical cousin, and best friend Beverly West, for her enthusiasm, insight, brilliance, humor, support, reassurance, and love. You're awesome, babe.

Contents

Introduction

As we women move through the landmark passages of our lives, books can be our best friends. We turn to books when we are working through the larger issues—when we're struggling to define ourselves, to sort out our spiritual beliefs, to take control of our relationships, to expand our horizons, to evolve a personal philosophy of life, or to answer once and for all that burning question: Am I a winter or a summer? Whatever paths we take, through triumph or adversity, success or failure, epiphany or embarrassment, we keep reading. We underline and highlight. We pass along copies of our favorite books to our friends, mothers, and sisters, and we gather together in groups to share our literary adventures. As we travel through our lives, our bookshelves fill with the dog-eared and yellowed paperbacks that have guided us on our personal journeys. And oh, if only we'd used all that money we spent on library fines to invest in Amazon.com!

Throughout the course of our experience, we turn to both fiction and nonfiction for guidance, validation, perspective, and communion. Books accompany us as we progress from the why-can't-I-get-a-date stage to the why-are-all-my-dates-jerks stage to the why-are-all-men-scum stage to the I'm-going-to-take-charge-of-my-own-happiness-and-just-forget-about-guys stage, and they are at our side when we start all over again back at the beginning.

Okay, so our progressions aren't always as linear as they might be. There are forty-year-olds still trying to assert their inner bitch (which some preteens have already mastered) and twenty-year-olds who are cynical, world weary, and experiencing existential alienation. But no matter what phase we're in, books help us confront our issues, remind us that we're not alone, and teach us about ourselves and our world. They also inspire us to try new things and then comfort us when our journeys into unknown territory don't work out so well. Armed with a book and a vivid imagination, we climb the Ngong Hills with Isak Dinesen, and roam the untamed moors with Emily Brontë in search of immortal love. We experiment with the hand-mirror examinations of *Our Bodies, Ourselves* or the I-think-this-works-better-as-a-fantasy-because-my-legs-just-won't-bend-that-way suggestions in *The Complete Kāma Sūtra*.

Of course, not all of our literary landmarks have been shining beacons leading us toward a more enlightened future. How often have we devoured the latest hot read only to discover that we're just not willing to feel the burn often enough to look like Jane Fonda in a pair of spandex leggings? And then, of course, there was *The Rules*, which taught us that if we want to hook a man, we don't need self-esteem, we just need to create the illusion of having a life. Frankly, we'd rather *have* a life.

Indeed, we've discovered through rereading some of the books that have influenced us the most that they are not exactly the enlightening tomes we remember. As Dorothy Parker once said, "This is not a novel to be tossed aside lightly. It should be thrown aside with great force." In our "Books to Be Thrown with Great Force" sidebars, we take a look back at these books that led us down blind alleyways. And in our sidebar series "Notes from Our Reading Journals," we revisit the books that have been instrumental in our becoming who we are.

We hope that no matter where you are in your life's journey, *Bibliotherapy* will help you discover new maps for your internal and external wanderings and guide you to your destination with a minimum of road rage.

—Beverly and Nancy
New York City, May 2000

P. S. If you'd like to share your literary journeys, e-mail us at *Nakape@aol.com*, or write to us care of the publisher.

Chapter 1

When You're Ready to Embrace Your Inner Bitch: Bad Girl Books

There's a reason good girls finish last.

Because a lot of times, doing what we think we're supposed to do means throwing the race.

Good girls are so busy paying the bills, getting dinner on the table, and maintaining the image of the archetypal mother, symbolizing unconditional love, selfless patience, and the compelling need for a refillable prescription for anti-anxiety medication, that they never even make it to the starting gate. With a job description like that, it gets pretty hard to imagine a walk around the block, let alone a race to the summit of our highest personal peak.

But what if we good girls started to give them all a taste of their own medicine? What if we found the courage to misbehave? What if we slipped into a pair of scuffed stilettos and stretch capris two sizes too small and, just for once, got really out of line?

The bad girl books in this chapter are about unmanageable women who pushed the limits and stood their ground. They're brash, bawdy, foul-mouthed, unladylike, and often on the wrong side of tipsy. But their misbehavior teaches us that if you want to be good—and we mean really, really good—you've got to be willing to be a little horrid.

■ *Who's Afraid of Virginia Woolf?* (1962)
by Edward Albee

George and Martha, sad, sad, sad.

Martha, the heroine of Edward Albee's *Who's Afraid of Virginia Woolf?*, is a blowzy, obnoxious, disappointed, desperate, and sadistic alcoholic, who is, despite her shortcomings, one of the most vicariously thrilling bitches in the history of the American theater.

What woman doesn't long to experience Martha's primitive abandon, if only for a moment—to be able to get drunk, and we mean really drunk—to loll about barking orders at our husband with a martini in our hand, gin trickling down our chin, stuffed into a catsuit two sizes too small stretched over our aging but profuse seductiveness?

Okay, so maybe most of us would stop short of doing the hootchy-koo with the history professor who is married and twenty years our junior. But which one of us wouldn't love to be able to toss off a line like "if you existed I'd divorce you" without batting a false eyelash?

Martha's not just a bitch, she is the bitch goddess—a plump, fickle, spoiled, foulmouthed, and irresistible Circe, randomly bestowing her favors or turning men into pigs, according to her whim. So while Martha is a pathetic, desperate, and drunken grotesque who brutalizes her husband because he has committed the unforgivable sin of loving her, Martha is heroic too. Her sheer unmanageability—her willingness to not only speak her mind but to slur it at full volume from the front porch in a sleepy suburb at midnight—is the act of defiance that liberates us all.

Read this one when you're feeling the need to perform a group exorcism. *Who's Afraid of Virginia Woolf?* chases all the demons into the light of day.

Points to Ponder

1. Discuss the use of flowers in Who's Afraid of Virginia Woolf? *For example, what is the significance of snapdragons and strolling Mexican flower-sellers in this play? (Hint: They are not just thrown in for set dressing and multicultural appeal.)*

2. *Putting the inevitable hangovers aside, do you think that* Who's Afraid of Virginia Woolf? *has a happy ending or an unhappy ending? Why?*

Bad Girls We'd Like to Have Over for Girls' Night

The Wife of Bath

Chaucer's classic bad girl taught us that things would be much better for everybody if husbands the world over just shut up and did what their wives told them for a change. She has a standing invitation to any of our get-togethers.

Lady Macbeth

Shakespeare's legendary power bitch would be fun to have around if we wanted to defy right reason and overthrow the divine right of kings. But there are hazards whenever you stand in opposition to nature. So if things go awry, and fair becomes foul and foul becomes fair, we wash our hands of the consequences.

Madame Defarge

It's always nice to have a motherly type around who can knit a secret code into an afghan, just in case you need to launch a spontaneous revolution, or the temperature drops suddenly.

Maggie the Cat

While a cat on a hot tin roof is not the most relaxing element to introduce into an evening of self-rejuvenation, something about that faded southern belle ambience just helps the hours, and the bourbon, flow sweetly.

continued . . .

Molly Bloom

James Joyce's symbol of eternal regeneration and the undiscriminating receptiveness of female fecundity is welcome at any of our soirees. You can ask Molly anything—she always says yes, yes, yes.

Salome

We'll invite this veil-dancing bad girl if we've had a bad day and are in the mood to serve somebody his head on a platter. ▪

▪ *Gone with the Wind* (1936)
by Margaret Mitchell

The green eyes in the carefully sweet face were turbulent, willful, lusty with life, distinctly at variance with her decorous demeanor. Her manners had been imposed upon her by the gentle admonitions of her mother and the sterner discipline of her mammy; her eyes were her own.

Sixteen-year-old Scarlett O'Hara knows from her mammy's and mother's teachings that her job in life is to be a graceful lady who quietly runs the business of her husband's plantation. But Scarlett also realizes that the real fun is in the husband catching, and at this she's an overachiever extraordinaire. When she's in her characteristic southern belle overdrive, Scarlett knows just when to show her dimple, how to sway her hoopskirt, and how to wrangle a marriage proposal out of a man and then keep him dangling while scoping out the other possibilities. And when we see her manipulate the entire male population of Clayton County that afternoon at the Wilkeses' barbecue, we realize that whatever her challenges, Scarlett's going to rise to the top and become the CEO of her own life.

So survival isn't always pretty. All of us who've been in that wretched and barren garden at dawn, rising from the spewing of our own bile to shake a fist at God and declare that we will never be hungry again, know that sometimes a gal has to lie, steal, cheat, and kill to get where she's going. It's just that most of us don't take that quite as literally as Scarlett does. She steals her sister's beau, backstabs her best friend, throws herself at a married man even though she's already got Clark Gable at home, slaps around the help, allows her sadistic foreman to starve and beat her workers, treats her children like annoying little rodents, and if you try to come between her and her goals, she'll blow your head off, search your pockets, and bury you out in the arbor. *So don't mess with Scarlett!*

Yet despite how much we love and admire Melanie, a well-bred good girl who, inspired by Scarlett, finds an inner strength to stand up for those she loves, it's Scarlett who draws us in. Frankly, we wouldn't trust Scarlett O'Hara with our man, our money, or our friendship, but somehow, we can't help loving her. She's the part of us that's the spoiled, selfish brat, who can't be bothered worrying about what other people will think or whether their feelings will be hurt. She moves full speed ahead, taking no prisoners, on a linear course to her own goals, unimpeded by kindness or grace.

Much as we embrace those two virtues, we know there are times when we've got to access our own inner Scarlett and go forth unapologetically. No wonder many of us return again and again to *Gone with the Wind*. Granted, some of us get more than a little obsessive about our Scarlett than others. This novel of survival is a touchstone that reminds us that we can't do it all and be a paragon of feminine nurturing at the same time. We may discover *Gone with the Wind* in adolescence, when it first hits us little Ophelias that being nice and achieving our goals are often mutually exclusive; or we may discover it later in life, when dealing with a great loss or betrayal that leaves us feeling furious and powerless. Either way, *Gone with the Wind* is there to remind us that the bitch prevails, and what's more, she deserves to be loved.

Points to Ponder

1. *Will Scarlett ever feel, like Rhett, that it's time to incorporate grace into her life? And do you even want her to?*

2. *What's the real reason that Scarlett is singing the morning after Rhett ravishes her?*

Notes from Nancy's Reading Journal

Personally, I finally recognized my addiction to *Gone with the Wind* after I'd read the book more than twenty-five times; don't even ask how often I've seen the movie. It all started when I was twelve and my grandmother brought me to a Saturday matinee. As soon as I got back to school, I checked out the book, read it straight through, took it all in for about five minutes, and started over again at page one. I was thrilled to discover that there was more to Scarlett and her world than the movie could begin to fit in, even at a four-hour length, and I learned one of the great truths about chick lit: The book is almost always more satisfying than the movie.

Another thing I learned from reading *Gone with the Wind* over and over is that a great book tells a story many different ways. I'd read it from Scarlett's point of view one time, and Rhett's the next; I'd read it to try to imagine what it was like to be a Confederate watching my world crumble, then I'd read it and identify with the slaves, whose choices were so limited. I'd put it aside for a few years, then rediscover it. I'd be disappointed at its racism, then I'd reread it and be amazed by Margaret Mitchell's psychological insights. The last time I read it I was shocked to realize what an incredible bitch Scarlett was. Hmm, where had I been? Probably envying her gumption so much that I was willing to overlook her mean streak. Maybe next time I'll just delight in her quintessential badness.

Which brings me to the most important thing I learned from *Gone with the Wind*: Depending on where you are in your life, a great book, even if you've read it so often you've memorized sections, will always have something new to teach you. ▪

■ *The Portable Dorothy Parker* (1944)
by Dorothy Parker

That woman speaks eight languages and can't say no in any of them.

Just like that little girl with the cute little curl right in the middle of her forehead, when Dorothy was good, she was very, very good, and when she was bad, she was usually about six sheets to the wind, evil-tempered, and had a tongue like a machete.

This is true of Dorothy's life as well as her writing. Both were either inspired or disastrous. Dorothy wasn't a great writer so much as she was a great character, and somehow the stories of her scathing wit and epic rudeness have become as complicated and important a masterpiece as any of the greatest works of her day.

Perhaps what is so captivating about Dorothy Parker for women, in her day as well as our own, is that while her bons mots are glib, her subject matter deals openly and honestly with our greatest heartbreaks—lost dreams, faithless partners, the sting of rejection, the folly of infatuation, the endless, unquenchable thirst for love, and of course, sex.

The Portable Dorothy Parker, a compilation of her poems, epigrams, and short stories, is a record of Dorothy's take-no-prisoners outlook on life. It is less a literary anthology than a reference book for bad girls in training. Dorothy Parker was desperate, indulgent, vengeful, and more often than not just on the wrong side of sober, but she was also passionate and brave and honest and intelligent, and perhaps most important, she was funny.

When you're feeling downtrodden, turn to Dorothy for a reminder that there is nothing that can't be faced down with a show of bravado and a really good one-liner.

Reality Check: Dorothy Parker's writing career began in 1916, when after several unsuccessful attempts to be published in *Vanity Fair*, she finally hit on the voice that would catapult her into the public eye and typify the rest of her professional and personal life. The poem was called "Woman: A Hate Song."

"Woman: A Hate Song" was a vicious attack against popular notions of femininity. The piece was so venomous that the editor convinced Dorothy to publish it under a pseudonym. Apparently the literary public's palate at the time tended toward the carnivorous, and Dorothy's provocative poem was a hit. Shortly thereafter *Vanity Fair* published the sequel. It was called, appropriately, "Man: A Hate Song." This time, however, Dorothy published under her own name, and an American bitch goddess was born.

Dorothy's Darts

You can lead a horticulture but you can't make her think.

I like to have a martini,
Two at the very most.
After three I'm under the table,
After four I'm under my host!

Look at him, a rhinestone in the rough.

Every year, back comes Spring, with nasty little birds yapping their fool heads off and the ground all mucked up with plants.

He is beyond question a writer of power; and his power lies in his ability to make sex so thoroughly, graphically and aggressively unattractive that one is fairly shaken to ponder how little one has been missing.

■ *Too Good for Her Own Good: Searching for Self and Intimacy in Important Relationships* (1990)
by Claudia Bepko and Jo-Ann Krestan

A lady can't even be appropriately assertive without feeling bad or being treated badly. If a lady gets too upset, she goes to a doctor who will give her tranquilizers that will help get her back to being calm, kind, and patient. If she gets too emotional, somebody will undoubtedly tell her to stop being hysterical. If she does get angry, she'll have to show it by crying. If she cries, somebody will tell her to calm down.

For those who were paying attention, the codependent's creed, first described in 1987 in the pages of *Codependent No More* by Melody Beattie, sounded an awful lot like the good girl's rule book: focus on others' needs, don't confront, lie in order to protect his feelings, and vehemently protest that you don't want to impose—why, you're perfectly happy sitting in that creaky wicker chair with the straw that pierces your back and smells faintly of cat. Many of us find that we don't need an alcoholic lover to inspire us to take on the role of doormat. We lower our heads and pick up our boss's theater tickets, readily forgive our friend for standing us up for the third time, and let our brother-in-law ruin every holiday by insisting on watching the football game on TV at full volume—all in the name of being nice. We smile, we apologize, we forgive seventy-times-seven times, and we allow everyone to stomp on our heads with their jackboot demands.

"We've seen too many women adopt the label codependent only to feel that they're sick for doing what they've been socialized to do," say the authors. "Codependency can sound like an indictment of who women are rather than how they behave. It implies that they love too much, that they make foolish relationship choices, that they are controlling, intrusive, martyrs. It tells them that they need to be improved." Probably we're all just a little tired of perpetually being on the self-improvement treadmill and are ready for the Jacuzzi, the sauna, and a massage. And while we're at it, a refill on the almond tea and jasmine aromatherapy, okay?

Too Good for Her Own Good may be a self-help book, but it's not aimed at making us better wives, mothers, lovers, workers, or friends. Instead, it's all about how to feel happier and more in control of our lives—the irony being that when we take care of our own needs, we find we have more energy for our relationships. It's refreshing to read a book in which the authors acknowledge our tendency to hand over a pound of flesh without its even being requested. Bepko and Krestan trash "the code" that tells us we must always be lady bountiful—attractive, in control, unselfish, endlessly self-negating, and working at all our relationships at all times, while never complaining or feeling overwhelmed. In its place, they give us guidelines that acknowledge our own needs: Be comfortable. Be direct and unapologetic. Be responsive and firm. And tell your brother-in-law that there's a TV in the basement for his viewing pleasure—and a lovely wicker chair for him to park himself in.

Read this book when you need to get back into the driver's seat of your life. Really, once you conquer your fear of being a bad girl, you'll be amazed at how much better you feel.

Points to Ponder

1. What part of no *don't they understand?*

2. Are you trying to be a good girl, giving in to codependency, or are you just turning the other cheek? And is there any difference?

Can I Get That Printed on a Coffee Mug?

Compulsions are a container for rage.
—Claudia Bepko and Jo-Ann Krestan

Bad Girl Bites

He had a big head and a face so ugly it became
almost fascinating.

—Ayn Rand

My specialty is detached malevolence.

—Alice Roosevelt Longworth

I'd rather be strongly wrong than weakly right.

—Tallulah Bankhead

I'd marry again if I found a man who had fifteen million dollars, would
sign over half to me, and guarantee that he'd be dead within a year.

—Bette Davis

The lovely thing about being forty is that you can appreciate twenty-
five-year-old men more.

—Colleen McCullough

If a man watches three football games in a row, he should be declared
legally dead.

—Erma Bombeck

Good girls go to heaven, bad girls go everywhere.

—Helen Gurley Brown

Lead me not into temptation; I can find the way myself.

—Rita Mae Brown

■ *Moll Flanders* (1722)
by Daniel Defoe

Nothing is more certain than that the ladies always gain of the men by keeping their ground and letting their pretended lovers see they can resent being slighted, and that they are not afraid of saying no.

Defoe's Moll Flanders was the ultimate at-risk youth in the days when being snatched by the gypsies was a step up in the world for a lot of poor kids from London. Born to a mother on death row in Newgate Prison, Moll is a gentlewoman at heart who manages to survive with a sense of dignity, honor, and self-awareness that's astonishing given how little her world seems to care about her. So can you blame anyone for her wicked, wicked ways? Sure, she boffs her patron's son, dumps her kids with the relatives when her first husband dies, goes on a mad spending spree the first time she gets a little gold in her pockets and ditches her creditors, turns whore and thief, and ends up mugging prissy little schoolgirls who ought to know better than to walk the streets without a chaperone or at least a little training in martial arts. Moll is, as she admits, quite a bad girl, but let's face it, the world of eighteenth-century England didn't offer her a lot of options, did it? And Moll *is* apologetic—sort of. Defoe's protestations that Moll's tale serves as a warning to young ladies everywhere may have satisfied his stodgier readers' objections to reading about a woman who defies all the rules of a so-called civilized society, but we aren't fooled. He revels in the hijinks of this totally lovable pickpocket and whore.

And for all Moll's excuses to the reader, you can't help being glad she had a chance to live life to the fullest and triumph in the end. Read *Moll Flanders,* and you'll realize you don't need to make up lame excuses to justify taking care of your own needs.

The Inferior Sex

The trouble with some women is they get all excited about nothing, and then they marry him.

—Cher

It is really asking too much of a woman to expect her to bring up her husband and her children too.

—Lillian Bell

When women are depressed, they eat or go shopping. Men invade another country.

—Elayne Boosler

Men are nicotine soaked, beer besmirched, whiskey greased, red-eyed devils.

—Carrie Nation

I love the male body, it's better designed than the male mind.

—Andrea Newman

▪ *Having Our Say* (1993)
by the Delany Sisters with Amy Hill Hearth

[E]ven as a tiny child, I wasn't afraid of anything. I'd meet the Devil before day and look him in the eye, no matter what the price.   —Bessie Delany

We believe it's the noblest of aspirations to want to grow up to be a feisty old lady. In *Having Our Say*, we meet two such people—centenarian sisters Sadie and Bessie Delany—but it's Bessie that really inspires a gal to develop her crotchety side.

The maiden ladies, as they call themselves, tell the story of their lives and how they experienced racist America in the twentieth century. As a piece of oral history, the book offers a fascinating glimpse of Jim Crow, Harlem in the 1920s, rural African American life, and how two professional women, one a home economics teacher and one a dentist, managed to carve out careers for themselves despite racism and sexism. Sadie and Bessie struck up friendships with the likes of Paul Robeson and Booker T. Washington, taught basic nutrition to the poorest of the poor, and managed their own home and finances until they were past one hundred years old. And you've got to admire women who not only refuse to be enslaved by the reach-me-anywhere-anytime attitude of our cell-phone-infested era, but who won't even install a telephone. If people want them, they can just make the time to drop by like civilized guests.

Now, as sisters, Sadie and Bessie got along so well because they complemented each other perfectly. Sadie, the teacher, led a life of quiet dignity, and when faced with blatant discrimination, she preferred to take the passive-aggressive route and play dumb, all the while secretly laughing at her tormenters. Her sister Bessie, however, refused to temper her emotions, despite the consequences. She confessed, "I'm afraid when I meet St. Peter at the Gate, he'll say, 'Lord, child, you were mean.'" That's because Bessie was always, to put it bluntly, quite the pisser.

For whatever reason, Bessie just didn't have the temperament to follow the lead of her hero Martin Luther King, Jr., and practice quiet nonviolence. Her favored forms of protest were to yell, scold, or accuse. She even nearly got herself lynched once when, after a drunken white lout insulted her, she told him where he could get off.

Bessie's strength came from an unshakable sense of self. "You see," she said, "I think I'm just as good as anyone. That's the way I was brought up. I'll tell you a secret: I think I'm better! Ha!" As her sister Sadie said, "She thinks it's her God-given duty to tell people the truth. I say to her, 'Bessie, don't you realize people don't want to hear the truth?'"

Having Our Say will show you that there is more than one way to fight oppression without losing one's dignity. For some, silent stoicism is the path. For others, it's choosing to be a bad girl. Sassing back without giving in to fear of reprisal allows them to fight for their rights and the rights of all people to be treated with respect. Both Sadie and Bessie Delany proved that a bad girl can be a very good thing, so read this when you need a little inspiration for your battles.

Points to Ponder

1. How are bad girls punished?

2. What's wrong with passive-aggressiveness? It works pretty well, doesn't it?

▪ *Auntie Mame* (1955)
by Patrick Dennis

Life's a banquet and some poor suckers are starving to death.

Auntie Mame is not really Mame's story at all. It's the story of young Patrick, the scion of an elevated but eccentric East Coast lineage, who is orphaned at ten years old. Patrick is shipped off to his auntie Mame to be brought up in a world far removed from the stolid, country squire life that he enjoyed with his conservative father.

Although this is Patrick's coming-of-age tale, Mame, characteristically, steals most of the focus. Well, how can you ignore a woman in an embroidered golden silk robe, jeweled slippers, and a bamboo cigarette holder? Like the cocktails she sips in startling quantities from sundown to sunrise, Mame is intoxicating, extravagant, and one hundred proof. Yet despite this epic bad girl's extravagant fashion sense, her unorthodox philosophical views, and her unquenchable thirst for bathtub gin, Mame still manages to excel at all of the traditional roles normally reserved for good girls—i.e., she's a great wife and mother—but of course, never before noon.

Read this one when you want to feel fabulous. Spending a few hours with Auntie Mame is like slipping on a pair of sequined slippers, pouring yourself a well-chilled martini, and nibbling bonbons.

Dorothy's Darts

On Katharine Hepburn's acting: **She runs the gamut of emotions from A to B.**

Dorothy Parker's suggestion for her own epitaph: **Excuse my dust.**

Notes from Bev's Reading Journal

My mother was an Auntie Mame wannabe. I swear she was. Although we lived in a hypercivilized bungalow in Stamford, Connecticut, circa 1965, and never rubbed elbows with the New York Gilded Age intelligentsia, I felt the atmosphere of Beekman Place nonetheless.

Sure, there was a swing set in the backyard, and one of those above-ground pools, and a front door with those little triangular inlaid windows, and avocado-colored appliances. But there was also chrome, and glass, and an Eames chair, and highballs, and of course, those cocktail dresses my mother used to wear with all those amazing sequins. And one Halloween I distinctly remember a bamboo cigarette holder.

My mom was mesmerized by the New York mystique, and she communicated her fascination to me, so Mame fit right in with our mutual fantasy life, and we resonated like wind chimes to this book, each in our own way. Well, we both had issues. I was adopted and transported to the suburbs, but I had been born in a hospital in New York City not far from Mame's pied-à-terre, and I had often dreamed that I was the exiled heir apparent of some exotic urban empress. And my mother had a bad girl streak a mile wide that her staunch Lutheran father did his best to restrain with stoic disapproval and a one-way ticket to a Lutheran college in North Overshoe. But my mother's rebellious spirit was unquenchable.

So Auntie Mame was right down my and my mom's alley, and we devoured the book together and saw the play twice, and Mame became an elemental part of our shared history.

For both of us, I think, Auntie Mame represented a more integrated view of womanhood. She helped my mother and me, and I'm sure many more

continued . . .

mothers and daughters just like us, to understand that we could be bad girls and still be good girls. Mame was a complicated, self-fulfilled role model who gave us permission to take off our sensible oxfords, thrust our feet into gold jeweled slippers, and feel fabulous without feeling guilty.

To this day, my mother and I still aspire to be Mame. And both of us, after our own fashion, have come pretty darn close. I live in a pied-à-terre in New York City (read: walkup), and while I don't make bathtub gin, the pyrotechnic-theme bacchanalias that I throw around my joint week in and week out are legendary in my eccentric circle. And lately, I've taken to calling everyone darling, and my friend's daughter Lily has taken to calling me Auntie Bev. And so will Nancy's son Dante, when he finally grows teeth and can get his mouth around hard consonants.

As for my mother, well, she works at the Denver Art Museum teaching kids how to appreciate alternative art, and some weekends she can be found tramping through the remote pueblos of northern New Mexico in search of a new and highly touted Native American potter.

Oh, and she still loves sequins. ▪

▪ *The Scarlet Letter* (1850)
by Nathaniel Hawthorne

Hester Prynne wasn't even a Puritan, but it was just her luck to end up living among that stiff-collared lot when she found herself a young widow with a major jones for that hot stud of a preacher boy, Dimmesdale. One short fling later, she's standing on a scaffold before a community of judgmental, dour, self-righteous men and women who heap scorn on her for daring to indulge in an illicit affair (which is a bit hard to hide when you're a single gal with a three-month-old in your arms). The New England townsfolk hate being faced with a woman who not only takes their punishment but flaunts it. A plain old scarlet A on her bodice won't do for Hester, so she embroiders a dazzling gold A on a piece of rich red cloth. What really infuriates them about Hester, though, is that she won't point the finger at her partner in sin. Without her help, they can't separate out the sinners from the saints and remain secure in their black and white world.

True, Hawthorne's eighteenth-century prose style can be daunting, but his story of a woman who refuses to play scapegoat for a community, and who takes responsibility without flagellating herself, is a terrific reminder of the power of individual conscience and the danger of groupthink. Read this when you need to remember that love means never having to say you're sorry.

Points to Ponder

1. *If there were a letter on your chest, what would it be, and what would it look like? And would you wear a sweater over it?*

2. *Why doesn't anybody notice that Hester's kid looks an awful lot like that new preacher who keeps babbling vaguely about his own failings?*

Chapter 2

When You Discover That Clitoris Is Not a Town in Greece: Exploring-Our-Sexuality Books

Let's face it, sex is not just like riding a bike. While it does require some of the same skills, like balance, cardiovascular endurance, and strong thigh muscles, it's a lot more difficult to master, and once you've learned, you can, on occasion, forget how.

Back in the days when the missionary position reigned supreme, being good in bed meant you had to close your eyes, lie back, and think of England. Nowadays we have to grapple with a whole host of confusing questions in our attempts to define ourselves as sexual beings—like is the multiple orgasm real or a myth? is a single orgasm real or a myth? and just where the heck is that pesky G spot anyway? These conundrums remain on our collective minds throughout the course of our sexual lives.

Whether you're just entering your sexual life and trying to figure out what all the fuss is about, looking for new techniques to keep alive the passion in your marriage, or rediscovering your sexual desire after a divorce or the breakup of a long-term relationship, the books in this chapter have helped us women to understand ourselves, put us in touch with our own sensuality, and answered the tough questions, like just how do you pronounce *clitoris* anyway?*

■ *Delta of Venus* (1969) and *Little Birds* (1979)
 by Anaïs Nin

The odor of her sex—pungent shell and sea odors, as if woman came out of the sea as Venus did—mixed with the odor of the fur, and John's suckling grew more violent.

Anaïs Nin is the grandmother of women's erotica. Fifty years ago, when she wrote these stories, she understood that language, setting, and psychology are crucial elements in raising pornography to the level of erotica. Unfortunately, her male patron, who was shelling out a dollar a page to get his rocks off, told her to cut the poetry crap and concentrate on "the good stuff." That's why you'll find, sandwiched in between her beautifully written pieces about women surrendering themselves to passion as they skinny-dip by moonlight, lots of blow-by-blow descriptions of who put what where and when. Nin would probably blame this mystery man not only for her stripped-down plotlines but for all her very un-PC pieces about dirty old men lusting after little girls and boys or indulging in erotic play with their daughters (in fact, both these collections start with such essays, which you may want to skip). But *Delta of Venus* and *Little Birds* are definitely worth dipping into when you want to generate a little heat.

■ *Lady Chatterley's Lover* (1928)
 by D. H. Lawrence

"What have yer done ter yerselves, wi' the blasted work? Spoilt yerselves. . . . Take yer clothes off an look at yourselves. Yer ought ter be alive an' beautiful an' yer ugly an' half dead."

* KLIT-er-îs.

It is ironic but not at all surprising that one of the great classics illustrating the awakening of a woman's sexuality was written by a man. But then again, D. H. Lawrence wasn't exactly your average Joe. In his day he was known as the priest of love. At first glance, this may seem like a surprising nickname for a callow, bookish, and intermittently tubercular son of the Midlands. But *Lady Chatterley's Lover*, the story of a young woman's sexuality unfolding like an O'Keeffian flower amidst the blight of industrial-age England, tickled the pistils of imminent female blossoms everywhere and set the laurel crown of Dionysian abandon on Lawrence's head once and for all.

The story of Lady Constance Chatterley's sensual rebirth at the hands of a sensitive and passionate gamekeeper was written as an indictment of the industrial age. Lawrence believed that the industrial revolution had murdered genuine human feeling and squelched the healthy, unfettered expression of human sexuality. The sensual gamekeeper, Oliver Mellors, is a symbol of a simpler time when people enjoyed a more intimate connection with nature, their own bodies, and each other. Lawrence's metaphorical male midwife was also a firm proponent of the idea that men should walk around in red tights so that their legs would be happy.

Despite the philosophical undercurrent in this famous and controversial novel, this is probably one of the sexiest books ever written. Pick this one up whenever you're feeling disembodied or out of touch with your natural cycles. The description of Oliver and Connie running naked through the rain across a meadow strewn with daffodils is guaranteed to cure even the most severe case of emotional industrial blight.

Notes from Bev's Reading Journal

I read *Lady Chatterley's Lover* for the first time in college. It was for a women's studies course, which I took on the rebound after a semester of Chaucer, Elizabethan and Jacobean drama, and Samuel Beckett. After a courseload like that, I was more than ready to run naked in the rain through the lily-strewn preserve of Lawrence's imagination

continued . . .

pursued by an ardent gamekeeper intent on burning away my shame with the consuming flame of his unbridled passion.

From the first, I fell head over heels in love with Lawrence's gamekeeper, Oliver Mellors. I loved his stillness, his isolation, his private pain, his gentleman's hands grown rough with hard labor, his broad vernacular, which he used like a weapon against the clipped and hollow life of the mind. I vowed to turn a cold shoulder to the paralysis of the ruling classes, long since grown dead below the waist. From that day forward I dated only ruddy laborers who called me lass, bathed naked in the woods, and wove wildflowers in my maiden hair. And it was the 1970s, so there were plenty of them around.

Unfortunately, my women's studies teacher did not share my feelings for Lawrence's male midwife. She resented the fact that it was a man, rather than a woman, who was chosen to embody the procreative powers of the universe, and she preferred to see only women in red tights. She found *Lady Chatterley's Lover*, along with most of the Western canon, to be a tool of the patriarchy that subordinated women with the weapons of insufficient character development and male-protagonist-driven plotlines.

I told her that if I couldn't dance, I didn't want to be part of her revolution. I felt that any system of belief that prohibited one from reveling in the ecstatic life of this novel was essentially sick at its center. This was my first significant departure from the often-taciturn philosophies of the radical feminist movement. While their position was technically different, I essentially saw them as being as restrictive as the forces that declared *Lady Chatterley's Lover* pornographic and banned it from U.S. publication until 1959, thirty-one years after it was written.

Clearly, I wasn't one of the star pupils in my women's studies class, but it was less a consequence of my pro-Lawrencian platform than the fact that the class met at nine A.M. After reading my assigned chapters of *Lady Chatterley's Lover* in bed with my boyfriend each morning, I rarely made it to class. Hey, it was spring semester, and there were a lot of wildflowers in bloom.

continued . . .

I have reread *Lady Chatterley's Lover* at various periods throughout my life. I read it out loud with my husband when we first started dating, and I read it again silently when my marriage ended. And I imagine that I'll read it once more when the next randy gamekeeper enters my life. Lawrence's novel is a kind of touchstone for me—a living symbol of the eternal resurgence of passion, and a reminder that no matter the duration or severity of my emotional winter, spring will always come again, the wildflowers will bloom, bathing the world in a riot of splendid Lawrencian color. ■

Like Crackers in Bed

Sex is the last refuge of the miserable.
—Quentin Crisp

There comes a moment in the day when you have written your pages in the morning, attended to your correspondence in the afternoon, and have nothing further to do. Then comes that hour when you are bored; that's the time for sex.
—H. G. Wells

Intercourse with a woman is sometimes a satisfactory substitute for masturbation. But it takes a lot of imagination to make it work.
—Karl Kraus

■ *Even Cowgirls Get the Blues* (1976) by Tom Robbins

The oyster, could it fancy, should fancy its excremental equipment a hot item, for what other among God's crapping creatures can turn its bodily wastes into treasure?

What, you may well ask, has hitchhiking got to do with sex? Particularly seeing as how you hitchhike with your thumb, which is traditionally one of the unsexiest parts of the human anatomy.

The thumb has played a rich and significant role in the annals of human history. Not only is our opposing digit one of the cornerstones of human evolution, but it is rich with metaphorical potential. We can give something a thumbs-up or a thumbs-down. We can thumb our nose, or thumb a ride to parts unknown. There are rules of thumb, and green thumbs, and of course, poor little Tom Thumb. But for all its multilayered anthropological and etymological history, the one thing that the thumb has never been is erogenous. Never, that is, until Tom Robbins introduced his phalange-fixated, hitchhiking heroine Sissy Hankshaw to the world in his ode to female empowerment, *Even Cowgirls Get the Blues.*

Sissy Hankshaw has the dubious distinction of having been born with two enormous thumbs, which extend pornographically, like prodigious dildoes, from the base of her unsuspecting palms. This accident of evolution, obviously, didn't do much for Sissy's desirability quotient in her small North Carolina town of origin. But Sissy, an indomitable spirit no matter the scope of her opposing digits, makes like an oyster and turns her crap into pearls, ultimately becoming the world's greatest hitchhiker and one of the few lesbian characters to take her place in the female canon of sexual self-discovery.

Even Cowgirls Get the Blues is Robbins's answer to the testosterone-fueled on-the-road epics of the 1950s and 1960s. Rather than featuring a restless, unshaven, leather-jacket-clad James Dean prototype, however, Robbins places a willowy feminine hygiene model at the center of his journey, who ends her quest in the arms of a cowgirl named Bonanza Jellybean on a lesbian dude ranch called the Rubber Rose. This, as you might imagine, is a highway of a whole different color, and it winds us up in an unencumbered female-identified sexual utopia that Kerouac's friend and muse Neal Cassady couldn't have imagined even in his wildest asphalt dreams.

Whatever part of your emotional or physical anatomy feels like a sore thumb on the rosy palm of life, *Even Cowgirls Get the Blues* is guaranteed to help you, like the oyster, turn your irritations into treasure.

Points to Ponder

1. *What part of your personality or anatomy would you compare to Sissy Hankshaw's thumbs?*

2. *What does hitchhiking have to do with sex, anyway?*

3. *Why is the Rubber Rose Ranch rubber?*

Been There, Done That

In our sexual journey over the latter half of the twentieth century, we've learned a lot about our sexuality, tried a few things that didn't work out, and come to realize that when it comes to sex, advice ought to be taken with an economy-size container of salt. Cases in point:

∎ *The Sensuous Woman* (1969)
by "J"

Oral sex is, for most people who will give it a try, delicious. It is part of the Sensuous Woman's bag of pleasures and has the added advantage, if you're a snob, of being a status style of lovemaking. (It's the preferred way with many movie stars, artists, titled Europeans and jetsetters.)

Back in 1969, nice girls didn't, so the author of this classic sex guide didn't even sign her name to it. Nowadays, of course, she'd not only have her name on the cover, she'd pose nude in *Playboy* to promote it.

continued . . .

Anyway, "J"'s advice was quite risqué at a time when white gloves and bouffants were on their last gasp and swinging was whispered about in middle America. That a woman should massage herself and then masturbate to orgasm so that she'll enjoy sex more is pretty time-honored advice, but the orgy etiquette sounds hilarious today. (To wit: *Don't* bring a nice chiffon dress, as they usually don't have hangers at the party; *do* expect come-ons from lesbians; *don't* expect any of the men to claim paternity if you get pregnant; *do* stay home if you are menstruating.) And how curious is it that "J" thinks anyone into S&M is a "sicko" but wife swapping is A-OK?

In the days before most women thought divorce was a viable option, "J"'s advice to married women on where to find a lover was almost practical—*almost* (take a look at hubby's business associates? Boy, is that playing with fire!). Probably the main reason this book was the hot read of 1969, however, was its graphic advice on how to perform fellatio and anal sex—scandalous revelations for the time, when, for all the talk, most orgies existed only in the fantasies of married men from suburbia. The book's most outdated advice? Learn to fake it in order to make him happy. Let's be grateful that *that* era is over, shall we?

Read this one when you want to take a surreal trip back to the days when the Pill meant freedom, not six pages of health warnings.

■ *Sex and the Single Girl* (1962)
by Helen Gurley Brown

If *The Sensuous Woman* brings to mind an image of Austin Powers, *Sex and the Single Girl* conjures up a Playboy Bunny with spiked heels, ears and tail, and thick black eyeliner. Unlike "Hooters girls," Bunnies, as they claim today, tolerated the torturous heels both on their feet and at their tables because they not only made great tips, they met some of the most important male movers and shakers in the country. Yes, in those days, the old boys' network

continued . . .

effectively shut out young ambitious women who wanted a career and a few years of "fun" (read: sex) before marriage and children, and if wiggling a bunny tail in a man's face nabbed you an audition, a secretarial job in a law firm, or some other entry-level opportunity, it didn't seem like exploitation so much as commonsense use of one's assets. In Helen Gurley Brown's world of the early 1960s, a single gal in the big city didn't know from sexism; she just enjoyed using her power to boost her lifestyle, nabbing a boyfriend (married or no) who could pay for a nice dinner and treat her like a lady. Her advice can be summed up as: First, find an apartment in a building with lots of eligible bachelors (have a friend giggle and ask your prospective landlord about the male population so that you don't look foolish); then put up some nice chintz curtains and find a matching bedspread; save your pennies so that you can buy some dynamite shoes for a hot date with a mogul; and don't get yourself pregnant.

Aren't you glad our agendas today are a little more ambitious?

Read this when you're up for a good laugh about the sexual mores of the past.

■ *Everything You Always Wanted to Know About Sex But Were Afraid to Ask* (1969)
by David Reuben, M.D.

Probably the most ripped-off title ever, and the basis for one of those broad-humored early Woody Allen flicks, *Everything You Always Wanted to Know About Sex But Were Afraid to Ask* was *the* hot read back in 1970. We were all just dying to know about those naughty underground subjects, whether it was homosexuality or prostitution or Spanish fly. And to his credit, Dr. Reuben, a forerunner of Dr. Ruth, did speak frankly and unapologetically about all issues sexual, with a wink and a smile that showed just how comfortable he was with his subject matter. Of course, all this candid discussion of what had been

continued ...

private matters also helped usher in the era of trashy confessions on Jerry Springer and Jenny Jones. But hey, we weren't perverts—we were just expanding our knowledge base by reading about one of the important topics of the day. And Dr. Reuben was a real psychiatrist, with thick black glasses and a sensible tie.

Yet there's a reason the title has outlived the book. Today, it's obvious that Reuben was sexist, homophobic, and laughably ill-informed. "Virtually every prostitute is in the business because she wants to be" is one of his more ridiculous claims. Male homosexuality merits an entire sneering chapter, while lesbians are confined to a couple of pages in the prostitution chapter (prostitutes hate men, lesbians hate men, therefore . . . well, that's his reasoning anyway). About the only time he's on the mark is when he's discussing the horrors of illegal abortions, which *were* pretty gruesome. Lucky for us, back-alley procedures and open contempt for "queers" are as outdated as his advice on birth control and venereal disease.

Reread this when you want a lesson on how far we've come in our understanding of all things sexual since those Swinging Sixties. ▪

Book lovers never go to bed alone.

—Anonymous

■ *The Complete Kāma Sūtra* (1994)
translated by Alain Danielou

If one wishes to, it is appropriate to pinch the gigolo's nipples although it is not becoming to clasp him in your arms.

It happens to us all eventually. Whether we're in the first throes of sexual discovery or trying to rekindle a stale love life, we all come face to face with the eternal question where sex is concerned: Just what is all the fuss about?

It is in response to this ponderous conundrum that we turn to the ancient and acrobatic wisdom of the *Kāma Sūtra*. Written in the first century by Vātsyāyana, a religious scholar, the *Kāma Sūtra* is an encyclopedia of gravity- and convention-defying sexual acts that would mesmerize even the most curious, jaded, or disappointed sensualist—if only we could figure out what the heck this guy is talking about.

The *Kāma Sūtra* documents, in excruciatingly elaborate detail (and often with full-color illustrations), just about every imaginable sexual possibility, and a few that defy even the most flexible of imaginations. Swapping, swinging, biting, slapping, sighing, and something called "sucking the mango" are just a few areas of focus in the first chapter alone. And then of course there are those cryptic instructions regarding the nipples of a gigolo. There is also a brief and spurious mention of something called buccal coition, which Vātsyāyana insists only people who live in the south engage in, then demurely refuses to say anything more on the matter. We shudder to think what is involved if even the *Kāma Sūtra*, which has mountains of theory devoted to the wooing of children, is unwilling to discuss the particulars.

Given the obscure acrobatics of the sexual acts themselves and the inaccessibility of the text, which reads a lot like the instructions that come with origami kits, it is surprising that generations of women continue to turn to the *Kāma Sūtra* to cure a bad case of sexual ennui. Regardless, there is no question that the *Kāma Sūtra* persists as the last word in sexual experimentation and continues to tease all of us with the elusive possibility that sexual nirvana really does exist, if only we can become double-jointed. Pick this one up the next time you're feeling disillusioned sexually. After making your way through the exhausting acrobatics of the *Kāma Sūtra*, three and a half minutes in the missionary position will sound like heaven.

Points to Ponder

1. What do you think the matter-of-fact and encyclopedic approach of the Kāma Sūtra means with regard to the Indian culture's attitude toward sex? How does it differ from ours? Which do you prefer?

2. Just what the heck is sucking the mango anyway? What are some of the things that you imagine it might mean? And what are you wearing as you imagine it?

Carnal Knowledge

If sex is such a natural phenomenon, how come there are so many books on how to do it?

—Bette Midler

The difference between pornography and erotica is lighting.

—Gloria Leonard

Fifty percent of the women in this country are not having orgasms. If that were true of the male population, it would be declared a national emergency.

—Margo St. James

If the world were a logical place, men would ride sidesaddle.

—Rita Mae Brown

Condoms should be marketed in three sizes, jumbo, colossal, and super-colossal, so that men do not have to go in and ask for the small.

—Barbara Seaman

■ *Pleasures* (1982) and *For Each Other* (1984),
edited by Lonnie Barbach, and
Slow Hand: Women Writing Erotica (1992),
edited by Michele Slung

The fucking was as soft as velvet and as hard as finality.
—from "And After I Submit" by Anonymous, from *Pleasures*

It's been said that romance novels are women's pornography, which accounts for the fact that they constitute 40 percent of all books sold in the United States. Women have never been much for visual porn: *Playgirl* magazine never really took off as *Playboy* has. True, that may be because it features boxy men with small, flaccid penises, who pose awkwardly with wineglass in hand—as if hunky heterosexual men ever sit around by the pool naked, sipping chardonnay. We wish! So maybe we're just all waiting for the right male image to turn us on. Like, say, the sight of Yul Brynner slapping a leather gunbelt over his lean, black-encased waist in *The Magnificent Seven*, which some of us feel is worth a hundred oiled bodybuilders in Speedos on the beach. But whatever gets you through the night, 'salright with us.

Anyway, what makes women get hot and bothered is exactly what a good romance novel captures—sex within a context. Whereas pornographers think a compilation of "best orgasmic moments" (to put it euphemistically) is hot stuff, women tend not to want to skip to the chase, at least in their erotica. Whether the context is a sultry scenario—say, a tropical rain forest redolent with wet, fertile smells—or a psychological setup, such as a flirtation with a forbidden lover, women's erotica captures more than just the highlights. In fact, sometimes it skips the highlights altogether, because while some women like their sexual reading material graphic, with lots of stage directions, others prefer subtler descriptions. (Although diffused sexuality has always left us cold, we suppose if you're feeling the urge to begin with, the right purplish prose describing a sunset ought to send you over the edge.)

In these classic compilations, which have turned on many a woman and her partner over the years, editors Barbach and Slung feature a mishmash of short erotic pieces. Some of the authors do a masterful job setting the scene for sex—for instance, we love that one in *Pleasures* about the teenage girl who loses her virginity to an Irish lad while on a work-study program picking fruit in Ireland. Give us cozy pubs and a fellow with a headful of brown curls, in a thickly-corded handknit sweater, with a brogue like Liam Neeson's, delivering lines like "Ah wont to hurt you, my luvly." Okay, it's cheeseball, maybe even as cheeseball as those chardonnay-by-the-pool shots, but somehow on the page it works—probably because there's something left to the imagination. You, for example, might cast Aidan Quinn in the role, while someone else might go for the alternative curls-and-brogue type, like Ewan MacGregor. There are endless possibilities.

The downside to women's erotica, however, is that the editors of these compilations are for some odd reason driven to explain why the stories are sexy. That's like explaining a joke before telling it. You become so aware of the structure and the correctness of it all that you can't enjoy it. (Slung is even more heavy-handed than Barbach in lecturing us.) In fact, some of these stories are soooo politically correct that it's hard to imagine them appealing to anyone. Barbach, for example, features in *Pleasures* a piece about an aging lesbian who makes love to her partner for the first time after having had a hysterectomy, carefully removing the belly band that the doctor put on. Frankly, we bet that an aging lesbian who makes love to her partner for the first time after a hysterectomy would find this as unerotic as we did. Listen, if you can't indulge in a little perfection and perfume on the page, why not just have sex without the literary crutch?

In a way, it's as if the editors are apologizing for women's base desires, dressing up these stories in a framework of art and women's empowerment. Why one women gets off on one type of story while another gets off on something entirely different is an interesting question but not one you want to contemplate when you want to get off yourself.

So if you're feeling the need to jump-start your engine or your weekend with a little read-aloud session with your lover, we suggest you skip the high-minded editorialization and go straight to the stories. And if one turns out to be a dud, stick it back in the box and keep sampling until you find the bonbon you're seeking.

Points to Ponder

1. What's the sexiest image that has ever popped into your head? And where on earth did it come from?

2. Which is hotter, a romantic scene observed through a gauzy lens with soft lighting, or one involving grunts, groans, and animalistic passions, seen through a handheld camera, under fluorescent lighting?

Books to Be Thrown with Great Force

▪ *How to Satisfy a Woman Every Time . . .*
and Have Her Beg for More! (1982)
by Naura Hayden

*I'm so grateful that God gave me my physical
collapse that led to my inventing the Dynamite
Energy Shake, that I decided to put all the money that
would have come to me from the sale of the Dynamite Energy Shake,
every penny, into a foundation—The John Ellsworth Hayden
Foundation—that I named after my father. The foundation is giving
free Dynamite Energy Shakes to people who can't afford it or wouldn't
be able to get it otherwise.*

The common wisdom in book publishing is that women buy books on
how to satisfy a woman and then leave them bookmarked and conspicuous
on the nightstand for "him" to discover. Probably that's the secret to the
success of Naura Hayden's bestseller, which has one of those winner titles
that editors spend many agonizing hours trying to dream up. In fact, the title
is the only thing good about this book. We can picture women seeing this on
the shelf in the bookstore, grabbing it, and stuffing it between their other
purchases, then nonchalantly browsing through the pocket-stuffer books and
clip-on reading lights at the register as the clerk rings it up. Let's face it:
Publicly purchasing sex guides is right up there with buying hemorrhoid
cream, lice spray, and *Weekly World News*.

And we can also picture women getting this book home and becoming
spitting mad when they realize that Naura Hayden is too interested in
blathering on about the importance of love, God, and positive thinking to give

continued . . .

more than the most basic sexual techniques. She devotes only thirteen pages to actual sexual advice and another thirteen pages to promoting her Dynamite Energy Shake and cookbook (adequate consumption of B vitamins and dolomite being especially important elements of good sex. Yeah, right). Not exactly a lot of bang for your buck, is it?

Oh, her advice is sound enough: Guys, slow down, and use a little bit of teasing rather than falling into the old wham-bam-thank-you-ma'am mode, and pay attention. But it's unfortunate that so many women think that skimming through sex books in a public place puts them in the same company with men in greasy raincoats browsing through titles at the porn video store; otherwise, charlatans like Hayden would have to write substantial books. ■

Points to Ponder

1. Can a man satisfy a woman every time?

2. Do California hardbodies and health food nuts have better sex?

■ *Rubyfruit Jungle* (1973)
by Rita Mae Brown

Let's stop this shit. I love women. I'll never marry a man and I'll never marry a woman either. That's not my way. I'm a devil-may-care lesbian.

There's more to sexual experimentation than trying out French kissing techniques on your pillow and winding up with a mouth full of lint. So often we women think of sexual experimentation as a tedious but required course in how to get somebody else's rocks off. But as Molly Bolt, the heroine of Rita Mae Brown's seminal lesbian coming-of-age/coming-out tale, demonstrates, the most important part of any journey into the sea of sexual response is learning what floats our own boat.

Molly discovers that she is a lesbian in the sixth grade when she kisses the cutest girl in school and notices that her stomach feels funny. From that first magical moment when their lips meet and Molly's upper gastrointestinal tract goes pitter-pat, Molly knows she's on to something good, and she doesn't let up, no matter what or who gets in her way.

If your sexual experimentation is beginning to feel like just one more chore on the laundry list, read *Rubyfruit Jungle* and let Molly show you how to squeeze every last drop from the rubyfruit.

Like Crackers in Bed

No woman needs intercourse; few women escape it.
—Andrea Dworkin

'Tis the devil inspires this evanescent ardor, in order to divert the parties from prayer.
—Martin Luther

It's Not Our Cup of Tea, But . . .

. . . somebody appreciates these S&M classics. Hey, we don't write 'em, we just review 'em. . . . Really, Mom.

- ***Justine* (1791)**
  by the Marquis de Sade

Justine, the Marquis de Sade's S&M classic about the triumph of vice over virtue, reads like a tour of the worst excesses of the prerevolutionary French aristocracy.

continued . . .

Cast out into the street at the tender age of twelve, Justine falls into the hands of one libertine after another, all of whom abuse her innocence with the most amazing array of sexual paraphernalia ever assembled in one town, era, or novel. There is no optimism in this book, just a sustained and lurid desecration of virtue at the hands of sexual profligates, so brutal in nature that they named sadism after the marquis. The next time you're contemplating Paris in the springtime, pick up this seminal novel and remind yourself that along with Bordeaux wines and truffle mousse pâté, sadism is one of France's most salubrious contributions to Western civilization.

Reality Check: Napoleon, outraged by *Justine*, ordered the marquis jailed after its publication. The Marquis de Sade spent the rest of his life in prison.

■ *Venus in Furs* (1870)
by Leopold von Sacher-Masoch

Just as you can't have a winter without a spring, or chocolate without vanilla, you can't have a Sade without a Masoch. *Venus in Furs*, Baron von Sacher-Masoch's S&M classic about a dominatrix and her willing slave, is the yin to De Sade's yang and gave birth to the term *masochism*.

Severin von Kusiemski, our protagonist, is an educated and devout man who develops a singular obsession for a cruel and naked goddess in furs with a whip in her hand and vengeance in her heart. Pick this one up the next time you're feeling dissatisfied with your partner's sexual imagination. There's nothing like an old guy in a truss getting his bum whipped to help you remember that there's no place like home.

Reality Check: The research for *Venus in Furs* was probably accomplished firsthand, because recent editions of this book include letters exchanged between Sacher-Masoch and Emilie Mataja, an aspiring writer who was also, apparently, a real artist with a cat-o'-nine-tails. ■

Freudian Slips, Jungian Archetypes, and Other Notes from the Collective Unconscious

No matter now how numbed we are by a superficial TV age, some stories resonate fathoms deep. When this happens—when the whole world collectively groans or moans, or recoils—it is usually a pretty good indication that something is going on way down deep, where the sun never shines.

The Exorcist (1971)

by William Peter Blatty

The Exorcist put the fear of the devil into just about everybody. Something about the vision of a pubescent girl possessed by the spirit of a demon who says things like "your mother sucks cocks in hell" in the voice of Mercedes McCambridge really got to us.

Perhaps *The Exorcist* registered so profoundly on the collective unconscious because it tapped into our primal fear of the power of women's sexuality. I mean, think about it. In *The Exorcist*, we come upon a virgin, fresh and unspoiled, barely pubescent in fact, with rosy cheeks and long red hair and a movie star mom, and an incredibly sweet disposition. The next thing you know, she's grabbing you by the balls, challenging your faith, sapping your strength with the superhuman effort it requires to control her, hurling you out of windows, and saying really nasty things about your mother.

For women, the scenario is equally frightening. Some guy shows up calling himself Captain Howdy and wants to play with the Ouija board in the attic. Next thing we know, he's tossed us on a bouncing bed, invaded our

continued . . .

body, and possessed us while we vomit pea green soup with our head rotating 360 degrees on its axis and our eyes rolling back in their sockets. Is this ringing any Freudian bells for anyone?

Let's face it, whether you're a man or a woman, *The Exorcist* is one big metaphor for all of our worst morning-after fears. Pick this one up when you need to remember that in a psychologically sophisticated post-Freudian age, a cigar is not just a cigar, so it might be a good idea to give up smoking. ■

■ *My Secret Garden* (1973)
by Nancy Friday

I sometimes think each woman goes through life secretly pursued by her own particular demon, representing her own particular brand of shame; a frenzy after her, not for anything real, but everything imagined. Shame and self-incrimination grow like mad in the dark.

If there's one dark little secret about women and sex, we don't think it's that women are faking it. Although some do, we've been hearing for thirty years that we owe it to ourselves and our lovers to direct him to the G spot—and the C spot—and we've gotten the message: We're responsible for our own orgasm. So these days the secret is, just what are we thinking about when we're knocking boots?

Ideally, we'd all be so overcome with passion in each encounter that we'd be completely present, totally in the moment, turned on by our partner and no one else. After all, this is how it happens in romance novels and movies and soap operas—and in our fantasies. And some women never resort to imaginary lovers. But the reality is that for many women, there are times when a little mental imagery helps keep the blood pumping. While he's running through the batting order of the local baseball team to keep from losing it, she's running a picture of Mel Gibson sucking her toes to keep the fires burning.

There's no reason to feel guilty about these or other seemingly bizarre images that come to us when we're doing it, says Nancy Friday. In this classic book, she collected the sexual fantasies of women from all walks of life, of all ages, presenting women with a randy read that serves to inspire our own imagination as well as to assuage any lingering guilt about needing a little erotic boost. Just because we are imagining ourselves being held captive by a group of native women about to perform a pagan rite of sexual initiation does not mean we do not love our man. Just because in our minds we are making love to the grocery delivery boy does not mean we are ready to rip our clothes off and give him today's payment and then some when he rings our bell. After all, acting out our fantasies, many women have found, defuses their power for good. As for sharing them with a lover, well, do you really want him to know about your secret desire to perform acrobatics with the grocery boy? And do you really want to know what your husband is thinking about your Pekingese?

Throughout *My Secret Garden*, Nancy Friday offers interesting insights into why particular women have latched on to particular fantasies, and why women who are getting plenty sometimes have the same fantasies as women who are currently celibate. Reading her comments may make you feel less weird about the movies running in your own head, but we bet some of the fantasies will make you feel even more prim. Once you get over the shock, you may even adopt them as your own. Then again, you may find yourself unable to look at a Pekingese ever again without feeling just a little creeped out. When it comes to sex, one woman's caviar is another woman's fish eggs.

Like Crackers in Bed

I've tried several varieties of sex. The conventional position makes me claustrophobic, and the others give me a stiff neck or lockjaw.
—Tallulah Bankhead

My own belief is that there is hardly anyone whose sexual life, if it were broadcast, would not fill the world at large with surprise and horror.
—W. Somerset Maugham

Can I Get That Printed on a Coffee Mug?

I will always thank the writers at Tampax for making perfectly clear how to stick one of those things in.

—Susie Bright

■ *Susie Bright's Sexual State of the Union* (1997) **and**
Herotica (1998)
by Susie Bright

Whenever our school showed those sex ed films to the girls in hygiene class, where the violins soar as young Debbie clutches her sanitary napkin belt to her breast, it was a message to us that this was a tremendous day, a day to feel like a woman instead of a girl.

If there's one subject the feminists of the Sixties and Seventies didn't address very satisfactorily, it's sex. They either ignored it or politicized it so that sexual intercourse became rape de facto (see Andrea Dworkin's *Our Blood*, page 123). Either way, hedonism got the shaft. Enter Susie Bright, cheerleader for a whole new wave of sexual feminists who don't fuss about gender identity or try to turn their sexual activities into metaphors. In Susie Bright's world, it's all just good dirty fun. In her essay collections, she takes on everything from the unenforceable Antioch College sexual conduct code, to amateur versus just-plain-bad porn videos, to the delights of "fisting." There are times when she seems less unfettered than twisted or confused, but her sense of humor prevents her from becoming just another self-appointed expert telling us what to do, whom to do it with, and how to feel about it. Refreshing and provocative—but not for the squeamish.

Read this when you're looking to expand your sexual horizons and shed your inhibitions.

Chapter 3

When You Still Think You Can Change Him: Bad Boy Books

He doesn't mean to misbehave. He doesn't mean to be surly, irascible, petulant, noncommunicative, emotionally inaccessible, and unemployed. Of course he doesn't. It's just that he wasn't loved as a child. He wasn't nurtured and encouraged. But with the transformative power of a woman's love, those injured eyes will shine with the beautiful light of self-confidence, and the hungry heart that beats beneath that impossibly skimpy T-shirt will feast on the banquet of self-acceptance and finally be healed.

Uh-huh. And pigs will sprout wings and cows will jump over the moon.

All of us, at some point or another, have labored under the misconception that we can change the man that we're in love with. Whether our guy is a perennially adolescent boy, a charismatic control freak, or a perpetual neurotic, we are all convinced that one day he'll wise up, get a clue, and change his evil ways.

Next to bust-development exercises and the multiple orgasm, changing our man is one of the fundamental myths of the female experience. Most of us have donated countless years and a wealth of personal resources to resurrecting the good guy we're convinced lurks behind the bad boy who doesn't help with the dishes or say please or thank you, and forgets our birthday on a regular basis.

The books in this chapter take a long, hard look at the phenomenon of the irresistible problem man/child, and at our own maternal instincts that keep us coming back for more.

▪ Bad Boys: Why We Love Them, How to Live with Them, and When to Leave Them (1997)
by Carole Lieberman

He flaunts his dilapidated hovel and his pitiful excuse for a career, well aware that they are an irresistible invitation for someone competent—like you—to step in and shore up his crumbling existence before it collapses completely.

Who was that masked man, the rebel without a cause who stole your heart, used it to polish his motorcycle, and threw it crumpled onto the floor? Why, it's your bad boy of the moment, a James Dean you plan on turning into a Tom Hanks, just as soon as you pay off the charges he put on your credit card.

Even if you haven't dated a man in a leather jacket, you may find bells of recognition ringing as you read this study of all the subspecies of bad boy. There's the wounded poet, whose gloom cloud casts a shadow that makes him look romantic instead of manipulative. There's Mr. Power Mad, the anal-retentive type who demands that you work your weekend plans around his Saturday morning laundry ritual because he has *always* done his laundry on Saturday mornings, and you'd better get used to it, even though it means you're going to hit traffic on the turnpike and arrive at the music festival after half the weekend's gone. There's the grandiose dreamer, whose résumé is four pages long but still hasn't nabbed him a job he can stay with for more than six months, unless you count his entrepreneurial stint selling T-shirts and bongs at concerts in the 1970s. And the rest of them are here too: the Compulsive Flirt, the Lethal Lover, the Self-Absorbed Seducer, the Man of Mystery—in all his guises, he's wildly attractive to you and a total drain on your energy and your sanity.

Of course, we all want to believe we can change the bad boy, or at least modify his behavior to the point where he can be tolerated by our friends and family. To that end, Carole Lieberman offers realistic expectations and advice for anyone who insists on staying with her manipulative Romeo. Even though he's costing you a fortune in therapy bills, you still hold out hope that maybe you'll be the woman who gets him to see the light, to accept once and for all that even artists have to pay the rent, and that weekends should not be shortened because of an obsession with neatly folded underwear.

Lieberman also delves a bit into archetype, using lots of frog-and-prince stories, and she muses about why Johnny Can't Commit—and why he can't stop treating you like his personal love slave. It's all very enlightening, and yes, after reading this book, all his stories about Mom and Dad and the time he lived on the beach in Monterey will finally make sense. And you'll probably use this newfound clarity to justify hanging in there in case things improve. We've been there, and all we can say is, if you're going to live out your Leader of the Pack fantasies, do yourself a favor—put your grandmother's jewelry in a safe-deposit box.

Points to Ponder

1. *Which would you rather do—date a bad boy or be a bad girl?*

2. *If your bad boy doesn't wear a leather jacket and ripped jeans, what is his costume? And could he go trick-or-treating in it?*

Let's face it, when an attractive but ALOOF ("cool") man comes along, there are some of us who offer to shine his shoes with our underpants.

—Lynda Barry

▪ *Wuthering Heights* (1847)
by Emily Brontë

"My love for Linton is like the foliage in the woods. Time will change it, I'm well aware, as winter changes the trees—my love for Heathcliff resembles the eternal rocks beneath—a source of little visible delight, but necessary. Nelly, I am Heathcliff." —Catherine Earnshaw in *Wuthering Heights*

Nowhere has the wild, unreclaimed, fiery-eyed, and raven-locked image of the bad boy been more lovingly and compellingly portrayed than in Emily Brontë's gothic classic, *Wuthering Heights.* The injured, misunderstood, passionate, fiercely handsome Heathcliff, stalking the lonely moors, bellowing his pain to the indifferent heavens as he searches for his lost paramour, is an image that has made more than one feminine heart go pitter-pat. And then of course, there are those amazing leather breeches, and that riding crop.

It's true—who can resist a man who patterns his destiny after the moorland skies, converses with the soul of the universe, and loves with a passion so forceful and uncompromising that it challenges death itself? Not us, that's for sure, as our Heathcliffian dating histories clearly demonstrate. Hey, we know it's a fairly simple concept, but until you've actually played with fire, it's hard to understand that you inevitably get burned.

On first glance, *Wuthering Heights* is an immortal love story about a communion between two like souls whose fundamental and almost supernaturally perfect attachment o'erleaps the bounds of the limited physical universe and finds union at last in a better and more heroic world beyond. On second glance, it's the recipe for a disastrous marriage, the destructive force of which kills one lover and twists the other into a substance so toxic that it pollutes the world around him for generations to come.

If you're defying the physical laws of the universe and standing on the brink of the abyss of pure union with a bad boy, read *Wuthering Heights* and revel in the gorgeous, heady, and terrifying sublimity of overleaping passion—while you still can.

Points to Ponder

1. What (besides the frock coat and those amazing leather breeches) makes Heathcliff seem larger than life and heroic?

2. In what ways do you believe that the great love between Cathy and Heathcliff managed to transcend death? Was it worth it?

Pearls from the Patriarchy

Regarding Hobbies

My hobbies are hooking up stuff to see if it works, and beer.
                                              —Joe Walsh

I spend money on, what—snakes, guitars, and cars.
                                              —Slash

I bit the head off a live bat the other night. It was like eating a Crunchie wrapped in chamois leather.

                                              —Ozzy Osbourne

■ *The House of the Spirits* (1982)
by Isabel Allende

[He] never knew the exact number of his children, and the fact of the matter was that he was not interested. He figured that when he was ready to have children he would find a woman of his own class, with the blessings of the Church, because the only ones who really counted were the ones who bore their father's surname; the others might just as well not have been born.

Now, now. He doesn't *mean* to be malevolent. But his fractured male self, untouched by the poetry of Robert Bly, lies by the pond of emotion, waiting for the lady of the lake to heal the mortal wound to his soul.

Okay, okay, *The House of the Spirits* is not a feminist interpretation of Celtic mythology, but any good ecofeminist will recognize the themes here. Esteban Trueba is the epitome of the desensitized male, brutalized by the patriarchy, clinging to his place on the hierarchy of a capitalistic system, terrified of the power of women. His wife, Clara, is his only hope for salvation. Clear-eyed, in touch with the mysteries of the world (it's one of those magic realism novels, you know—lots of spirits floating around and magical powers and stuff), Clara waits for him to throw off the cloak of masculinity and embrace his feminine side. In the meantime, Trueba destroys the life of his ever-sacrificing sister, tries to murder his daughter's lover, abandons his illegitimate children, and sows the seeds of discord that result in a violent military coup to overthrow the government.

Really, if only guys would learn a little respect for the feminine force, maybe we'd have paradise on earth instead of police states and exploitative capitalistic hierarchies. Men!

Read this one when you want to believe, if only for a few hours, that it's all society's fault, not his.

Pearls from the Patriarchy

Regarding Genius

If there is such a thing as genius—which is what . . . what the fuck is it?—I am one, and if there isn't, I don't care.
—John Lennon

Of course we revel in our own fucking genius. Why the hell not? Self-indulgence is what we're full of and we're proud of it.
—Johnny Rotten

■ *The Peter Pan Syndrome* (1983)
by Dan Kiley

They fly away from reality, get high on the natural herbs of the land, cavort with fairies, and cop out on mature responsibilities.

We don't think it's coincidence that *The Peter Pan Syndrome* was published—to great success—in the 1980s, a decade in which cocaine-fueled self-indulgence and unbridled greed were all the rage. It was a time when a Hollywood actor thought he could get away with playing a serious political observer by day and an X-rated video star by night. Yes, Rob Lowe's antics at the 1988 Democratic National Convention kicked off the era of the Man Boy, guys who wanted to live in never-never land, free from the confinements of commitment, maturity, and sobriety. Those of us who were dating in that era can probably think back to at least one Peter Pan we played Wendy to, thinking that if we just showed enough patience and unconditional love, he'd grow up and act like the lover we deserved.

Ha!

Even today, plenty of women are pinning their hopes on a slightly less sexually am-biguous Leonardo DiCaprio type, waiting for him to stop chasing bimbos and hanging out with his brat pack morning, noon, and night, and settle into the dignified life of an adult male. But if you're dating a Peter Pan, you'd better find yourself some magic fairy dust, because it's going to be a loooong wait.

Psychologist Dan Kiley draws a picture of how these eternal boys are created and nur-tured by their dysfunctional—and usually middle-class suburban white—parents (al-though, as Terry McMillan would tell you, there is clearly an African American variety as well, and we bet they come in all colors and shapes). These Man Boys are lonely, irre-sponsible, anxious, confused about their sexual role, narcissistic, chauvinistic, and socially impotent—but at the same time intoxicating. And sure, he drinks a little—okay, a lot—and is more married to his loser buddies than to you. Sure he sees women as madonnas or whores, wants you to play Mommy and then resents you, and thinks your love should be unconditional even when he lies to you, cheats on you, and smashes up your car after partying on your good liquor when he was supposed to be out looking for a job. But oh, that view from the back when he's in those clingy Calvin Kleins! Isn't that worth giving him the healing balm of your acceptance?

Kiley offers a lot of do's and don'ts for anyone involved with a Peter Pan, and for parents of potential Peters (don't you wish that you could go back in time and hand this to his mom and dad?). Of course, the biggest "do" is to leave him and let him solve his own damn problem, but if you insist on trying to make it work, take off your Mommy halo, read this book, follow Kiley's advice, and stop letting your Peter Pan manipulate you.

Women Who Love Men Who Hate Women Who Love Men Who Hate Women . . .

We women must've had it bad for those bad boys in the mid-1980s, because suddenly several books on the phenomenon were driven to the top of best-seller lists. There was *Women Who Love Too Much* (1985) by Robin Norwood: thousands of women recognized themselves in Norwood's gut-wrenching stories of women who enslaved themselves to someone who was clearly bad news. Norwood promised that we weren't crazy or stupid for turning into obsessed martyrs. There was hope, she claimed, as long as we worked a 12-step program and admitted we couldn't break our "addiction" to bad boys all on our own. Histrionic? Yes, but it sure struck a chord.

Then came *Men Who Hate Women and the Women Who Love Them* (1986) by Susan Forward, which devotes most of its pages not to understanding the roots of nasty male behavior but to developing your personal plan for regaining sanity, pride, and peace of mind—a crucial foundation for women caught in abusive relationships who need to get out. But it didn't discuss why there were so many misogynists in the dating pool. And finally, there was *Smart Women, Foolish Choices* (1985), by two men (Connell Cowan and Melvyn Kinder) who urged women to get real about their expectations of men. We were intimidating the good ones and conning ourselves into believing that

continued . . .

we could change the bad ones, the authors warned. We had to forget about "marrying up," that is, finding men who could make more money than we could—and at the same time we had to accept that many men would be intimidated by the fact that we made as much or more than they did.

Really, it seemed we couldn't win. And in retrospect, a lot of those 1980s experts' advice sounds far too ominous and ridiculously nonconfrontational— 12-step programs don't address practical tactics, like throwing his stuff in the hall and changing the locks. But just what was going on? Had we women collectively developed the same deep-rooted psychological problems, or were we picking up on an insidious cultural message: that we'd better stop being so picky if we ever wanted to get married? And couldn't it be that the jerk-to-nice-woman ratio was way off?

Maybe our main problem was that we were just a little too lonely and/or horny for our own good. Didn't we women who loved too much all know deep down that it wasn't *him* we were nuts about, but the *idea* of having a lover or husband? Suddenly, we were grappling with a new and scary concept: that we might have to learn to enjoy our lives without having a significant other for a long stretch. We wanted to get married someday to a wonderful guy, but along the way we wanted someone to have and to hold for a while, until something better came along. Or maybe we panicked and married quickly lest we find ourselves turning into one of those lonely old ladies with a houseful of cats.

What many of us came to realize was that a woman who dates a jerk *can* find herself a terrific man and never go back to bad boys. We decided that being with someone just for now wasn't such a terrible thing. And we discovered that it helps a lot to just get pissed off, write him a scathing letter, compose a vicious rock 'n' roll song about him, evict his sorry ass, and go out with our girlfriends and celebrate our freedom. ▪

Pearls from the Patriarchy

Regarding Ambition

Lack of understanding is a great power. Sometimes, it enables men to conquer the world.

—Anatole France

Feel slightly, think little, never plan.

—Benjamin Disraeli

Whenever a friend succeeds, a little something in me dies.

—Gore Vidal

■ *A Clockwork Orange* (1962)
by Anthony Burgess

Me me me. How about me? Where do I come into all of this? Am I like just some animal or dog? . . . Am I just to be like A Clockwork Orange?

A Clockwork Orange is a vividly brutal depiction of the can of worms we pop open when we decide to reform a bad, bad boy.

The hero of Burgess's novel, Alex, is a violent, homicidal, drug-addicted sociopath who steals, rapes, maims, and kills for pure enjoyment. But somehow we forgive him—almost love him—because he accomplishes his craft with artistry, because he's misunderstood at home, and because he harbors a deep and abiding passion for Beethoven. Oh, and he has a boyish grin . . . And a dimple . . . And he wears a codpiece.

In this novel, society attempts to reform this unreclaimed and terrifying enfant terrible with a refined musical sensibility by strapping him in a chair, propping open his eyelids, and administering a nausea-inducing drug played over montages of misbehavior under-scored by Beethoven's "Ode to Joy."

While these medieval methods are partially effective and Alex never again resorts to arbitrary violence and always remembers to take out the garbage and do his dishes, he also gets sick to his stomach every time he hears his beloved Beethoven, and thus what is truly special and beautiful about Alex is extinguished along with his annoying bad habits.

Read this book the next time you're contemplating a systematic brainwashing to re-form your juvenile offender. It might give you some creative ideas—although if you're considering ipecac and involuntary snuff flicks as an option, you ought to be real careful about choosing your soundtrack.

Points to Ponder

1. *Why is the loss of Alex's love of Beethoven in this novel considered a loss to the world?*

2. *What is the metaphorical significance of a codpiece?*

Notes from Bev's Reading Journal

I was introduced to *A Clockwork Orange* by the very first bad boy I ever dated. He was the first of many and set a pattern that was to haunt and frustrate most of my ro-mantic life. . . . But he wrote his love letters with such artistry, he was misunderstood at home, and he held a deep and abiding passion for Marcel Duchamp. And yes, he had a boyish grin—but no dimple. And I don't remember a codpiece, but you can see where *A Clockwork Orange*'s amoral aesthetic can lead you.

To be truthful, I'm not sure Burgess had a dysfunctional relationship between a good girl and a bad boy in mind when he penned *A Clockwork*

continued . . .

Orange. But when you think about it, a bad boy's relationship with society isn't much different from his relationship with his girlfriend or his wife.

Despite their rich latent potential, clockwork oranges like Alex scoff at helpful suggestions, defy explicit instructions, and ignore ultimatums just for the fun of it. And if we take our cues from Burgess's novel, the only way to get through to these committed bad boys is to equip ourselves with a full-service medieval torture chamber and a good selection of highly sophisticated psychotropic drugs. And even then, at best, our efforts at reform will result only in tragedy. In the 1986 Norton edition of the novel, Burgess included a final chapter in which a reformed Alex, who has grown up, now finds senseless violence boring and is ready to settle down, but I'm not buying that. The message of *A Clockwork Orange* was plenty clear to me, even then, although I didn't heed its warning. *A Clockwork Orange* taught me that while we may, through extreme and pornographic measures, manage to impose our will and transform a bad boy's behavior, we do so only at the risk of offending nature and giving birth to perversion. ▪

Pearls from the Patriarchy

Regarding Women

I hate women because they always know where things are.
—James Thurber

I must not write a word to you about politics, because you are a woman.

—John Adams

In point of morals, the average woman is, even for business, too crooked.

—Stephen Leacock

Women are like elephants to me; they're nice to look at but I wouldn't want to own one.

—W. C. Fields

On one issue at least, men and women agree: they both distrust women.
—H. L. Mencken

I have a tendency to get really drunk and then I get to the hotel and I'll pick the first chick that I can get . . . you'd be surprised at some of the chicks I've picked up. . . . What you do is to go up to the room and just drink till they look good.

—Slash

Women have more imagination than men. They need it to tell us how wonderful we are.

—Arnold H. Glasgow

■ *Men Are from Mars, Women Are from Venus* (1992)
by **John Gray**

When a man grumbles it is a good sign—he is trying to consider your request versus his needs.

It sure sounds simple, doesn't it? Men are one way, women are the opposite, and a few basic behavior changes will end the battle of the sexes once and for all. No wonder *Men Are from Mars, Women Are from Venus* has sold more than eight million copies in hardcover, making it the most influential book of the 1990s. Yes, with a few "advanced relationship skills," the worst male-female dynamic can be fixed, and the most emotionally frozen male can be thawed like some perfectly preserved Cro-Magnon from the Alps—brought back to life and suddenly, inexplicably, able to spout key supportive phrases like "Gee, sounds like you had a terrible day, honey" on cue.

Problem is, fixing your relationship, like most home-improvement projects, turns out to be a lot more complicated and expensive than originally planned. Men, says Gray, need the freedom to say no. So even if he hasn't done the dishes since Bob Vila first began renovating *This Old House*, you have to be willing to nicely ask, "Would you help me with the dishes tonight?", accept his "no" with grace, and refrain from, say, hurling a salad plate at his head. You must also listen to his rumblings and grumblings about your requests and not give in to seething silently or asking, "Ya got a problem with that, buddy?" If you are resentful, Gray says, you should work through your feelings by writing a "love letter" to him that ends with "but I forgive you." If this sounds rather like using bubble gum to patch that huge crack in the foundation of your house, *Men Are from Mars* will probably just make you a hell of a lot testier than you already are.

On top of that, careful readers will note that should you not fit into Gray's black and white world and identify more with the opposite sex's way of processing stress or taste in leisure activities (hatred for shopping is clearly some sort of Venusian birth defect), his advice gets awfully fuzzy.

Still, if the male/female dynamics Gray describes fit your relationship (and the older and more conservative you are, the more likely it is that you'll find yourself a purebred Venusian), his advice actually does work. Yes, you've got to undertake a major renovation project on Hubby's attitude, but Gray is full of acknowledgment of women's strength and competence, and he calls for us to allow men to do for us, even if their efforts seem inept or incompetent. And there's something empowering about being told that men really do respond better to simple, direct commands than they do to long-winded, roundabout ways of asking them to do something. Frankly, we've been confidently barking out orders to the men in our lives a lot more often since reading *Men Are from Mars*, and we are pleased to announce that it actually results in action on their part. A pop psych book that can help a woman get a man to modify his behavior, even on the smallest of scales? No wonder it's a smash hit.

Points to Ponder

1. How the hell did we end up on Venus?

2. What happens if your passport incorrectly states "Citizen of Mars"? Hey, is there a supervisor you can talk to?

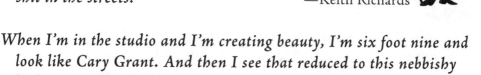

Regarding Self-Image

I'm a Sagittarian—half man, half horse with a license to shit in the streets.
                              —Keith Richards

When I'm in the studio and I'm creating beauty, I'm six foot nine and look like Cary Grant. And then I see that reduced to this nebbishy little guy with a double chin.   —Billy Joel

A man without a woman is like a neck without a pain.
                              —Anonymous

■ *Secrets About Men Every Woman Should Know* (1990) by Barbara De Angelis

Well, in case you haven't figured it out yet, the aliens have landed and are living among us—they're called "men."

Men, the final frontier. We women boldly go forth and try to forge relationships with them, but though we have all spent countless hours discussing their every nuance with our girlfriends, for all our budget psychoanalysis, they still remain a total mystery. Like peeing in the snow—is that some sort of primitive marking instinct? And why can't he sit with his back to the door in a restaurant? Is he afraid the James Gang is going to come in and do a quick draw before he can turn around? And can someone explain the Three Stooges thing? 'Cause we're not getting it.

Barbara De Angelis doesn't answer all of these eternal questions, but she does clue us in to a lot about what men want and why they act the way they do. They have a hard time thinking and acting at the same time, which explains why he can't discuss your vacation itinerary when he's tinkering with the carburetor, even though you can formulate Plan B while packing, cooking dinner, braiding your daughter's hair, and watching the Weather Channel. Men are brought up to feel they are responsible for fixing things, which is why he won't just take the car in to the dealership and have it checked out before you hit the road for the weekend. And men equate their self-esteem with accomplishment and expertise, which is why he can't bring himself to admit he has no idea how a carburetor works in the first place.

Armed with this info about the male species, we should be able to build fulfilling relationships with them without making ourselves crazy trying to figure them out—yeah, *should* be able to. In real life, De Angelis has been married and divorced several times over, including once to relationship expert John Gray (hence the overlap in their books—the jury's out on who came up with the different planets metaphor), so apparently we cannot assume that knowing how men operate makes it easy to work with them. Kind of like knowing how gravity operates doesn't result in our being able to counteract it.

Just as you may find that you have to reconfigure the dilithium crystal processor before you are permanently stranded in a time-space continuum, you can't get a man to notice, act, and efficiently follow up just because you've told him a thousand times over to get a tune-up and alignment. Training a husband to modify his behavior or express his emotions clearly is a science women have yet to master. With books like this to clue us in, however, we have a fighting chance of attaining the relationship we desire—and getting to the summer cottage without having to call AAA from the cell phone.

▪ *Waiting to Exhale* (1992)
by Terry McMillan

"The ones that are good for us we find dull and boring, like Michael, for instance, and then we pick the assholes, like Russell, the ones who won't cooperate, the ones who offer us the most challenge and get our blood flowing and shit. Those are the motherfuckers we fall in love with."

—Robin Stokes in *Waiting to Exhale*

In Terry McMillan's *Waiting to Exhale*, four friends join a charitable group dedicated to enhancing the status of black women in the community. Unfortunately for them, they all need to learn to take the old adage "charity begins at home" to heart, because each one is a poster girl for dysfunction.

If black men come off as jerks in this book, which many reviewers and readers complained about, the women come off as fools for putting up with them. Somehow, no matter where they look, the men they find are plain old bad news (except one, of course, who redeems his entire gender).

But how perfect do we want our heroines, really? Don't we all find ourselves doing stupid things, like considering—or even having—affairs with married men? Or trusting our man to the point that we don't have a clue whether our names are on the bank accounts or what his true assets are? Or sleeping with a man whose breasts are larger than ours because, well, he's available and we haven't been laid since Whitney Houston just wanted to dance with Miss Demeanor? At the heart of *Waiting to Exhale* is the story of girlfriends who support each other even though they are inwardly groaning at each other's stupidity and naïveté. Because, of course, a true friend is one who will listen to you dissect your latest pathetic relationship and interject things like, "No! I can't believe he did that!" even though of course she's warned you that that's exactly what he'd do. Even if your girlfriend does drive you nuts sometimes, you listen patiently because you know that next time it'll be you sailing down the river of denial.

Frankly, for all that the four friends in *Waiting to Exhale* can seem ridiculous or desperate or badly in need of a reality check, there's something empowering about reading a story in which, however badly the men behave, the women never get so caught up in their lovers' little psychodramas that they lose their sense of self. These women are holding out for the best before they kick back, relax, and exhale. And if he doesn't show up, it won't be the end of the world—an incredibly soothing message when you've gone out with every loser in the book.

Points to Ponder

Whose neurotic behavior bothers you more, your man's or your best girlfriend's?

Doomed But Inspired Heroes

■ *No One Here Gets Out Alive* (1980)
by Jerry Hopkins and Danny Sugerman

To be a poet meant making a commitment: to embrace the tragedy fate has chosen for you and fulfill that destiny with gusto and nobility.

It is often said that the more things change, the more they stay the same, and that's true for bad boys. The nineteenth-century conception of the bad boy was the tragic figure of the romantic poet who pushed the envelope of sensation with wine, women, and verse. But take off the tragic poet's ruff and waistcoat, slap on a pair of snakeskin hip-huggers, and put a tambourine and a microphone in his hand, and you've got today's quintessential representation of the bad boy—the rock god.

Nowhere is the image of the rock 'n' roll outlaw more opulently and rhapsodically illustrated than in *No One Here Gets Out Alive*, Danny Sugerman's biography of rock's tragic poet, Jim Morrison.

continued . . .

Right from the get-go, Sugerman makes us aware that we are not in the presence of a mere mortal. Sugerman draws Morrison as a modern-day Pan, a ballad-singing Bacchus, making use of the ritualistic powers of backbeat, and a very good pipe organ, to set the souls of his audience free. In the introduction alone, Sugerman discusses Morrison as an embodiment of the myths of Dionysus, Persephone, Bacchus, Orpheus, Mithra, Antinous, Adonis, and Pan, and likens his artistic contributions to those of Nietzsche, Plutarch, Artaud, Blake, Aristotle, Rimbaud, Van Gogh, Baudelaire, Huxley, Coleridge, Sartre, and somebody called Saint John of the Cross.

Now, we like Jim Morrison and all—and we understand that he was a really good rock singer, with the soul of a poet and a very sexy pair of leather pants, who died tragically before his time from a chronic desire to rearrange the senses. So we can understand the Arthur Rimbaud parallels. And we get the thing about Blake and Huxley and *The Doors of Perception*. And we suppose, given Morrison's mythic appetite for the fruit of the vine, that the Bacchus allusions ring true. But Aristotle and Nietzsche—and Saint John of the Cross? Hello.

Clearly, women are not the only ones who are just a little bit giddy over the specter of the rock 'n' roll outlaw. Truth be told, men are more head-over-heels in love than women with the lyrical leather-clad rock star, pushing the limits of experience with the force of his passion, a really good haircut, and those amazing hip-huggers.

In this sense, *No One Here Gets Out Alive* is a source of valuable insight because it gives us a bird's-eye view of the mechanism that allows men to elevate bad behavior to the level of the divine through the power of poetic imagery, classical allusions, Homeric references, and an epic capacity for alcohol.

Every aspect of Jim Morrison's life in this book is gilded with mythic resonance. An unfortunate encounter with the back end of a truck full of migrant workers becomes a metempsychotic visitation with the spirit of a shaman. Falling off the stage drunk at the Hollywood Bowl becomes a cathartic ritual

continued . . .

designed to loosen the primitive soul of the universe. Jim's not drunk, he's Dionysian. Jim's not ill-tempered, he's iconoclastic. Jim didn't drop out of school, he embarked on a spiritual journey into the dark heart of chaos.

Every time Morrison gets a hangnail in this biography, it somehow ultimately tugs at the delicate web of life. Given the pervasiveness of this brand of alchemy, which transmogrifies the crude metal of self-destructiveness into gold, it's easy to understand how our own bad boy's refusal to secure some visible means of support can seem like a counterculture stance that will ultimately bring about a revolution of the collective unconscious and a revitalized connection with the soul of the universe.

But you know, the truth is, it probably won't.

Tragic poets are called tragic poets for a reason. Basically, they're tragic. And just like comedy, tragedy is not pretty.

Jim Morrison wasn't really a beautiful young Bacchus, spilling his young blood on the ancient earth in order to revitalize the life-force, reaffirm the eternal cycle of death and regeneration, and ensure the bounty of the coming harvest. Jim Morrison was just a guy looking for love and understanding who never found it and died drunk, bloated, and unhappy in a bathtub at twenty-seven years of age.

It's apparent that even a bad boy disciple like Danny Sugerman has had to wrestle with the way Jim Morrison died in order to try to find its mythic meaning. He falls on a whole gallery of ancient mysteries and Nietzschean circumlocutions about pity and terror and the eternal joy of becoming, and affirmation and negation. Well, it takes a lot of classical allusions to transmogrify such a bleak conclusion.

Jim Morrison, like Achilles before him, made the hero's choice. He opted for a brief but glorious life instead of a long and unremarkable one. This is the Hellenic version of "Live fast, die young, and have a good-looking corpse," and I've never been a proponent of the Judeo-Christian and distinctly masculine worldview that exalts suffering and condemns longevity. I have always felt

continued ...

that there should be a few other options. I'd like to make this eternal true-or-false conundrum a multiple-choice question. What's wrong, for instance, with a long and heroic life? Why do our heroes have to be tragic in order to be relevant? Why do we have to suffer to be beautiful? Why do we have to die in order to live?

Jim Morrison didn't die from an excessive thirst for life or death. He died from an excessive thirst for bourbon. And while it's a wonderful thing to say yes to life in all of its many forms and to expand the horizons of our experience, when it came to the eighty proof, I think Jim should have found a way to just say no. If he had, who knows, he might have found a way to get out of there alive. ■ —B.W.

Pearls from the Patriarchy

Regarding Peace and Love

Like, peace and love, motherfucker, or you're gonna die!
I'm gonna kick your ass if you fuck with my garden.
—Axl Rose

Chapter 4

When You're Ready to Make Your Own Kind of Music: Hearing-Your-Inner-Voice Books

For a lot of us, the end of the rainbow keeps getting further and further away. We are so busy struggling through our formative years to achieve the goals that society has set before us—career, marriage, children, beauty, brains, perpetual youth—that we can become deaf to the tiny voice within that is asking if this is really the dream trip we signed up for. Until we can tune out those external voices with all their demands and tune in to our authentic selves, we will find ourselves on a cruise to nowhere.

If you've arrived at the end of the rainbow and found that the pot of gold is made out of fourteen-karat tin, these hearing-your-inner-voice books can help you to slow down, take a deep breath, and hear what your heart is telling you.

▪ *A Tree Grows in Brooklyn* (1943)
by Betty Smith

Miss Garnder handed her the "sordid" compositions and the play, saying, "When you get home, burn these in the stove. Apply the match to them yourself. And as the flames rise, keep saying: 'I am burning ugliness. I am burning ugliness.' "

We suspect there are a lot of Francie Nolans in the world—you know, the kind of girls who assign themselves noble tasks like reading all the books in the local library from A to Z and who then wait in vain for the librarian to notice their diligence. Like Francie, many psychologically precocious teenage girls see the fears and insecurities that adults try to hide underneath a façade of confidence and cruelty, and they get the message, loud and clear, to pretend that what you see is what you get. Then they become either Junior Leaguers or junior nihilists.

But part of growing up is coming to understand that we all have to embrace both the darker *and* the lighter sides of life. You've got your Wynonna Judd and you've got your Nico and the Velvet Underground, and there's room on the CD rack for both.

The choice to see the truth in all its complexity is at the heart of Betty Smith's *A Tree Grows in Brooklyn*. The heroine, Francie, is the apple of her father's eye. Johnny Nolan is a charming and handsome Irish waiter with a tenor to die for, but he's not exactly a practical money manager, and he's a little too friendly with the whiskey bottle. Francie's mother, Katie, is a sensible and hardworking janitor, whose infatuation with dreamers and artists has grown as cold as her tenement in winter. Caught between the world of imagination and harsh reality, Francie chooses to write about joy, beauty, and hope, putting a positive spin on the life of the poor Irish in pre–World War I Brooklyn. But when her beloved papa freezes to death on the street, drunk and unemployed, Francie's writing gets a little, well, Sylvia Plathian.

The new, edgier Francie is chastened by her teacher, Miss Garnder, loses her way, and gives up writing altogether. It's only when she begins to come to terms with the end of her childhood and the beginning of her womanhood that she can imagine herself writing again, expressing a truth that is neither simplistically bright nor self-consciously dark but comprising many tones and hues.

Many of us discovered *A Tree Grows in Brooklyn* back when we were teens—it's a classic coming-of-age tale—but we'll bet that if you reread it at a time in your life when you're having trouble connecting to your authentic self, it will resonate even more for you. That's because Francie represents a commitment to one's inner voice, a voice that, if we're not careful, can be drowned out by the Miss Garnders of the world.

Points to Ponder

1. Was Keats right—is it true that truth is beauty, beauty is truth? And is beauty always pretty?

2. If you were a tree, what kind of tree would you be?

▪ *The Awakening* (1899)
by Kate Chopin

She turned her face seaward to gather in an impression of space and solitude, which the vast expanse of water, meeting and melting with the moonlit sky, conveyed to her excited fancy. As she swam she seemed to be reaching out for the unlimited in which to lose herself.

What happens to a married woman who yearns to savor the freedom of independence and the passionate embraces of an illicit lover, and yet is forced by social convention to deny her feelings or lose all? Will she risk losing her position, custody of her children, all her friends, and her husband, who is her sole means of financial support? What choices lie before a fallen woman? Aside from throwing herself on the train tracks or disappearing into the ocean depths, that is.

Thank goodness those days are over! A century after the publication of *The Awakening*, it's a given that passion invites recklessness, and that recklessness can be a really cool thing. Nowadays a woman who explores her sexuality outside the confines of proper behavior for ladies not only doesn't have to lose all, she can capitalize on her fall from grace through movie and book deals; arrange a Barbara Walters interview designed to reconstruct her public image, thereby maximizing profits from subsidiary projects; and utilize the services of a good PR person to maintain her visibility in an increasingly saturated celebrity market. At the very least, flouting social mores and revealing sexual indiscretions can lead to a trip to the big city and fifteen minutes of fame on a talk show, with all hotel accommodations and plane fare covered. And if you're really lucky, you can get a makeover to boot (if the topic for the day is, say, "My momma's a hootchie and needs to get real"). Okay, so it's not as romantic as engulfing oneself in the vastness of the ocean, but it's a lot more fun, isn't it? And you get to live afterward.

In the pre–Jenny Jones era, though, women's options were a lot more limited, as Edna Pontellier discovered. Her sensual self is awakened one summer vacation on an island off of New Orleans. Then, brought to life by her experience of the waves, the sun, and the flirtatious attentions of a young man, she realizes she has to find a way to redefine her life. As soon as Edna gets home, it's ship the kids to Grandma and Grandpa's, rent a room of one's own, dabble in oils, and start hanging out with bad boys and cantankerous musicians who are ruled by their hearts. Edna's husband is none too pleased with her new lifestyle, of course, but she clings to it as long as she can, until the inevitable moment occurs when she must climb back into her gilded cage or destroy any chance of a place for herself in the world.

A century ago, the fact that Kate Chopin offed her heroine, rather than allow her a happy ending with a suave lover and a darling bungalow populated by an array of fascinating friends, wasn't enough to satisfy critics or her St. Louis neighbors. Her novel was shunned, her name scratched from dinner party lists, and poor Kate never wrote another novel, shamed by the scathing criticism of those uptight Victorians. But thanks to feminists of the 1960s, who recognized that Edna Pontellier's dilemma has been experienced by women all over the world throughout the ages, *The Awakening* was rediscovered and given its due at last. Modern-day readers may chafe at Chopin's unwillingness to let Edna spread her wings and fly, but let's be honest—isn't death in the service of orgasm a lot more provocative?

Read this when you're feeling trapped by everyone's expectations of you.

Points to Ponder

Have you ever been awakened by an encounter with nature? And what did you do once you got back home?

Literary Heroines We'd Like to Go Bar Hopping With

Nora in Glenn Savan's novel *White Palace* is a middle-aged, not particularly striking, and extremely sloppy White Castle waitress, who wins the heart of a young, handsome, wealthy, and impeccably accessorized ad exec named Max Barron. Without lifting an unmanicured finger, Nora convinces this upwardly mobile man-about-town to choose her gritty, unvacuumed world of genuine feeling over his thoroughly Dustbusted and sterile reality. Any literary heroine who can elevate fading youth and deplorable housekeeping habits to the level of a sexual goddess is definitely somebody we'd like to bring along when we're slumming it in the dive bars downtown and in the mood to get dirty.

Scarlett O'Hara in Margaret Mitchell's *Gone with the Wind* is a pouty, spoiled, and self-involved daughter of the antebellum South, whose epic sense of entitlement is the only part of Dixie that refuses to be driven down. Plus, she's a boyfriend-stealer. But we'll take Scarlett along when we're pub crawling on a budget, because with that southern belle charm of hers, and that seventeen-inch waist, she's probably good for a lot of free drinks.

Moll Flanders, Daniel Defoe's prison-born heroine, has an astonishing ability to reinvent herself—from orphan to eligible bachelorette to vulgar rich woman to whore to landed gentry. If there's one thing Moll could lead us to, it's a new adventure. But we'd prefer to go hopping with her when she's on one of her financial upswings rather than her running-from-the-cops phases. We just hate to leave a bar before we've finished our drink.

Bridget Jones, Helen Fielding's neurotic British thirtysomething plagued by an eccentric mother, a string of sexy but elusive boyfriends, and a social life filled with uptight Brits in ugly sweaters, may beat her head against the wall after counting up the calories the next day, but we know she'd be a hoot and a half telling us all about her fresh hells. ■

■ *Revolution from Within* (1992)
by Gloria Steinem

Empathy is the most revolutionary emotion.

Feeling put upon? Carrying the whole world on your shoulders? Tired of trying to change the laws of physics, captain? Thinking that it's time to turn your energy inward and recharge your batteries before you sputter to a halt? If so, this is the book for you.

When Gloria Steinem first published *Revolution from Within*, the general critical consensus was that America's most famous feminist had gone soft. Okay, maybe that's not the best metaphor to use when discussing a book written by a woman. Anyway, the critics' ridicule of Steinem's focus on self-esteem sure sounded like some cranky male authority trying to dictate how a proper activist ought to conduct herself. You've got to wonder whether those accusations of having gone all squishy in the head would've been hurled at her if she were male. After all, Steinem always claimed the personal was the political, so why all the fuss about her addressing the issue of personal power? Was this just another case of guys squirming when some woman starts to talk about feelings? Or had Steinem gone Marin County on us, trading in her intelligent insights for platitudes about hugging trees and tuning in to higher vibrations?

Listen, you can take the gal out of Toledo, but you can't take Toledo out of the gal. Steinem is at heart a sensible midwesterner. You won't find advice here about carrying around teddy bears in order to symbolically nurture the wounded inner self. You also won't find any jargony talk about "being in process" or avoiding "shame parfaits." She just writes in a straightforward way about how real political change can come about only when the downtrodden recognize their own complicity in their oppression and raise the level of their self-esteem. Without a sense of rightful entitlement, she says, no one, man or woman, will find the courage and perseverance to fight for their rights.

So what's with the histrionic backlash against self-esteem? What are we all supposed to do, prove our humility by scraping our heads against the sidewalk? Now, it's true that there are a lot of annoying Stuart Smalleys in the world, who equate self-discovery with self-indulgence and reduce great truths to insipid, pedantic free-form poetry that makes that 1960s shellacked-plaque classic "Desiderata" look like a Shakespearean sonnet. And we can sympathize—to a point—with conservatives who break out in hives at the very mention of the self-esteem movement, which reached its height of absurdity in California when improving self-esteem became part of school curricula. There *is* something unsettling about kids spending their limited classroom time reciting simple-minded affirmations of their specialness and being praised to the heavens for successfully existing. Talk about lowered standards.

But unlike those William Bennett types who claim that a few good licks with a hickory stick will build the kind of character that will allow anyone to overcome anything, Gloria Steinem understands that, for large numbers of people, achieving the great American dream, or for that matter, any dream whatsoever, starts with the basic perception that you deserve to achieve it. We don't have to be worker bees, as men traditionally have been, divorced from our emotions. We also don't have to be submissive and afraid to claim our place in the world, and men don't have to become emasculated. Gloria explains how we can develop core self-esteem through such empowerment exercises as forming consciousness-raising groups, communing with nature, or dancing wildly in our living rooms with the CD player cranked to full blast. Then, once we've become unstoppable forces, we'll be able to take on the patriarchy, abolish our exploitative economic system, reinvent human interpersonal dynamics, replenish our exhausted ecosystems, and reject linear and hierarchical thinking.

Girlfriend, count us in!

Points to Ponder

1. Who told you you could?

2. Who told you you couldn't?

3. What's your preferred method for jump-starting your self-esteem?

Learn to say "No"; it will be of more use to you than to be able to read Latin.

—Charles Haddon Spurgeon

Books to Be Thrown with Great Force

▪ *On Your Own* (1985)
by Brooke Shields

On Your Own by Brooke Shields, America's favorite pretty baby turned Princeton coed turned earnest yet awkward canceled-sitcom star, is a guidebook for college girls attempting to negotiate independence for the first time. This is an unusual launch point for a book that focuses mainly on the proper angle to place your mirror while applying mascara and how to avoid putting on the "freshman fifteen." Brooke seems to feel that independence is little more than learning how to maintain a hyperscrupulous beauty regimen even though you've finally freed yourself from the control of an autocratic and unyielding parent who is used to making a bundle on your good looks.

If we take it from Brooke, our landmark rite de passage is to learn how to say no to everything that even remotely smacks of a good time. We must say no to staying up late, no to pimples and bloat, no to rebellion against an overly invasive and dysfunctional parent, no to matte foundations, drugs, sex, and rock 'n' roll, and most important, no pizza or chocolate ice cream—ever.

But don't despair, being on your own Brooke-style does let us say yes to some things. We can say yes to daily exercise, to fruits and vegetables and poached fish. We can open our pores with a steam bath, or close them with a splash of ice water, and every so often, on a very, very special occasion, we can say yes to one glass of champagne.

One wonders, after reading this book, how Brooke managed to come of age at all, because, as we all know, exploring our own independence means breaking a few rules so that we can establish a new order that makes sense for us.

continued ...

But Brooke's reflections of a codependent daughter masquerading as a coming-of-age tome can't be blamed entirely on her. Once again she's only doing what she was told, by a parental publishing company and an obedient, adolescent public, who perennially confuse the siren song of celebrity with the voice of authority.

Read this one the next time you need to be incited to launch a personal revolution. ■

■ *Out of Africa* (1932)
by Isak Dinesen

When the Gods want to punish us they answer our prayers.

Jilted by her paramour, Danish aristocrat Karen Blixen, the heroine of Isak Dinesen's saga *Out of Africa*, finds herself without any marriage prospects and in danger of a future populated with all the earmarks of Victorian spinsterhood: social isolation, limited financial means, and failing health. Rather than accept the meager lot appointed to unmarried Victorian ladies, Karen strikes an unorthodox bargain with her lover's brother and moves to Africa to start a dairy farm.

But as with most best-laid plans, things don't turn out quite as Karen had expected when she trades her civilized life in Denmark for the wilds of Kenya. For one thing, the dairy farm suddenly becomes a coffee plantation. And her lover's brother–turned-husband, whom she had hoped would at least provide some amicable company, winds up spending most of his time on lengthy hunting expeditions into the heart of the African savannah, without sending even so much as a postcard to alleviate Karen's isolation. Karen, however, gives up the need for a man's protection and sets out into the rich tapestry of turn-of-the-century Kenya, finding love, meaning, and self-fulfillment on her own terms. And then of course there's the Aryan god Robert Redford played in the movie, who drops by from time to time.

If you're feeling claustrophobic and have been daydreaming about trading your nine-to-five job and bungalow in the 'burbs for a farm in Africa at the foot of the Ngong Hills, then Isak Dinesen's *Out of Africa* is the book for you. This lyrical account of her safari toward self-actualization will set even the most hypercivilized heart beating to an unfettered African rhythm.

Me, Myself, and I

It is ironic that the one thing that all religions
recognize as separating us from our creator—
our very self-consciousness—is also the one thing
that divides us from our fellow creatures. It was a bitter birthday
present from evolution.

—Annie Dillard

People often say that this or that person has not yet found himself. But
the self is not something one finds; it is something one creates.

—Thomas Szasz

You have for company the best companion you will ever have—the
modest, defeated, plodding workaday self which has a name and can
be identified in public registers in case of accident or death. But the
real self, the one who has taken over the reins, is almost a stranger.

—Henry Miller

▪ *Backlash* (1991)
by Susan Faludi

Although the backlash is not an organized movement, that doesn't make it any less destructive. In fact, the lack of orchestration, the absence of a single string-puller, only makes it harder to see—and perhaps more effective. A backlash against women's rights succeeds to the degree that it appears not to be political, that it appears not to be a struggle. It is most powerful when it goes private, when it lodges inside a woman's mind and turns her vision inward, until she imagines the pressure is all in her head, until she begins to enforce the backlash too—on herself.

Many of us keep getting the feeling that no matter what our personal and professional successes may be, we are supposed to be miserable, driven mad by our biological clocks, and longing to quit our jobs and make homemade yogurt while raising babies out in the boonies. And we're supposed to be furious at the feminists for ruining the great deal we women had for lo those many centuries. *Huh?* We don't think so.

Backlash strikes a resounding chord with many of us who may feel occasional pangs of disappointment but are basically happy with the choices that feminism has provided. True, the more choices you have, the harder it is to figure out what you want for yourself and the easier it is to live in the land of regret, but few of us are ready to take a giant step backward into the barefoot-and-pregnant, feminine-mystique, give-me-Librium-or-give-me-meth days. If anything, we have listened to our hearts and are now ready for the real gains of feminism, which, frankly, we thought were going to come along a little more hastily. Where are all the men who do their half of the housework and child care without prompting and who celebrate our successes instead of being threatened by them? Where are the day care and birth control options? When will we make as much as our male counterparts, dollar for dollar? And dammit, where are all the size twelves come Presidents' Day sale?

Our search for bread *and* roses—that is, social and economic parity as well as reasonably priced, comfortable clothing that looks really cute even if you're a little broad in the beam—does sometimes preoccupy us. But despite what our inner voices say, the media and all their experts seem to insist that we're all man hunting and baby hungry. We are unhappy and resentful, they say, and kicking ourselves for not settling down and popping out puppies back when we had a chance—back when we didn't even need a shelf bra in our bathing suits, much less an underwire. We are old maids—and ready to string up Gloria Steinem and her ilk.

Oh, hardly. So where did this crazy idea come from? Well, like many lies, it is rooted in truth. We career women do have our lonely moments, days when we are convinced the grass is greener on the other side of the fence. And then we baby-sit our nieces and nephews for the weekend and get a reality check.

But the main source of this pervasive lie, that women regret feminism, comes from the media, which pick up on our fleeting insecurities and blow them up to poster size. Reviewers of *Backlash*, who may have lacked the time to trek through a 460-page tome and seem to have closed the book before finishing the introduction, claimed that Faludi blamed this backlash against feminism on some sort of male conspiracy. In fact, Faludi says that a backlash is the typical reaction of large groups of people who feel change is happening a little more quickly than they can digest. Her portrayal of self-appointed social experts—journalists, writers, activists, and sociologists such as Camille Paglia, Betty Friedan, and Warren Farrell—whose personal baggage makes their advice and interpretations highly suspect—is particularly revealing and a great reminder for us to kill our Buddhas.

Now, it's true that *Backlash* is overly long and dated in some ways (does anyone really care about the impact of the movie *Fatal Attraction* anymore?). And Faludi just plain doesn't get it when it comes to working 12-step programs or secretly wearing sexy underwear, both of which some card-carrying feminists have found empowering. But she understands that there is often a chasm between the media interpretation of women's feelings and what's really going on in our hearts and heads. If you're struggling to balance your life and are feeling guilty about the choices you've made, *Backlash* will help you get those pundits and alarming magazine articles out of your head so that you can hear your own voice.

Notes from Nancy's Reading Journal

■ *Rebecca* (1938)
by Daphne du Maurier

*I was too young for Maxim, too inexperienced,
and more important still, I was not of his world.
The fact that I loved him in a sick, hurt, desperate
way, like a child or a dog, did not matter. It was
not the sort of love he needed.*

When I was going through my awkward and invisible stage somewhere in my twenties, I became completely sucked in by *Rebecca*, the story of a wallflower who, once she is able to muster up her dignity and develop a little confidence, triumphs over the perfect woman.

Now, if you haven't read *Rebecca*, the most curious thing about the story is that the narrator, the main character in the book, is so insecure, so overshadowed by the powerful persona of Rebecca (her husband's former wife) that she never even reveals her name. As someone who changed her surname twice in her twenties, and considered changing her first name too, I recognized the significance of du Maurier's choice to leave her narrator anonymous. Without a name that one can embrace and say loudly and clearly, we forever wander about the west wing of our lives, wondering how the hell to get back to the front room.

In *Rebecca*, "the girl," who has no family, no friends, and no life, quickly seizes the chance to marry a man with a title, a position, an estate, and self-hood, a man who looks a lot like Laurence Olivier in his prime with that perfect pencil mustache and a raised eyebrow that just sends me (okay, okay, that was the movie—but in the book, Maxim is still pretty hot). She spends

continued . . .

the first year of her marriage trying desperately to please him and to live up to her notion of how the mistress of Manderley ought to behave. What sort of sauces ought Cook prepare with tonight's meal? Is it okay to light a fire in the morning room in the afternoon? And what's with Mrs. Danvers, the omnipresent, omniscient, and omnivorous head servant who floats down the hallway and speaks of Rebecca as if she were Mother Mary?

Somehow, when I was in my twenties, these questions seemed not so far from those I asked myself daily: Can I carry off miniskirts, or will I look like I'm still in high school? How do I exude confidence when I am utterly directionless? Will my adult acne go away before I start getting laugh lines? And will I ever stop dreaming about being locked out of my childhood home? "The girl," like me, had no one in whom to confide her anxieties and feelings of ineptness. And also like me, she tried her best, but no matter what she did, she always ended up making major social blunders.

When I first read *Rebecca*, I thought the novel ended happily. I overlooked the airless, lifeless marriage the girl ended up with, and the fact that we never do learn her name. I now think that what Daphne du Maurier was trying to say to us was that when women's choices are limited to society's constricted vision of the good girl and the bad girl, there are no happy endings. We have to come to terms with our whole selves and embrace both the good girl and the bad girl within. Only then will we find ourselves comfortable occupying the Manderleys of our own lives. ▪

▪ *Roots* (1976)
by Alex Haley

As if Kunta were sleepwalking, he came creeping slowly back up the driveway—when an African remembrance flashed into his mind, and near the front of the house he bent down and started peering around. Determining the clearest prints that Kizzy's bare feet had left in the dust, scooping up the double handful containing those footprints, he went rushing toward the cabin: The ancient fore-fathers said that precious dust kept in some safe place would insure Kizzy's return to where she made the footprints.

When we are unaware of the forces that shaped us, it's very hard to chart a life path for ourselves. When we don't know who we are or where we came from, we are so discombobulated that we don't know whether we're facing east or west, uptown or downtown, much less how to get to our lunch date without having to trust some cab driver who wants to take a shortcut through the warehouse district. So we remain frozen in time and space, wishing we'd paid more attention in Girl Scouts to finding our way out of the woods.

Some of us figure it out pretty quickly, but others have to do a lot of exploring before they discover enough about themselves and their place in the world to be able to move forward. It took Alex Haley the bulk of his middle years—and cost him a marriage—to discover his source. But driven by what some would call an obsessive need to research his ancestors, he made discoveries that paid off big time not only for him but for all Americans as well. *Roots: The Saga of an American Family* was a huge cultural force in the 1970s, first as a bestselling book and later as a wildly successful miniseries. It unleashed a flood of genealogical searching. Suddenly, we all wanted to know where we came from, whom we belonged to, what we were a part of. All right, some of us had to accept the reality that our family trees yielded nothing more exciting than a few Bulgarians and a Swedish nobleman who emigrated in a hurry after he knocked up the maid. But at least we didn't feel quite so isolated.

For African Americans, *Roots* was an especially powerful book, because the vast majority of them have ancestors who survived the excruciating and violent ordeal of being taken prisoner, strapped to a plank in a ship for months during an ocean voyage, stripped of their cultural identity, and enslaved with no hope of ever seeing family and homeland again. How can any African American help feeling enormous pride about her ancestry after reading this book?

But as anyone, black or white, who reads *Roots* discovers, even the most iconoclastic individuals belong to something larger than themselves: a family. When we explore our family histories, we discover the roots of our talents, our temperaments, our flaws, our dreams, our inability to follow directions. Missing pieces of ourselves fall into place, and we find that the unsettled feeling that has haunted us has dissipated. We've come home. Don the kente, whip up the fruit soup, and celebrate, baby.

Now, *Roots* is a long book, but don't let that discourage you, because it's a richly woven tale. Even if your own family's past does not include life on the dark continent or being involved in that "peculiar institution," read this when you're feeling disconnected, and you'll find that the story of Kunta Kinte, who refused to surrender his heritage, his identity, or his culture, even though these treasures cost him dearly, will inspire you to reclaim yourself.

Points to Ponder

1. Who is your family?

2. Who are you?

The Writer's Life

America is no place for an artist: to be an artist is to be a moral leper, an economic misfit, a social liability. A corn-fed hog enjoys a better life than a creative writer, painter, or musician. To be a rabbit is better still.

—Henry Miller

There never was a good biography of a good novelist. There couldn't be. He is too many people, if he's any good.

—F. Scott Fitzgerald

Writers are really people who write books not because they are poor, but because they are dissatisfied with the books which they could buy but do not like.

—Walter Benjamin

*Every secret of a writer's soul, every experience of his life, every quality
of his mind is written large in his works.*

—Virginia Woolf

■ *Silent Spring* (1962)
by Rachel Carson

*Those who contemplate the beauty of the earth find reserves of strength that will
endure as long as life lasts.*

If you are feeling like destiny has lost your phone number, bear in mind that a lot of
times divine callings arrive when we least expect them, and history is often made in the
most unlikely places.

Rachel Carson, for example, was a shy biologist who worked for the U.S. Department
of Fisheries penning pamphlets about trout and stuff. In her free time, she waded in the
tide pools of New England and wrote about what she saw there. Destiny, however, was
not put off by the smallness of Rachel's life, and at fifty-five years of age, while suffering
with breast cancer, Rachel Carson published *Silent Spring* and became the mother of the
modern environmental movement.

Published in 1962, *Silent Spring* documented the devastating effects of DDT on the
natural world and questioned the government's indiscriminate use of the pesticide.
Carson's poetically logical account of the vulnerability of nature suggested that human
beings are an inseparable part of nature and first introduced the idea of ecological balance
into popular culture.

Silent Spring created a lot of hubbub when it was published, and the chemical compa-
nies called Rachel Carson everything from a spinster to a crackpot in order to discredit
her in the eyes of the American public. But Rachel's romance with the natural world,
which she expressed so compellingly in *Silent Spring*, won out over the bottom line, and
Silent Spring became an instant bestseller.

Now, we realize that a literary summary of scientific evidence about the bad behavior of a pesticide doesn't exactly sound like a day at the beach. When you're in the midst of an identity crisis, you don't really want to sit around reading stuff about brittle eagle shells. You've got bigger problems.

Or do you? When it feels as if the universe begins and ends with your problems, *Silent Spring* is a good reminder that there's something out there bigger than we are, that there's beauty all around, and that life has a way of resolving itself—as long as you don't poison the groundwater.

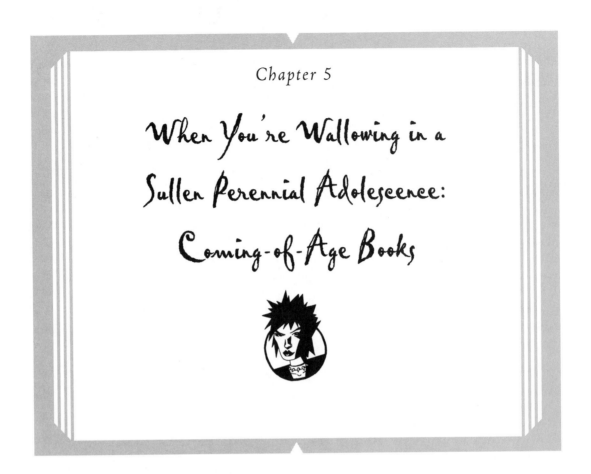

Chapter 5

When You're Wallowing in a Sullen Perennial Adolescence: Coming-of-Age Books

Adolescence is more than a sudden onset of hormones coupled with a compelling need for braces and a good reliable antidepressant. Adolescence is a state of mind that flares up, like a case of emotional acne, for the rest of our lives.

Although we have to live through physical adolescence only once, we go through spiritual and emotional puberty all over again each time we make a major change in our lives. Divorce, a career change, and having a baby are just a few of the times when we experience growing pains on the way toward emotional maturity. While the process of adolescence is not always pretty, it ultimately leaves us with a new set of life skills and a stronger sense of confidence and independence.

So whether you're poised on the cusp of womanhood, experiencing that first magical premenstrual bloat, or going through one of those phases when you're beginning a new life's chapter and feeling a little awkward, angry, or misunderstood, these perennial adolescent classics will put you in touch with the eternal teenager within and help you come of age.

■ *Go Ask Alice* (1971)
by Anonymous

Then I talked to Alice, who I met sitting stoned on a curb. She didn't know whether she was running away from something or running to something, but she admitted that deep in her heart she wanted to go home.

Nowhere are the perennial eruptions of adolescence more searingly portrayed than in the diary of a teenage girl known only as Anonymous, who plunges into a series of addictions, first to french fries, then to boys, then to class-one narcotics, and ultimately dies of an overdose of all of the above. Despite the "is this fact or fiction?" controversy that surrounds the book, millions of women, spanning the generations and the globe, have resonated to the teenage tribulations of this quintessential pubescent.

Not all of us respond to *Go Ask Alice* in the same way. Many interpret its message to mean that any step off the straight and narrow will result in being locked in a closet during an acid flashback, while garish mood lights flash and a supersynthesized 1970s theme wails disconsolately in your head. After reading *Go Ask Alice*, this camp generally vows to live flawlessly clean lives and to just say no. Others used Alice's adventures in the counterculture of cool as a springboard into an extended experimentation with handmade beaded jewelry, hallucinogens, and the Jefferson Airplane at full volume.

Whatever your feelings about beaded jewelry and mood-altering substances, however, Anonymous speaks to the perennial adolescent in us all. *Go Ask Alice* is a compelling and inspiring reminder that if you can make it through adolescence, you can make it through anything.

Points to Ponder

1. After reading Go Ask Alice, *do you find yourself just saying no or asking "Anybody got any mushrooms on them"?*

2. Is Anonymous really Alice, or an adult with a right-wing moral agenda and a total lack of appreciation for acid rock?

■ *The Bell Jar* (1963)
by Sylvia Plath

> To the person in the bell jar, blank and stopped as a dead baby, the world itself is
> the bad dream.   —Sylvia Plath

There's nothing like a little sardonic patriarchal imagery to satisfy the dark appetites of inner female teenagedom. And nobody does sardonic patriarchal imagery like the high priestess of the interior female wasteland, Sylvia Plath.

The Bell Jar is the autobiographical tale of a young and talented writer who goes to New York on a five-month scholarship to work at *Mademoiselle*. While in New York Esther encounters most of the landmark coming-of-age experiences that we all have to face: building a professional wardrobe, working for a living, figuring out what to order at a bar . . . oh, and having sex for the first time.

In every instance, Esther's rites of passage result in unparalleled horror, not to mention pure disillusionment. This is a great book to read when you're in the midst of an emotional goth phase, reveling in the beauty of the night, because Sylvia is the real deal. She dwells in a perpetual darkness, and there is no dawn at the other end of her poetic midnight. This stuff is a masochist's caviar.

Reality Check: On February 11, 1963, Sylvia Plath, a casualty of perennial adolescence, killed herself with cooking gas at the age of thirty, just three months after the publication of *The Bell Jar*. But her character Esther lives on, bearing brave, brilliant, and breathless witness to the terrifying beauty of emerging womanhood.

Notes from Bev's Reading Journal

I first read Sylvia Plath's *The Bell Jar* while living with my parents in the foothills of Boulder, Colorado. It was a beautiful bedroom community sheltered in the cleavage of the Front Range, and our house had been built by the coach of the 1972 U.S. Olympic ski team. It was rumored that the whole team had lived there, and the bar in the family room downstairs was papered with a blow-up photograph of Olympic skiing star Spider Sabich mid-slalom. We had a view of the whole Boulder Valley from the floor-to-ceiling living-room windows, and no room in the house was perfectly square. I had my own bedroom, my own sauna, and a horse in the backyard. . . . But I was fourteen, so it was hell.

I, like Sylvia Plath's Esther, was a goddess of despair. All of creation disappointed me, and that included my horse and the sauna. It did not, however, include the Spider Sabich bar. I always got a real kick out of that. I imagined that my bedroom had been his, and the night that Claudine Longet shot the Spider, I swore I felt his presence in the room. But that's the thing about us teenage goddesses of despair—our suffering is pregnant with romance and motivated by a voracious, albeit perverted, appetite for the richness of experience.

This is perhaps what made *The Bell Jar* so irresistible to my pseudo-pathological teenage palate. I, and many teenage goddesses of despair like me, pretended a dispassion that we did not actually feel. Our contempt was skin deep, but Sylvia was the real deal. She was walking on the bottom of the oceans, exploring abysses that we as merely despondent teenagers could only dream about.

Read this when you're scuttling across the floors of silent seas and remember, *it's only teenage wasteland.* ■

▪ *The Outsiders* (1967)
by S. E. Hinton

I lie to myself all the time, but I never believe me.

If you're struggling unsuccessfully to appear in control even as you're careening down the expressway of life straight into an emotional guardrail, then this is the book for you. *The Outsiders* is a study in the art of looking cool, which, as anyone who has ever worn facial glitter, teetered around on platform shoes, or pierced a body part can tell you, is a very exacting science.

The world of *The Outsiders* is divided into two distinct camps, with two distinct and opposing philosophies about what is, and what is not, cool. For the greasers, the guys on the wrong side of the tracks, cool is all about long hair, leather jackets, and Brylcreem. For the socs, the privileged jocks from the right side of the tracks, cool is all about the dry look.

As one would expect, the socs and the greasers go together like oil and fire, and this tonsorial antipathy ultimately results in a conflagration that engulfs both camps, and incinerates the protective trappings of apathy and false bravado that divide us from each other and from ourselves.

Okay, so plotwise this book didn't exactly reinvent the wheel. But it does make you feel a whole lot better about being a geek.

 Reality Check: S. E. Hinton, the author of *The Outsiders*, a seminal male coming-of-age tale, was a sixteen-year-old girl.

 ## Points to Ponder

What was cool when you were a teenager? Were you cool? Are you cool now? If you answered yes, who told you that, and what were they smoking at the time?

■ *Diary of a Young Girl* (1947)
by Anne Frank

It's really a wonder that I haven't dropped all my ideals, because they seem so absurd and impossible to carry out. Yet I keep them, because in spite of everything I still believe that people are really good at heart.

How many of us began confessing our souls to our journals when we were teenagers? No one—not our mothers, our fathers, our sisters, or our best friends—could possibly understand us, probably because we were confident one minute and brooding the next, passionate on Tuesday afternoon and disdainful by dinnertime. We needed to be close to Mom and Dad one moment and a hemisphere away from them the next. Hey, even *we* couldn't keep up with our moods. No wonder our parents were a wreck.

Poor Anne Frank not only had to deal with the turbulence of adolescence and ever-changing needs for privacy and intimacy, she had to do it within a confined space that she shared with seven other people, including four strangers. Now you can understand why she was spending so much time with her diary—who wouldn't go stir crazy being cooped up in a room with Mom, Dad, and a perfect older sister for two solid years?

Anne, like so many of us, found solace in journaling. She wrote of the daily trials of hiding out from the Nazis, of the course of the war, of her longings to walk in nature again. She wrote about her anger at her mother and her guilt at pulling away from her, of her disappointment with her father, and of her crush on Peter, the teenage boy who lived with the Franks in the Secret Annex. ("Peter has taken possession of me and turned me inside out; surely it goes without saying that anyone would require a rest and a little while to recover from such an upheaval?") She wrote of adult hypocrisy, and of her own dreams for moving beyond the limited world of her mother's life—of having a career as well as a family. And she wrote about her hopes for the future, when, she believed, the madness around her would settle and she could step out into the sunshine and start constructing a new life.

Well, we all wish Anne's optimism had been warranted. But unlike most girls who fill books with their pubescent musings and gushings, fearing and yet sometimes secretly hoping that someone else will read their words and pronounce them writers of the highest merit, Anne actually did have her diary published, albeit posthumously. And reading

Anne Frank's diary, we come to appreciate the intensity with which all of us feel and dream when we are in an adolescent transition. Her optimism puts us in touch with our own and makes us realize that even if life takes us in a completely different direction from what we expect, we still have a choice about our attitude. And when we choose to embrace what is instead of what isn't, then no matter how small our lives may seem to the outward eye, no matter what happens to those dog-eared journals, we create a legacy of spirit.

Mystifying Morsels from Tween-Age Goddesses

Regarding Sex, Drugs, and Rock 'n' Roll

I have these really bad mood swings too, and I thought that if I stopped eating sugar they would go away, but they didn't. I had a serious ice cream habit, a serious ice cream problem. . . . I used to be able to eat people under the table.

—Juliana Hatfield

As far as I'm concerned, selling marijuana is one of the most respectable things anyone can do. I think everybody should smoke it, because it teaches you a lot about yourself.

—Sinead O'Connor

■ *The Catcher in the Rye* (1951)
by J. D. Salinger

If you really want to hear about it, the first thing you'll probably want to know is where I was born, and what my lousy childhood was like, and how my parents were occupied and all before they had me, and all that David Copperfield kind of crap but I don't feel like going into it if you want to know the truth. In the first place, that stuff bores me, and in the second place, my parents would have about two hemorrhages apiece if I told anything personal about them.

Thus begins the story of old Holden Caulfield and his lousy escapades living in some cheap goddamn hotel and dealing with all the phonies and crap in crumby old New York. And never has the monosyllabic marshland of male adolescence grunted more compellingly than in Salinger's modern-day fable.

The Catcher in the Rye reads like a guy's version of *The Bell Jar*. Holden, like Sylvia Plath's Esther, is disgorged from school and left to wander the mean streets of New York in search of genuine feeling in the artificial world of adulthood. And Holden, like Esther, never finds it.

Despite the in-your-face, distinctly male first-person voice of Salinger's narrator, many of us iconoclastically inclined perennial adolescents will really resonate to the message that is at the core of this novel—kids are the genuine article and all adults are phonies.

Generally speaking, we perennial teenagers don't like adults. Adults are an embodiment of the journey's end, and to many of us our parents' final destination didn't look quite like the utopia we had in mind. It was less Shangri-La in May than Boise in February, and many of us have thought very seriously about getting off the developmental train before reaching the destination of maturity. This, at any rate, is Holden Caulfield's solution.

If you're in a phase where you're feeling like a disgruntled idealist, and are reluctant to let go of the past in order to embrace an uncertain future, then read *The Catcher in the Rye* and celebrate stagnation. Through Holden we can revel in the thought of pulling the emergency handbrake on the railroad of our own development and, for a few moments anyway, experiencing the bliss of maturational stasis. But it might be wise to make sure, before you do, that there aren't any fast-moving trains approaching from behind, or you, like Holden, might risk permanent derailment.

Notes from Bev's Reading Journal

A lot of my friends read *The Catcher in the Rye* as
teenagers and aspired to become Holden. I, however,
didn't so much want to become Holden as to love him
and protect him, just as his little sister did. I aspired
to be Phoebe.

Holden Caulfield is the prototype male misfit, the
ur–bad boy. He's surly, unpredictable, misunderstood,
injured, and savagely intelligent. He's adrift in a world that has bitterly disappointed him, and constantly under siege because he doesn't know how to ask
for love properly. He tries to appear tough, but in actuality, like a horseshoe
crab, underneath the spikes of his protective plate, he's soft and painfully vulnerable. Holden feels superior and inferior all at the same time, displays
nothing but contempt for social norms, and wears a goofy hat. This sounded
like a teen god to me.

But the problem is, Holden never grows up. He chooses instead, in the
end, to live off the fat of his sister's uncomplicated, presexual devotion and her
prodigious piggy bank. In other words, the resolution that Holden finds is
stagnation. And while *The Catcher in the Rye* is certainly an attempt to energize
adulthood with the vitality and integrity of youth, it also begs a very important
question—a question that I didn't ask myself when I read the book as a teenager, but that for me now is perhaps the central question of the novel.

Phoebe, Holden's little sister and the embodiment of his purest ideal, is
unequivocally the heroine of this story. She's smart, self-contained, beautiful,
willful, and uncompromising. My guess is that Phoebe would go far in
this world. I wonder, though, what happens when the engine of Phoebe's
development slams into Holden's stalled caboose.

What happens, in other words, when sweet, pure, devoted, presexual little
Phoebe is ready to grow up? ▪

■ *Lisa, Bright and Dark* (1969)
by John Neufeld

Naturally we talk about everything in the world from civil rights to sex. And movie stars, and hippies, and free love, pot, potato pancakes, and Paul Newman; the Doors, censorship, Sly and the Family Stone. Strobe lights and see-throughs, Ethel and her kids, Paul Newman, Mia Farrow, the Iron Butterfly, and Paul Newman.

Lisa, Bright and Dark is a cautionary tale about the value of friendship, the importance of attentive parenting, and the inherent lunacy of teenagedom. Lisa Shilling is sixteen years old and knows she is losing her mind. But her parents think that she is faking, despite the fact that she is either exuberantly loquacious or morosely silent, and that her wardrobe vacillates wildly between black matte and luminous pastel.

Even when Lisa starts employing more method performance techniques, like using her forearm as a pincushion or walking through plate glass windows, she still can't get her parents to acknowledge the obvious—nobody can be Farrah Fawcett-Majors one day and Edie Sedgwick the next, and still be said to be sane, even if she is a teenager.

In response to the tenacious denial instinct in the adults around them, three of Lisa's friends, each in her own way a shining example of wholesome, psychologically simplistic, distinctly unadolescent young womanhood, form a therapy group to cure Lisa of her perilous pubescence. And because this is a 1950s-style morality play, unmuddied by the pregnant waters of psychoanalytic theory, Lisa is restored to a normal, french-fry-eating, Paul Newman–loving teenager through the love of her friends, the cooperation of her parents, and a yearlong stay at a rest home upstate.

Despite the naïveté of *Lisa, Bright and Dark*, which plays like a dated *Beverly Hills 90210* episode—and defines bipolar depression in terms of a lack of fashion consistency that can be solved in forty-five minutes not including commercial breaks—there is something important at work here. This is a great book to read when we're vacillating wildly between light and dark ourselves, because it's a reassuring reminder that no matter the mercurial extremities of our current spectrum, with just a few short months upstate and a few 1970s-style parenting techniques, we too can be restored to our normal appetites and once again crave empty calories and Paul Newman. Phew!

Mystifying Morsels from Tween-Age Goddesses

Regarding Priorities

There are cities with arugula, and cities without arugula. I just can't live in a city without arugula.
—Cindy Crawford

What I have to say is far more important than how long my eyelashes are.
—Alanis Morissette

Plucky Prepubescents We'd Like to Invite to a Tea Party

So many of us started reading in earnest when we were barely out of single digits and were inspired by heroines who taught us that tomboys can triumph and brainy girls have more fun. We're still in awe of the following power page girls.

Nancy Drew

Whether wearing athletic shoes (in her current incarnation) or sensible heels (back in her blue roadster days in the 1930s), Nancy showed us that intelligence, curiosity, and bravery are not just the domain of adult male heroes. We'd love to pick up more tips from her on getting out of dilemmas like being in the path of a speedboat or locked in the trunk of a car, all the while maintaining the affections of loyal Ned Nickerson for most of a century.

continued . . .

Harriet M. Welsch

While we'd prefer to prepare the sandwiches for our little get-together (we're not too keen on tomato on white), we'd love Harriet the Spy to come along and remind us to trust our instincts and value our own perceptions. We just wish she'd share some of the dish she's got recorded in her notebook.

Jo March

In *Little Women*, Jo taught us two key lessons: (1) tomboys who are more interested in writing adventure novels than attending formal dances end up living the most interesting lives, and (2) when long hair is all the rage, a low-maintenance bob is a delicious statement of freedom. We figure she'd be a fascinating conversationalist over tea and biscuits.

Pippi Longstocking

Pippi Longstocking, the redheaded Swedish latchkey kid with the perpetual bad hair day, is a girl who just wants to have fun and knows how to do it—skipping school, staying up late, and washing the kitchen floor with scrub-brush skates strapped on her feet. Pippi believes that rules were made to be broken, which puts her at the top of our guest list.

Mary Lennox

Mary Lennox, the heroine of *The Secret Garden*, at first sight seemed an unlovable spoiled brat, but we came to realize that, just like ours, Mary's contrariness could be soothed by spending hours upon hours in a lovely, hidden-away English garden. Mary teaches us the secret of rebirth, and we know she's got the perfect spot in mind for our chamomile and cookies—next to the azaleas.

continued . . .

Sarah Crewe

Sarah, the princess in *A Little Princess*, may seem like a goody-goody with her preternaturally regal bearing, but we're amazed by her self-possession and her ability to spin fantastical stories. Definitely an entertaining guest.

Anne Shirley

Anne of Green Gables is, let's face it, a weirdo, but she's just the kind of weirdo that we'd love to hang with. She's refreshingly honest, totally in the moment, downright Buddhist in her appreciation of the little things, and in awe of the magic of life. She'll cure any traces of cynicism before you can say "two sugars please."

Charlotte the Spider

Normally we'd prefer not to have insects invading our turf, especially spiders, but we'll make an exception for Charlotte of *Charlotte's Web*. She's the perfect nurturing, maternal pal, and she has a way with language too. We'd be thrilled if she'd spin a little web for us, although the afternoon's motto, "Carpe diem sistah friend," might be a little too exhausting for her.

Claudia Kincaid

Given her organizational, planning, and budgeting abilities, we'd like the heroine of *From the Mixed-Up Files of Mrs. Basil E. Frankweiler* to do the shopping and menu planning for our little party (although we won't ask her where she got the money to buy all the goodies). Then Claudia can kick back and discuss art with us—we'd be particularly interested in her observations about Michelangelo's sculpting.

continued . . .

Caddie Woodlawn and Laura Ingalls

Both of these pioneer girls from pre–Barbie's Dreamhouse days know how to have fun in the natural world, whether picking berries or finding secret swimming holes. Because they live in a preconsumer age, they are so enthralled with the world around them that they can make the simplest things, like a Christmas orange, seem magical, and our Mattel- and Ideal-cluttered world seems pale by comparison. We'd not only invite Caddie and Laura, we'd lend them some twenty-first-century duds to replace those nineteenth-century button-up dresses and shoes they both loathe.

Ramona the Pest

Any girl who can manage to get suspended from kindergarten because of her bad, bad ways is always welcome at our tea parties.

Eloise

It's always useful to have somebody around with connections at the Plaza, and a charge account with room service. ■

Pearl of Perennial Adolescent Wisdom

Sometimes you have to look with the eyes of a teenager if you want to see what's really going on.

Notes from Bev's Reading Journal

▪ *Zen and the Art of Motorcycle Maintenance* (1974) by Robert Pirsig

The study of the art of motorcycle maintenance is really a study of the art of rationality itself. Working on a motorcycle, working well, caring, is to become part of a process, to achieve an inner peace of mind. The motorcycle is primarily a mental phenomenon.

I first read *Zen and the Art of Motorcycle Maintenance* in my junior year of high school. My math teacher, Jim, assigned it as required reading for algebra lab (I went to one of those 1970s-inspired "experimental schools"). Anyway, Jim was ahead of his time. He was the very first cybergeek—sort of like Bill Gates with a Dan Fogelberg haircut and John Denver glasses—and he had this adorable mole just below his left nostril that almost made logarithms tolerable. Almost.

Jim explained to us, in hushed, reverent tones, that *Zen and the Art of Motorcycle Maintenance* was the instruction manual for a new world order, where the classic and the romantic, the technical and the natural, truth and illusion, the 1970s and the 1980s, would finally find harmony, balance, and peaceful coexistence.

Whatever this may have meant, it sounded good to me. I dove into *Zen and the Art* expecting a major reality shift. Hey—I was fifteen, okay? Anyway, I did fine with the parts about life being about the journey and not the destination. I liked thinking about my life as one long road trip, and I adored antithesis and sustained ambiguity on general principle. But I think my whole class started to run into a little trouble with the motorcycle metaphor.

continued . . .

For one thing, it was an all-girls school, and somehow changing spark plugs on a vintage Harley just didn't resonate for us as a restorative communion with the divine soul of the universe. Then we hit the part about a priori as opposed to experiential knowledge, and the roadside analysis of Kant's *Critique of Pure Reason*, and it began to look a lot like what it was—a guy thing.

Jim wasn't entirely misguided, though. He had evidence to suggest that his experiment might work. Even though it was all girls, my high school was a fertile breeding ground for Pirsig's science of ambiguity. The place was a sink of contradictions.

I went to a boarding school that was nestled at the foot of Pike's Peak and housed in a gold-rush-era mansion that was an exact replica, in miniature, of the Grand Trianon in Versailles. I know . . . and it gets better. . . .

My child developmental psychology classroom, appropriately, was called Versailles. All the rooms had names. Versailles bordered the Terrace Room, which had a view of the fountain and held a chandelier that was said to have once belonged to Czar Nicholas II. It was chipped and somewhat lopsided and the wiring was bad, but it captured my imagination and added a spark of romance and mystery to Piaget's theory of cognitive development.

So, inherent in the very structure of my school was the union that Pirsig had postulated—a marriage of the romantic and the scientific. And here it was, perfectly realized in a broken-down but elegiac old chandelier that intermittently illuminated the pages of my psychology textbook.

Despite the Gilded Age motif of my school, the curriculum was rustic. Outward Bound was a required course, and nobody graduated until she had camped in the woods solo for three days and three nights, equipped only with a tent, a rain poncho, a lamp, a tin of hot chocolate, a copy of *Zen and the Art of Motorcycle Maintenance*, Thoreau's *Walden*, and a few bags of gorp.

But despite the fertile nature of the environment, and that adorable mole on Jim's upper lip, Pirsig's great experiment failed, at least where I was concerned. Not only was I a hopeless mechanic, but to this day I do not

continued . . .

drive. I developed mono to get out of the solo wilderness experience, and it took me four full years to get through algebra. I barely graduated.

And I suspect that I wasn't alone. Because as far as I could tell, the sum total of Pirsig's pop culture movement nationwide was a generation of journey- as opposed to destination-oriented travelers, who could never quite decide where they were going but who nevertheless knew how to change their own oil. I don't know, but I don't think this is what Pirsig, or Jim, had in mind.

Despite the fact that the arguments at the core of *Zen and the Art of Motorcycle Maintenance* went soaring right over the heads of a generation gone intellectually flabby with excess, free love, and far too many Fleetwood Mac hits, the book left skid marks across the highway of my adolescence that are discernible to this day.

Thanks in part to *Zen and the Art of Motorcycle Maintenance*, I am able to see my life as a journey to be enjoyed, I can endure chaos in the service of a better order, and I can entertain ambiguity. I'm also proud to say that while I still have not completed an oil change, I have successfully installed a new motherboard in my computer, a machine to which I have grown passionately attached. I'm not sure, but I think my math teacher Jim would be pleased. ■

Points to Ponder

1. *Do you change your own oil, and if so, why?*

2. *Do you characterize your worldview as scientific or romantic?*

3. *Just what the heck is a priori knowledge anyway?*

Mystifying Morsels from the Popular Dialogue

Regarding Dreams and Ambition

I want to get a house someday, and I want to have a room set aside, a totally empty room for smashing things.

—Juliana Hatfield

In high school I took an aptitude test that said I was ninety-eight percent guaranteed to be a mechanic.

—k. d. lang

I feel if I were to organize it correctly, I would try to sing like a Mexican and think like a German. I get it mixed up sometimes, anyway. I sing like a Nazi and I think like a Mexican and I can't get anything right.

—Linda Ronstadt

I won't be happy until I'm as famous as God.

—Madonna

A Horse Is a Horse, Of Course, Of Course

What is it about adolescent girls and horses? When we're in that hormonally fueled nether realm between presexual passion and puberty, there's no experience quite like straddling a great heaving beast and driving him on at heart-racing speeds with a gentle touch of a crop on his neck and the pressure of our thighs, until he breaks into a sweaty lather  and his mouth begins to foam. And then afterward the slow walk home to cool off, the currycomb across his chest, and that mane, combed into submission and fanned out across that slick, strong, graceful neck like a coarse flaxen waterfall. And then later, after dinner, curling up under the sheets with a flashlight and one of the horsy classics in this sidebar, and then falling asleep and dreaming of adventures atop our fiery, powerful, magnificent stallion.

There's no question that a breathless canter through the honey heather atop a valiant literary steed is the next best thing to the real deal, and it doesn't require relationship skills, auxiliary power, or putting up with his mother.

Black Beauty (1945)

by Anna Sewell

What kind of a person could ever be mean to a horse? Especially Black Beauty, an elegant carriage horse who was the apple of his beloved first master's eye? But life and the treatment of animals being what they were in the nineteenth century, Black Beauty is sold by accident into a fleet of cab horses and is cruelly mistreated and overworked, until he is rescued and restored to his former glory by a kind and loving family. Aside from the

continued . . .

sadomasochistic psychosexual implications, this book is a heartwarming reminder that even the most magnificent stallions need love and a good stable family life.

National Velvet (1935)

by Enid Bagnold

Velvet Brown, a fourteen-year-old girl living in pre–World War II England, forms a lifelong friendship with an untamed piebald horse. Velvet wins her horse in a raffle and in spite of her family's skepticism—they think that the horse is a commoner and a rube—Velvet puts the Pie through his paces. In the end, she exposes a diamond in the rough when she rides her steed to victory in the Grand National steeplechase. Read this one when you need to remember that even the most mangy of mounts can be a champion with a little loving attention and a good currycomb.

Misty of Chincoteague (1947)

by Marguerite Henry

If one horse is good, how about a whole herd of wild ponies that still roam the marshy grasslands of Chincoteague Island? Phantom, the wildest mare on Assateague Island, has eluded capture for years. But Phantom's a single mom now, and she's got to give up her wild ways and settle down. She has a foal to think of, after all. And so Phantom relinquishes her freedom to two children, Paul and Maureen, and settles down in a nice paddock in the suburbs. Okay, so it's a far-fetched morality tale, but it's nice to know that a Freudian archetype can end happily ever after once in a while, isn't it? ▪

Chapter 6

When the Mom Tapes Are Looping and You Can't Find the Eject Button: Mother Issue Books

There you are, standing proudly and competently at the helm of your own life. You've braved the open ocean, explored foreign and exotic lands, and emerged unscathed and victorious, a well-seasoned and competent mariner in the vast sea of life. Then just when you're ready to head full-tilt for your home port and some much-deserved rest, that critical inner mom voice kicks in and takes all the wind out of your sails.

No matter how old we are or how far we've come, even if we're mothers ourselves, sometimes we feel we aren't living up to what Mom expected of us—that is, to what we *think* Mom expected of us. Reading the books in this chapter can shed some light on our mysterious relationship with Mom, help us to understand where she's coming from, and hopefully lead us to discover that she's a lot happier with us than we thought. Hey, maybe that critical mom that we hear in our heads isn't actually her voice after all.

If the Mom tapes in your mental cassette player are reminding you to finish your vegetables and get married already instead of congratulating you on a job well done, read these critical inner mother tomes, and make peace with the mom within—and the real mom without.

■ *Divine Secrets of the Ya-Ya Sisterhood* (1996)
by Rebecca Wells

That old-lady sedan came with my second baby. I had nothing to do with picking it out. It appeared in the driveway with a note from Shep, and I was supposed to say thank you. Didn't my husband remember my Jeep? Didn't he remember I was the queen of the road, roaring through the night with the Ya-Yas, my bare foot heavy on the pedal, my painted red toenails bright as the dials on the dash?

The Ya-Ya sisterhood is a group of zany southern women who, in the vein of *Steel Magnolias*, share tears, fears, and rollicking good times. And indeed, within *Divine Secrets of the Ya-Ya Sisterhood* you will find a message about how friends can save your life and your sanity. But the Ya-Yas' divine secrets go beyond how to band together and stage a small-scale revolution at a Shirley Temple look-alike contest, or how to bust a friend out of convent school, or how to mix the perfect martini. What you will find here is a message about mother-daughter dynamics that completely transcends regionalism, religion, era, and choice of beverage.

Reading Wells's book, many of us discover that our own mother is Viviane. She doesn't have to be Catholic or southern, or carry around Bloody Marys in a Thermos marked "cough medicine." But like Vivi, many of our moms remain a mystery to us. It isn't until we learn the secrets of their darkest days that we can truly appreciate how hard they had it, and how hard they tried to be good mothers to us.

At the heart of *Divine Secrets of the Ya-Ya Sisterhood* is a story about a woman, Sidda, who discovers that while we as daughters may never know all our mothers' secrets, nor their motivations, it's our job to find within ourselves the ability to forgive, and to have faith that if Mom could've been all that we needed her to be, she would've been.

Read this book when your mom's unreasonable and inexplicable behavior is making you nuts. Maybe you'll start looking at her in a more flattering light.

■ *My Mother, My Self* (1977)
by Nancy Friday

Whenever we come across this book at a thrift shop, a used book store, or on the street where someone has spread out a handful of rummage from well-used potholders to hardcover first editions of classic self-help guides, we notice one thing: The book seems brand new, as if no one had ever cracked the cover. Frankly, just the title alone is enough to send shudders of fear down the spine of all women. My mother, my self? AIEEEEEEE!!!!!

Now, of course, it's irrational to fear turning into one's mother, because it's inevitable. No one could have that much influence on you without your starting to sound or act like them after a while. So why fight it? And why is mutating into Mom such a terrifying thought for so many women?

Because, Nancy Friday says, we have this powerful need to differentiate ourselves from Mother in order to forge our own identity. Thus we want to claim to be nothing like her, even when we hear ourselves spouting words like "Do you think I need to bring a sweater just in case?" or cutting the end off a roast because that's the way Mom did it, only to discover that this family tradition started three generations back because Great-grandma's roasting pan was on the short side. It's a knee-jerk thing, this imitation of Mom.

Of course, most of us overcome our Electra complex eventually. We learn to accept Mom as she is and to smile at our mirrorlike behavior, and even to be proud of it. She's the one we have to thank for things like an appreciation for a good wool winter coat and the usefulness of matching Tupperware. She's the one responsible for our inherited ability to let the house go to pot and enjoy a good double matinee instead.

But it also seems that every mess we make in our lives and every hell we go through can be attributed to Mom. Okay, Friday admits, we can't actually *blame* Mom, as if she messed us up on purpose, but on some sort of deep Freudian level, Friday says, our entire karma can be ascribed to what Mom did or didn't do. Somehow, if she'd just been able to describe to us the intensity of orgasm, we wouldn't have ended up dropping out of college and getting pregnant by a would-be rock star with a cocaine habit. Reading this book, you get the distinct impression that somehow every sexual mistake we've ever made is attributable to Mom's inability to embrace her own sexuality.

Today, a lot of Nancy Friday's assumptions about mothers don't ring true for many of us. Certainly, there are entire generations of women whose moms were anything but asexual (see *Our Bodies, Ourselves*), which pretty much blows that cosmic climax theory out of the water. And most of us recognize that Dad often had a stronger influence on certain aspects of our selves, such as how we deal with our competitive drive, or our financial wheelings and dealings, or whom we decide to marry. But Nancy Friday's groundbreaking book does capture the essence of the repetition compulsion, of our inability to break out of textbook-case behavior when we have no insight into our parents' influence on us.

Read this when you want to explore that hard question: What is it about turning into Mom that makes me shudder?

Points to Ponder

1. Have you ever borrowed your mom's clothes? Has she borrowed yours? And do said articles of clothing have any red-wine stains that were passive-aggressively acquired?

2. Do you have any interest in discussing with Mom the intensity of your orgasms?

All women become like their mothers. That is their tragedy. No man does. That is his.

—Oscar Wilde

▪ *The Glass Menagerie* (1944)
by Tennessee Williams

Tennessee Williams's memory play about his emotionally and physically fragile sister who is shattered by the sledgehammer of her mother's disappointed expectations is a classic mom issue tale that has captivated glass-animal-identified daughters for generations.

Laura is a shy and rarified young girl with a limp that is not nearly as noticeable as her crippling self-esteem issues. Amanda, Laura's mother, is a former queen of the Delta with more gentleman callers than you can shake a jonquil at, who chose badly and married a telephone worker who "falls in love with long distances," which is a charming antebellum euphemism for abandoning his family. And her son Tom, based on Tennessee Williams himself, experiences his own version of the repetition compulsion by following in his father's footsteps.

Frustrated and penniless, Amanda looks to her limping, stammering, chronically nauseous daughter to attract a suitor who can rescue them from penury and despair. Of course, such a clear case of mother-daughter transference is a shoo-in for a dysfunctional holocaust, which leaves the entire family gasping amid the rubble of Amanda's broken dreams and Laura's fractured ego.

Despite its grim content, this is one of the most beautiful plays ever written, and it is one of the best depictions of how a toxic mother's love, when crossed, can very quickly become something else entirely. Read this one when your own mother's shattered expectations are giving you an emotional limp, and remember, sometimes those who live in glass houses still throw stones.

▪ *The Joy Luck Club* (1989)
by Amy Tan

"She bring home too many trophy," lamented Auntie Lindo that Sunday. "All day she play chess. All day I have no time do nothing but dust off her winnings."

She's impossible, isn't she? I mean, there's no pleasing her: You can't just play piano, you have to be a concert pianist. She's always blatantly fishing for compliments on her steamed pork and preserved vegetable dish, insisting that artificial flowers are better than real ones because they last forever, and asking why you can't be more like all her friends' daughters, who are always obedient, astonishingly gifted, and utterly perfect.

Of course, you know that somewhere, buried in your mother's past, is a poignant and moving story of how a spirited, innocent child got twisted around until she turned into the mysterious matriarch before you. Her priorities baffle you, and while Mom's pearls of wisdom sound great when you read them on a needlepoint pillow, they never seem to shed any light on why she's driving you bonkers, do they?

In Amy Tan's collection of interwoven short stories, four Chinese-American daughters come to realize that for all their mothers' annoying peccadilloes, deep down, Mom loves them more than she will ever be able to express. Reading the stories of how these women survived soul-annihilating experiences that faded into painful, secret memories is a good way to remind yourself that everyone's mom is a woman first, with a history that could make even her most irritating behavior completely forgivable—or at least understandable.

No matter how old a mother is she watches her middle-aged children for signs of improvement.

—Florida Scott Maxwell

■ *A Yellow Raft in Blue Water* (1987) by Michael Dorris

Michael Dorris's redemptive intergenerational mom saga *A Yellow Raft in Blue Water* features a mom who has a few annoying tics—like a chronically terminal disease that never quite kills her, a Percocet habit, and a predilection for disappearing for months at a time without leaving a forwarding address. But once we hear Mom's side of things, we understand that all her behavior springs from her love and concern for her teenage daughter.

Dorris's story begins with Rayona, the youngest member of a matriarchy of Native American women living on a reservation in New Mexico. Rayona, who is half black, struggles to come of age with her erratic, depressed, and terminally ill mother, Christine, who ultimately heads for the hills, leaving her daughter with an emotionally remote grandmother and a membership for a video club that she can't use.

Thus, Rayona is forced to negotiate reservation life, her own half-breed status, and the emergence of womanhood all on her own because her mother, Christine, couldn't hold her temper and had to tell her own mother to screw herself and stomp off like a teenager without thinking about the consequences.

Sound familiar? Okay, so maybe the mother-daughter conflicts in this book are a little more extreme than most, but we're all familiar with the lapses of maturity that occur when we come face to face with our mother issues.

Mothers, much like God, move in mysterious ways, and sometimes they do the darnedest things that leave us daughters standing in amazement, scratching our heads, and licking our wounds. But maybe if we could see things from Mom's point of view, we'd understand the method behind the madness. Maybe we'd understand that Mom is just doing what she has to do to survive.

This at least is the theory at work in *A Yellow Raft in Blue Water*. Through the narrative device that Dorris employs, we get to hear three separate accounts of the same story, and as we listen to each version, we begin to realize that what seemed like the inexplicable and cruel acts of an unconcerned mother are actually an expression of affection.

A reassuring message about the underlying goodness of motherhood.

The Fiercest Love

Now that you're a mom yourself, you're just a bit chagrined about all those complaints you used to make about your own mother, aren't you? You know the joys of colic and leaky diapers and shopping mall tantrums, not to mention the delights of living with a sullen and moody adolescent, and you're a bit more sympathetic. So why not try these books on being a mom, and get in touch with your own maternal instincts?

▪ *Not Without My Daughter* (1987)
by Betty Mahmoody

Back in the 1980s, nothing was a more resonant metaphor for a threat against the security of Mom and apple pie than those Iranians. They all

continued . . .

seemed to be patriarchal and fanatical, ready to kidnap, bomb, and terrorize innocents faster than you can say "Death to the Shah and American Satan!" No wonder Betty Mahmoody's memoir about trying to escape Iran and her abusive Iranian husband with her sweet little daughter was so compelling. Talk about Mom's worst fear—having a big bad evil daddy destroy the sacred bond between mother and child. Well, that and being stuck for weeks on end with your new in-laws and their atrocious housekeeping habits and intense resentment of you. Poor Betty Mahmoody had to sneak out of the house in the dead of night, outwit the police and soldiers, and climb the mountains to cross the border in order to ensure that she wouldn't lose her daughter to her evil ex-husband.

Read this when you're facing an afternoon with a half dozen second graders at Chuck E. Cheese—that'll seem like a minor sacrifice compared to Mahmoody's ordeal.

■ *The Good Mother* (1986)
by Sue Miller

It's an agonizing choice: eroticism or momhood. Sort of like deciding between a thrice-marked-down party dress that fits as if it were designed for you and the perfect pair of funky yet comfortable shoes. There's no compromise—you simply have to have both.

Anyway, like many of us, Anna Dunlap, a very, very good mom, focuses on her daughter's needs and works hard to provide a good life for her—to make up for the absence of Dad, who gave up custody in the divorce. But then who should show up in Anna's life but a charming painter who slips into her little family ever so perfectly—until she realizes that he's taken this family closeness thing a bit too far. Reading this one will churn up all those single-mom dating issues.

continued . . .

▪ The Broken Cord (1989)
by Michael Dorris

All right, so Michael Dorris was a father, not a mother. But in this memoir about raising an adopted son who suffered from fetal alcohol syndrome, Dorris beautifully and lyrically captures the highs and lows of being a parent, the fierce loyalty we feel toward our children, the pride, and the frustration—as well as the agony that rips us apart when they are suffering. Dorris tells the story of how he poured a father's healing love onto his son Adam, thinking that with enough determination, not to mention the right teachers and doctors, he'd be able to cure his son's seizures, learning disabilities, and extremely poor judgment. Instead, Dorris's journey took him in another direction, and he had to learn the hardest lessons we parents face: acceptance of our limitations and gratitude for who our children are—whoever they are.

Read *The Broken Cord* when you are ready for a sober look at what it means to be a parent.

▪ Reviving Ophelia (1994)
by Mary Pipher

"I'm not going to let fear rule my life again," she told me. "I'll stay and fight rather than run. Next time I won't pretend that my stomach hurts when my life is hurting."

Losing one's way in the woods of adolescence is pretty much a given in our culture, but Mary Pipher believes the journey toward womanhood is getting more and more treacherous for young girls. They can't seem to win—they're either too tomboyish or too girly-girly, too pretty or too ugly, "stuck up" or nerdy. And so begins the descent of formerly confident prepubescent

continued . . .

girls into the pit of self-loathing, where angst-filled young women writhe to the soundtrack of Fiona Apple while planning their next body piercing.

Pipher says we should blame most of these woes on our sexist society, which is holding girls to more and more impossible standards, whether it's airbrushed, underfed fashion models or Miss Americas who can carry off a swimsuit and spiked heels combo while spouting solutions to America's economic woes utilizing Keynesian economics. And along with the impossible physical standards to meet, girls today are also intimidated by the violence that threatens them, from harassment on the school bus to wackos with automatic weapons opening fire on the playground. No wonder they act out.

Even if you aren't a mom, check out *Reviving Ophelia* when you're feeling maternal. It will bring out the mother lioness in you, and inspire you to try to make the world a better place for young women. ▪

▪ *The Thorn Birds* (1977)
by Colleen McCullough

A Kennedy-esque family saga unfolding on the sweeping outback of Australia seems an odd setting for a book about mother issues, but it just goes to show you, you can ride, but you can't hide. Though you may flee to the other side of the international dateline, you can't get away from the repetition compulsion.

The Thorn Birds captured the imagination of America with its epic Australian vistas and its story of the forbidden love between Father Ralph, a Roman Catholic priest, and Meggie Cleary, his young virginal charge. Once Meggie comes of age, the two fall in love and eventually consummate their affection in some removed and exotic island locale that resembles an ecumenically enhanced Gilligan's Island. The fallout from this moment of weakness twists the next three generations of Clearys in the smelting furnace of their unlawful passion. Fortunes are lost, farms burn, and most male members of the family wind up gored by wild boars, extinguished in forest fires, or incarcerated.

Every plot point in the book is motivated by the magnum force of Meggie's homicidal mother. It's Meggie's mom who brings Father Ralph into the picture in the first place, because she herself is in love with him. It's Meggie's mom who neglects Meggie and favors her eldest son, leaving her daughter vulnerable to Father Ralph's own brand of maternal ministrations. And it's Meggie's mom who has twisted Meggie's conception of love to the extent that she retains a lifelong attachment to an unavailable man. Mother and daughter do make peace at the end of the novel, but not before Meggie has been doomed to a life without love.

This paints a pretty bleak picture for us conflicted daughters of the world. But take heart, there is a redemption of sorts in the end.

This book is a stunning illustration of how we grow to hate what we do not take the time to understand, how we become what we fear, and how the whole world can take on the contours of our own maternal outback, unless we make peace with the mother without and the mother within.

Points to Ponder

1. How is the natural environment of the Australian bush reflective of the emotional themes at play in the novel?

2. Why is red Father Ralph's favorite color?

3. What is your favorite color? And why? What was your mother's favorite color?

A Freudian slip is when you say one thing but mean your mother.

—Anonymous

■ *Mommie Dearest* (1978)
by Christina Crawford

Shaking me by the hair of my head she screamed in my ear, "No wire hangers! No wire hangers!"

Many have done it since, but few have come close to serving up a spicier dish of steaming hot revenge than the original matricidal memoirist Christina Crawford. In *Mommie Dearest*, Christina manages to deconstruct an American film icon and strike a blow for revenge-seeking daughters everywhere.

Now, few of us have mom horror stories as memorable as Christina's—the demands that she scour the bathroom floor in the middle of the night, or wear the same pathetic pinafore for weeks on end, or fix perfectly mixed cocktails for the revolving cast of daddies that come in and out of Mommie Dearest's life—and bedroom. And then there's that gut-churning anecdote of pure Freudian homicidal mother mettle when actress Christina, ill in the hospital, tunes in to the soap opera from which she has had to take leave, only to discover that her aging mother has usurped her role as the sweet-faced twentysomething ingenue.

Reading this scathing memoir, most of us realize that our own moms' meanest moments pale by comparison, but the adolescent within loves to identify with the tortured Christina, who despite everything still never got over her desire to win her mother's approval. Joan Crawford faked a truce in her later years, only to cut her adopted daughter out of her will with the cryptic explanation that she was disowning Christina for reasons she well understood. But Christina's classic tell-all, ripping Joan Crawford's beloved public image to shreds, indeed gave her the last laugh.

Read it and gasp—and don't be surprised if you find yourself just a touch more appreciative of your own mommie dearest.

Mothers, food, love, and career: the four major guilt groups.
—Cathy Guisewite

▪ *The Girl in the Photograph* (1998)
by Gabrielle Donnelly

Are you happy now that you know? And the weight that she knew she would carry for the rest of her life dropped, settled, and made itself comfortable on Allegra's heart.

Unlike *Divine Secrets of the Ya-Ya Sisterhood*, the secrets about Mom that this novel's heroine wants to uncover require major detective work, and they carry the aroma of something sinister. But Allegra O'Riordan just does not take a hint. Every time she presses someone for information about her mother, Theresa, who died years ago when Allegra was just a child, they suddenly become absorbed by a discussion of the cilantro in the pork marinade. And the only person who probably does know the real story, Helen, is senile and prone to wandering off into some convoluted anecdote about Ernest Hemingway visiting her bookshop all those many years ago. About all poor Helen can remember of Theresa is that she was as Irish as Paddy's pig, which, believe me, Allegra has already figured out. Will she ever learn what happened that day at the beach, when her mother posed in her bikini for one of the few photographs Allegra ever saw of her—the only photograph in which she was smiling? And given how cagey everyone is about Theresa, does Allegra really want to know what was behind Mona Lisa's smile?

If you're obsessed by the need to know more about who Mom was, *The Girl in the Photograph* will remind you that it's easy to let our fantasies and dreams overpower us, and that in real life, moms are never picture perfect.

Points to Ponder

1. Have you ever discovered something about your mom that you wish you hadn't?

2. Be honest—didn't you sort of know already?

I found out why cats drink out of the toilet. My mother told me it's because the water is cold in there. And I'm like, how did my mother know that?

—Wendy Liebman

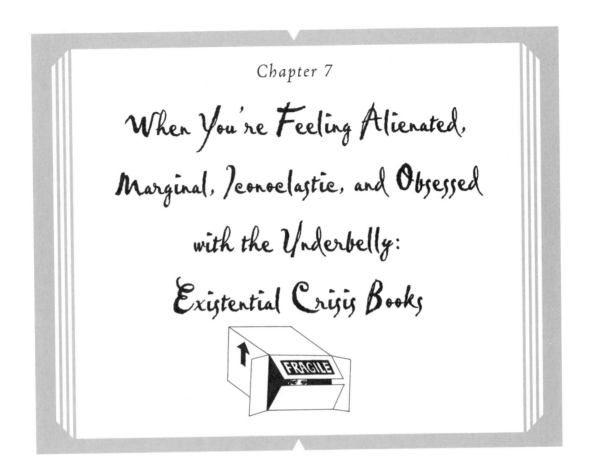

Chapter 7

When You're Feeling Alienated, Marginal, Iconoclastic, and Obsessed with the Underbelly: Existential Crisis Books

"**Who am I?** Why am I? To be or not to be? What is the meaning of it all, and why have people stopped inviting me to their cocktail parties?"

There comes a time when all of us good-natured, agreeable Ophelias enter the Hamlet phase, stepping away from the crowd to ask ourselves the difficult questions.

Sometimes the answers can bring us resolution and spiritual relief; then we right our wrongs and step back into the mainstream. Sometimes the answers can really piss us off, leaving us alienated, disillusioned, politically passionate, or downright unfit for polite society. And of course, sometimes, we just pick up and move to Paris. Hey, it happens.

Whether you're suffering the slings and arrows of outrageous fortune, or taking arms against a sea of troubles, these existential crisis books can be good company on that stretch of the road that runs through the wrong side of town, and they can help you appreciate the special beauty of the dark side.

Alienation Primers

■ *Post Office* (1971)
by Charles Bukowski

Somebody at one of these places asked me: "What do you do? How do you write, create?" You don't, I told them. You don't try. That's very important: not to try, either for Cadillacs, creation or immortality. You wait, and if nothing happens, you wait some more. It's like a bug high on the wall. You wait for it to come to you. When it gets close enough you reach out, slap out and kill it. Or if you like its looks, you make a pet out of it.

No tour of the underbelly would be complete without spending a few hours with the undisputed king of the antiheroes, the lowlife laureate himself, Charles Bukowski. Bukowski is more than an author, he's a myth. Buk's epic drinking, whoring, gambling, and palling around with rough trade has made him a counterculture icon who elevates inebriation, hopelessness, and bad plumbing to the level of divine.

Henry Chinaski, Bukowski's literary alter ego, who appears in *Post Office* as well as many of his novels, poems, and short stories, is a disenfranchised outcast, at home with hangovers and whores, chiselers and cheap booze. Bukowski relates Henry's exploits in the hard-bitten byways and dive bars of Los Angeles in his characteristically stark but warm-hearted and sardonically giddy poetry of the street, which has made him a Beat-Generation-style prophet of the outland.

If *Post Office* is any indication, Charles and Hank earned their cult status the hard way. Bukowski was a writer of early promise who was first published in the 1940s. But guided by his evil and drunken muse, he gave up writing to drink and drift, finally settling in a job working for the U. S. Postal Service. And like many who are in constant contact with the U. S. Postal Service, he became preoccupied with themes of madness and death.

Twenty years later, driven to the brink by the mind-numbing, spirit-squelching repetition of his work in the post office, he wrote a novel called *Post Office*—and the legend of Hank was born.

Post Office is a great novel to read when you're feeling down and out, because Bukowski illuminates the beauty and poetry of even the most squalid settings and reminds us that even when we're at our most down and out, at least we can be grateful that we don't work at the post office.

Words to the Wise: If you do work for the post office, it might be wise to skip this one, particularly if you are licensed to carry a firearm.

▪ *Tropic of Cancer* (1934)
by Henry Miller

Life moves on, whether we act as cowards or heroes. Life has no other discipline to impose, if we would but realize it, than to accept life unquestioningly. Everything we shut our eyes to, everything we run away from, everything we deny, denigrate or despise, serves to defeat us in the end. What seems nasty, painful, evil, can become a source of beauty, joy, and strength, if faced with an open mind. Every moment is a golden one for him who has the vision to recognize it as such.

Henry Miller's *Tropic of Cancer*, the first volume of an autobiographical trilogy about the author's life in Paris, isn't too heavy on plot or character, but Miller's anecdotal and meandering philosophizing on the hollow pretense of social and moral convention will make even the most marginal pariah feel less like a boil on the bottom of the body politic and more like a disciple of a new and unfettered order.

The richness and color of Miller's prose, as well as the variety of imagination in the descriptions of his sexual exploits, makes his life seem so exuberant and sensual and noble that we even forgive the fact that he's basically a homeless, versifying mooch living off his friends (and sometimes his friends' husbands) and, worse yet, cheating on his wife.

Read Miller the next time your controversial views start eroding your sense of national identity as well as your basic support systems. There's nothing like spending a few hours with a sexually compulsive, poetic, and picaresque expatriate in Paris to make you feel better about being on the outs with your own emotional country of origin, and your landlord.

Points to Ponder

What is the latitude and longitude that best describes your life?

Beat Bites

Show me a man who lives alone and has a perpetually clean kitchen, and 8 times out of 9 I'll show you a man with detestable spiritual qualities.

—Charles Bukowski

I don't know, I don't care, and it doesn't make any difference!

—Jack Kerouac

▪ *Crime and Punishment* (1866)
by Fyodor Dostoyevsky

Taking a new step, uttering a new word, is what people fear most.

Nobody illustrates the haunting beauty of the underbelly as well as Dostoyevsky, the undisputed king of the underground. *Crime and Punishment* is the story of a sensitive and brilliant young man whose isolation and punishing intelligence drive him over the brink, and he murders his landlady and her daughter. Once the deed is done, his moral confusion lifts, and he spends the rest of the novel hunted by his own unspeakable guilt, a sinister and sarcastic embodiment of the Nietzchean Übermensch, and the unconditional and redemptive love of an impoverished maiden.

Reading *Crime and Punishment* is like spending a few hours in the warm, musky embrace of a spiritual tomb, or that really dark cigar bar, with all the exposed steam pipes and no windows in the basement of the Morgan Hotel—when the tobacco growers' convention is in town.

Dostoyevsky hurls you down to the very bottom of the abyss, only to snatch you back up again at the last minute and disgorge you suddenly into the fresh morning air. Read this the next time you've been taking the fundamentals of life for granted. You can take it from us—after a few hours in that Dostoyevskian Morgan Hotel cigar bar, breathing fresh air feels like a gift from God.

I'd Rather Have a Bottle in Front of Me Than a Frontal Lobotomy

 Have you noticed if for some reason you want to feel completely out of step with the rest of the world, the only thing to do is sit around a cocktail lounge in the afternoon.
—Jay Dratler, *Pitfall*

The important thing is the rhythm. Always have rhythm in your shaking. Now a Manhattan you always shake to fox-trot time, a Bronx to two-step time, a dry martini you always shake to waltz time.
—Dashiell Hammett, *The Thin Man*

I distrust a man that says "when." If he's got to be careful not to drink too much, it's because he's not to be trusted when he does.
—Dashiell Hammett, *The Maltese Falcon*

▪ *The Stranger* (1942)
by Albert Camus

I opened myself for the first time to the tender indifference of the world. Finding it so much like myself—so like a brother, really—I felt that I had been happy and that I was happy again. For everything to be consummated, for me to feel less alone, I had only to wish that there be a large crowd of spectators the day of my execution and that they greet me with cries of hate.

The Stranger is not merely one of the most widely read novels of the twentieth century but an unparalleled portrait of the terrible things that can happen when you are traveling and don't obey local traffic laws. Camus's world is one where events are stripped of their redemptive purpose—where belief in "right reason" is replaced with spiritual doubt, where existence is meaningless, and where salvation is possible only through an acceptance of the brutality and purposelessness of life. Okay, so *The Stranger* is not a light and frothy romp through the festooned streets of Paris on a sunny morning in May. But it is one of the cornerstones of existentialist literature and is worth reading for that reason alone.

The plot of *The Stranger* is very simple. A young Algerian named Meursault, who is plagued with a sort of inert modern malaise, stumbles unintentionally into committing a meaningless murder that ultimately gets him executed at the guillotine. He is condemned not for killing another man, however, but for the far greater crime of offending polite society—sort of like being caned for jaywalking in Singapore. Chief among his crimes are the fact that he didn't cry at his mother's funeral, that he smoked in the mortuary, and—one shudders to even imagine it—drank a café au lait and laughed at a comedy while his mother lay cold and buried in the ground. Ultimately Meursault is executed for his capital insensitivity, his only comfort being that before his death, he finds communion with the rest of humanity through a shared condemnation of himself.

The Stranger is a good reminder that in the court of original guilt in a postexistentialist age, we are all our own judges, juries, and executioners. So we might as well acquit ourselves and move on.

Hard-Boiled Homilies

Experience has taught me never to trust a policeman. Just when you
think one's all right, he turns legit.
—W. R. Burnett, The Asphalt Jungle

My guess might be excellent or it might be crummy, but Mrs. Spade
didn't raise any children dippy enough to make guesses in front of a
district attorney, and an assistant district attorney, and a
stenographer. —Dashiell Hammett, The Maltese Falcon

I don't mind if you don't like my manners. I don't like them myself.
They're pretty bad. I grieve over them on long winter evenings.
—Raymond Chandler, The Big Sleep

In my case, self-absorption is completely justified. I have never
discovered any other subject quite so worthy of my attention.
—Vera Caspary, Laura

■ *Ulysses* (1922)
by James Joyce

Leopold Bloom ate with relish the inner organs of beasts and fowl.

James Joyce's masterpiece about two epic outsiders, Stephen Dedalus and Leopold Bloom, is touted as one of the greatest works of art in the Western tradition. Not just literary art, mind you, but art, period. *Ulysses* has been canonized by academia, and as an academic sacred cow, it has been the butt of more editorially obscure, supersophisticated, hyperattenuated essays than *Hamlet* and *Moby-Dick* combined.

Judging by the number of companion volumes that have been published to try to help readers unravel Joyce's somnambulant stream of consciousness and subaquatic classical allusions referring to just about everything ever sunk and buried beneath the snot-green sea, we imagine we're not alone in our confusion over such obfuscated interpretative essays as "Ulysses: Chaos and Complexity," "Homeric Parallels in Ulysses," "The Cybernetic Plot of Ulysses," "The Power of Reading: Belief and Justice in Ulysses," and something called "The Litani Schema."

Ulysses is about everything and nothing plotwise; it touches on death, life, mothers, fathers, sons, daughters, Irish civil servants, and the meaning and significance of the Catholic Church's stance on transubstantiation. Joyce, in his efforts to revolutionize the novel and give birth to a fiction that spoke with the free-associative and idiosyncratic voice of the subconscious, invented a new language with which to tell his story. In other words, he made up words as he went along.

This made Joyce something of a misunderstood and lonely exile, haunting the periphery of proper punctuation. It also made him a role model to a whole school of form-over-content revolutionaries who used him as an excuse for bad writing. Joyce's unique and eccentric style, however, created a new and enhanced English language that could express the expanded consciousness of a psychologically enlightened age, and it is a good reminder that those who exist outside of the boundaries of our current understanding are really just insiders ahead of their time.

Points to Ponder

1. What is the ineluctable modality of the visible?

2. What is the significance of Leopold Bloom eating with relish the inner organs of beasts and fowl?

3. How can you close your eyes and see?

Can't Live with 'Em, Can't Shoot 'Em

When you've entered your radical female separatist phase and are ready to hurl abuse at anyone with an XY chromosomal pairing, these rabid feminist tomes will appeal to the raging she-devil within you. You may want to note that leaving these in a conspicuous place, like on top of your coffee table or sticking out of your beach bag, is the equivalent of citronella for men.

■ *The Women's Room* (1977)
by Marilyn French

Bitterness closed her in. She had lost her life. She would live out a half-life, like the rest of women. She had no choice but to protect herself against a savage world she did not understand and by her gender alone was made unfit to deal with. There was marriage and there was the convent. She retreated into one as if it were the other, and wept at her wedding.

Your relationship was working for a while, wasn't it? You repressed all your instincts, rationalized away those uneasy feelings, and put on a happy face. Now you're awake, smelling the coffee, and realizing this ain't Starbucks and he is *not* somebody you want in your kitchen in the morning. In fact, it would be nice if he would leave the planet.

If you're in a rabid I-hate-men mood, you'll love Marilyn French's infamous novel about men who run and ruin women's lives. There's not a salvageable male here: Even the politically correct professor who seems to be ready to redeem his entire gender proves completely self-centered in the end, leaving his girlfriend Mira to realize that no man can fulfill her the way a graduate degree from an Ivy League college can. In fact, there are a lot of Ivy League grad students in this book, all of whom have come to the same conclusion: Dissertations are a breeze compared to tolerating any man on any level at any time.

Doing away with the distraction of a real plot, Marilyn French shares these women's stories of how they got to Harvard, having survived the sheer hell of marriage in the 1950s. She tells horror story after horror story about suburban housewives who had nervous breakdowns, slit their wrists, downed handfuls of sleeping pills, turned radical lesbian feminist, or became addicted to Valium because their husbands were A-1 creeps who annihilated their wives' sense of self. Then, of course, those nasty men did things like run off with younger women, jump state lines to avoid child support payments, and live happily ever after, having sated themselves like vampires on their wives' lifeblood.

Scathing—you'll need to wipe the foam off the corners of your mouth after reading this one.

Been There, Done That

▪ *Our Blood* (1976)
by Andrea Dworkin

It will not be easy for us to establish values which originate in sisterhood. For centuries, we have had male values slammed down our throats and slammed up our cunts.

If we credit Andrea Dworkin for one thing, it's for creating the "femi-Nazi" stereotype that strikes terror in the hearts of the Rush Limbaughs of the world. In this typical collection of her essays and speeches, she rails against the patriarchy, claiming that "phallic supremacy" is at the root of all our institutions and that in order for women to regain power, a full-fledged revolution is called for. Now, granted, she wrote her most famous pieces in an era when women were earning less than half of what men made in the marketplace, abortion was illegal, rape victims could be grilled about their sexual behavior, there was no Title IX providing for girls' and women's sports, and the sight of a woman wearing pants was still a major shocker. No wonder Andrea was pissed off, and in retrospect some of her arguments have a real "duh" factor: Isn't it amazing that equal pay for equal work wasn't a given all along?

But one thing that makes reading Andrea Dworkin so fascinating today is the way she dressed up pretty tame demands (by our standards) with all sorts of high-falutin' rhetoric. Is it any wonder the average Jill didn't find herself moved by such statements as "it is necessary to understand that under the sexual system of male positivity and female negativity, there is literally nothing in the act of fucking, except accidental clitoral friction, which recognizes or actualizes the real eroticism of the female, even as it has survived under slave

continued . . .

conditions"? Back in the day, it wasn't enough to just have some provocative ideas: You had to make them sound as if they came out of a think tank. Andrea, babe, give it a rest or give it a melody. Somehow, Bikini Kill and their Riot Grrrl friends were a lot more fun.

Now, most of us have a hard time with the idea that we can't even have good old-fashioned sexual intercourse without betraying all women throughout history because Dworkin insists that the "pleasure in being fucked is the masochistic pleasure of experiencing self-negation." But if you've just discovered he's had another woman in the picture all along, such pronouncements make you want to punch your fist into the air and scream, "Right on, sistah!"

The thing about radicals like Andrea Dworkin is that they always go for the most extreme examples to prove their points (like Chinese foot-binding as a metaphor for oppression, an image Dworkin loves to trot out in every conceivable situation). But radicals serve a very important purpose: They make moderates' ideas seem so much more palatable by comparison. So you see, in a roundabout way, we can thank Andrea for everything from the Family Leave Act to unisex bathrooms, which make the line move infinitely faster.

But maybe the best thing about reading *Our Blood* today is to enjoy how absolutely enraged Dworkin was back then. As women, we hit a collective boiling point in the early 1970s, about the time Bobby Riggs openly ridiculed Billie Jean King, who struck a blow for all womanhood when she quietly and gracefully beat the pants off him in a battle-of-the-sexes tennis match. We were damn tired of being treated like a joke: by newscasters who giggled at those "kooky women's libbers," by male coworkers who just couldn't understand why those nice "girls" in the office didn't like their bottoms pinched, and by our husbands and lovers who chuckled at our anger and our serious demands. Well, we gave those fellas the boot, took our macramé wall hangings and lopsided ceramic expressions of selfhood, and moved into apartments all our own.

continued . . .

Today, we women seem to have simmered down as a group, but if you've just woken up to the extent of sexism throughout history and across cultures and have just about had it with the men in your life, it's sort of refreshing to get back in touch with the rage of the rad fems, isn't it? So open up a beer, park yourself on the sofa you paid for (even if it's only a futon or a Goodwill special), and let yourself feel just a bit self-righteous. ■

Points to Ponder

1. *Is the orgasm a biologically programmed adaptation designed to perpetuate the species, or an act of violence against women?*

2. *Are you acting out your victimhood by smashing your feet into Manolo Blahniks, or do you just like how they make your ankles look thin?*

Is That Why They Call Them Militant?

My feelings about men are the result of my experience. I have little sympathy for them. Like a Jew just released from Dachau, I watch the handsome young Nazi soldier fall writhing to the ground with a bullet in his stomach and I look briefly and walk on. I don't even need to shrug. I simply don't care.

—Marilyn French, *The Women's Room*

■ *Dolores Claiborne* (1993)
by Stephen King

I'm gonna tell you three a hell of a lot starting right about now, and a hell of a lot of it prob'ly could be used against me in a court of law, if anyone wanted to at this late date. The joke of it is, folks on the island know most of it already, and I'm just about half-past give-a-shit.

There are solutions, you know. We could replace our capitalistic system with a socialist one that recognizes and rewards the unpaid labor of those doing work of social value. We could embrace a feminine spirituality that emphasizes the connection between all living things, reclaiming our sacred bond with the forces of nature. We could march on Washington and demand government subsidies for child care and elder care, rather than letting women struggle on their own to patch together a way to meet their own needs as well as their loved ones'. Or then again, we could smash a cream pitcher upside the head of the nearest man and hold a hatchet over him until he agrees to our demands.

Feeling a little less than diplomatic? Tired of the soft sell? Ready to attack like a cornered mama bear? Then you'll enjoy *Dolores Claiborne*, Stephen King's tale of a salty working-class woman with a powerful sense of justice and an endless supply of one-liners. True, she does have two murder raps hanging over her, but sometimes a woman has to take a more direct route to even up the score. Dolores's fierce loyalty, maternal instinct, and truck driver mouth compel her to walk a different path. And yes, the death of her drunken, child-molesting, wife-beating lout of a husband is quite timely. As for the unfortunate accident that killed her abusive employer, well, there's a very good explanation for all that as well. Dolores will fascinate you, shock you—and if she inspires you, you'd better find a damn good lawyer.

The Flip Side: How the Other Half Lives

▪ *Why Men Are the Way They Are* (1986)
by Warren Farrell

*Anyone—woman or man—who wishes to change another person
has to ask first whether the desire to change the other is basically
a desire to reinforce the "he or she needs help—I'm the better one"
syndrome.*

Just what do men want? Don't you wonder why Sigmund Freud didn't pose
that question? Because while some of us may be inconsistent about whether
we want a mate who is vulnerable or tough—somewhere in between seems to
about do it for most of us—there are certain things all of us are crystal clear
about. We want a man who understands that grunting does not count as par-
ticipating in a conversation. We want a mate who does not believe that the
uterus is a homing device that enables a woman to pinpoint exactly where he
left his keys, his favorite pen, or the remote. And we want a man who understands that the toilet needs to be cleaned regularly, and who acts upon that
knowledge by finding the Lysol and the brush and taking care of it already.
Are these not simply stated requests?

But men, Warren Farrell claims, are emotionally crippled by all the
demands we women place on them. As potential romantic partners, they
must be financially successful, attractive, charming, confident, *and* unmarried.
In our experience, you can garner the attention of a lot of women if you're
simply unmarried. And we don't really think that's all that much to expect
from a potential husband. But according to Farrell, under the weight of
women's expectations, men shut down emotionally, become workaholics,
and die early of stress-related illnesses. *And it's all our fault!*

Excuse us, but did we tell him he has to be a corporate lawyer and make

continued...

senior partner rather than steer himself into a less demanding career? Or did old Warren just assume that's what his first ex-wife wanted?

Basing his argument on magazine ads and 1980s prime-time soaps, Farrell claims that women all want men to turn into Willy Loman and sacrifice themselves on the altar of our desires. But he never accounts for all the women who date starving artists and con artists who just need a little encouragement and some financial patronage until they get their big break. And what about the women who are comfortable making more money than their male partners do?

We guess Farrell hasn't met a lot of women we know, who lower the bar until it's underground. If men choose to work themselves into a state of hypertension because of delusions about women's expectations, why is that *our* fault?

All things considered, however, there is *some* redeeming value in the book. Part 5 gives excellent, hard-hitting advice on how to negotiate a change in your mate's attitude and behavior. The key, as you might guess, is that realistically, the person wanting change (you) is the person who has to change first. *You've got to put aside your resentment that he just doesn't get it. So forget about smashing the patriarchy already—do you want a man or not?* Oh, okay Warren. If the guy we end up with thinks anything like you do, we'll take "not." ■

Alienation Lite

So you're not big on images of torturous despair, blinding nihilism, and destruction of the male species, but instead feeling just a bit lonely? You can remain isolated, or you can celebrate your unique gifts. Check out these alienation lite reads, and you'll rediscover your pride in standing out from the crowd.

■ *Maybe the Moon* (1992)
by Armistead Maupin

I was more or less adopted by a space in downtown Los Angeles, where I was in great demand by artists doing pieces on alienation and absurdity. They were gentle, surprisingly naïve kids, who took endless pains to guard against what they referred to as "the exploitation of the differently abled." This got to be old fast, so I pulled two of them aside one day and told them not to sweat it, that I was an actress first and foremost, that of course I would play an oil-slick mutant for them, that I would sit on a banana and spin if it was in the goddamned script and they paid me something for it.

In the end, we're all different, and we all feel like outsiders at times. But it's our attitude toward our difference that is the core of our character. We can remain alienated, or we can celebrate our specialness and demand that the world around us love us and accept us for who we are. And with perseverance and determination, we can be anything we set out to be, even if we are a thirty-one-inch midget who aspires to be a leading lady of film and television. In *Maybe the Moon*, Cady Roth is as dogged as she is diminutive, and dammit, she wants her career and her made-for-TV movie about her life (starring, of course, herself), too. And if she has to play a jar of anticellulite cream in an infomercial to pay the bills meanwhile, well, so be it.

Okay, so Cady is totally deluded. But aren't we all? We truly want to believe that we will be accepted on our own terms, that we'll be embraced for our uniqueness, that our richness of character—our quirks and our flaws—will be deeply cherished by everyone who meets us. Luckily, most of us aren't as far gone as Cady is, thinking Hollywood actually cares about the woman behind the rubber extraterrestrial mask (unless you count the fleeting moment when the *People* magazine profile is on the stands—and then it's on to the guy who belched the alphabet in that dot-com commercial, or some such). But Armistead Maupin's *Maybe the Moon*, based on the real-life story of Tamara De Treaux, the tiny woman who played E.T., is an allegory about how we all want love, recognition, and acceptance (not to mention great sex, which Cady manages to find, courtesy of a studly fellow with a creative streak). Cady's struggle teaches us to love ourselves enough not to be hurt by those who can't embrace us, and to appreciate those who support us unconditionally, even if they are Fabric Barn salesgirls who confuse Scientologists with scientific researchers, or aging Munchkins living off the former glory of their yellow-brick-road days.

Read this when you're feeling downtrodden and ignored. It'll reassure you that you're due your moment in the sun, even if takes climbing into a rubber suit to get the world's attention.

Points to Ponder

1. What's wrong with denial? It works, doesn't it?

2. Name three historical triumphs that would never have occurred had the heroine faced facts.

▪ *The Clan of the Cave Bear* (1980)
by Jean M. Auel

It wasn't exultation she felt, not the excitement of a first kill or even the satisfaction of overcoming a powerful beast. It was something deeper, more humbling. It was the knowledge that she had overcome herself.

Feeling that you're not just an outsider but of a different species—and a more advanced one at that? Then you'll identify with Ayla, the heroine of Jean Auel's *The Clan of the Cave Bear*. Orphaned and picked up by a passing band of Neanderthals (and we mean that literally—this takes place in the Ice Age), Ayla suffers years of abuse, neglect, and humiliation at the hands of these jealous, stoop-shouldered, low-browed people. These awful creatures just don't appreciate the special gifts of a blond-haired, blue-eyed Cro-Magnon teen who can bring down large animals with her slingshot and discover where babies come from thousands of years before anyone else does. Well, if that's the way they want it—living in smoky, firelit caves and communicating by grunts—then Ayla will just have to strike out on her own, that's all. And don't you worry—she'll be back, a perfect specimen of Nordic maleness on her arm, her lion totem at her side, to claim her due.

All right, you've probably noticed that something here smells a bit like the eugenics movement, with the dark people portrayed as inferior to Christie Brinkley-esque Cro-Magnon Aryans. And you may find it tempting to skip those long-winded descriptions of Ice Age flora and fauna. But don't feel guilty. This rich story of a spunky gal who refuses to conform to the rules of a bunch of cretins will remind you that eventually, you will find where you belong. Read this when you want to feel a little smug and are telling yourself they're all a bunch of yahoos.

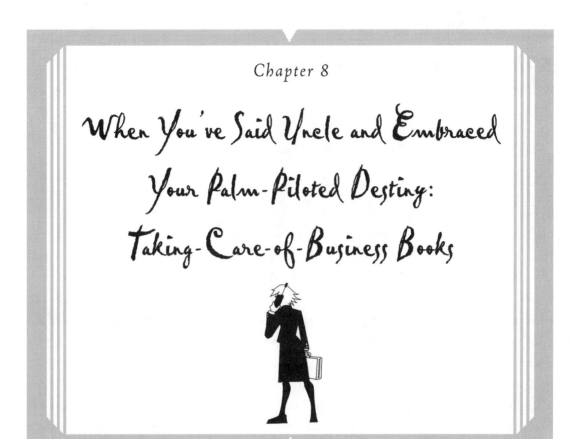

Chapter 8

When You've Said Uncle and Embraced Your Palm-Piloted Destiny: Taking-Care-of-Business Books

Yes, it's a pity your advanced degree in Romantic poetry as it relates to twentieth-century performance art didn't result in a feature film contract. But does that mean you can't be a contributing member of society? Of course not. You can always grow up and get a real job and work too many hours for too little money for the rest of your life. Or you can hold on to your dream and hope that maybe someday Romantic poetry performance art will come into vogue. Or you can go back to the drawing board. You can head out into uncharted territory, armed with a dollar, a dream, and these taking-care-of-business books—and completely reinvent yourself. The books in this chapter can help direct, inspire, organize, and motivate your journey on into the unmapped frontier of your professional future.

■ *The 9 Steps to Financial Freedom* (1997)
by Suze Orman

Money itself cannot make you financially free. Only you can make yourself financially free, and you can do it—and so much more. You have that power.

In the 1990s, it wasn't enough to be frugal, or to invest aggressively, or to know the difference between a CD that you play and a CD that yields interest. If you were going to be money smart, you had to be *spiritual* about it. Prosperity thinking begins with a respect for your money and for yourself. Orman, for example, says that if your wallet is a mess, you are a financial mess. But I don't think she lives in New York City, where everyone's in such a rush that no one has time to neatly place their bills and coins in the proper pouches of their wallets. Hey, when you've got a line of people behind you, your stylist is backed up once again, and you've got to get across town for a drinks date with a multimedia producer, smoothing out your singles just isn't a priority.

Anyway, the most compelling part of Orman's nine-step take-charge-of-your-finances plan, the one that captured the imagination of so many readers, is Step 1, in which she exhorts you to dig deep into your past and come up with your personal money mythology. What incidents from your childhood taught you about money, and what were the lessons? Whether Mom and Dad made it clear that you should never buy retail, or insisted that if you have to ask the price, you can't afford it, your youthful lessons about money permanently color your attitude, turning you into either the type to buy a round for the whole bar or iron all your used gift-wrap. All any of us have to do to start wresting control of our spending is to question these deeply embedded beliefs and start developing new, healthier habits.

Unlike a lot of spendaholics looking for a financial savior, however, those of us who long ago mastered the fine art of bouncing credit-card debts won't find Suze Orman's specific suggestions terribly helpful. As for all that advice on how much insurance and savings one really needs, some of us get into a blue funk just thinking about it. If we had the money, we'd certainly all be insured up the wazoo, and we'd probably know the difference between a living will, a revocable living trust, and a durable power of attorney, because it would matter. Until then, a lot of us are just trying to figure out where the hell it all goes.

Anyway, *The 9 Steps to Financial Freedom* is a great tool for anyone looking to get over their money fears and ignorance and start feeling in control. Even if you take only a few of Orman's suggestions, you'll feel empowered. So give this book a try, and maybe you'll find you've got a little extra at the end of the month—or at least not so many bounced-check charges.

When You're Sick of Your Career and Are Seriously Considering Taking Up Alpaca Ranching in Peru:

Books for Career Burnouts

A Small Farm in Maine (1988)
by Terry Silber

This firsthand account of how one couple built a self-sustaining life in the country is like a country breeze to the soul of stressed-out urbanites who are longing to find a world without gridlock. Read this one when you just can't take it anymore.

How to Have a Green Thumb Without an Aching Back (1955)
by Ruth Stout

Another urban escapee who has managed to solve all of life's complexities with a good mulching system. Read this one when you're up to your eyeballs in compost, and make your flowers bloom.

continued . . .

Downshifting (1991)

by Amy Saltzman

The most famous in the spend-less-so-you-can-work-less school of burnout management. This is a great book to read when you're feeling stretched too thin and overaccessorized.

Voluntary Simplicity (1981)

by Duane Elgin

This book started an ideological movement away from the complexity of consumerism and toward the spiritual value of doing without. Read this one when you're feeling like just saying no. ▪

▪ *Trust Me on This* (1988)
by Donald E. Westlake

Jack was on the phone, helpless with rage. "Whadaya mean," he demanded, "incest isn't interesting? Incest has always been interesting. So what if they're giraffes?"

Native New Englander Sara Joslyn had a liberal arts degree in her back pocket and a promising career as a journalist, but then she had to go and get ambitious. Lesson number one: When they're paying twice the salary of any other entry-level position, there's got to be a catch somewhere. First, there's that location, the backwaters of Florida, a land fit only for mosquitoes and aluminum-siding salesmen. Then there's the paper: *The Weekly Galaxy*, a tabloid that even Rupert Murdoch would be ashamed of (well, then again, maybe not). Before you can say "aliens have impregnated my poodle," Sara finds herself trying to manipulate doctors into giving quotes like "sex cures gallstones," stalking television celebrities, and faking photos of hundred-year-old twins. It's not like there isn't a great story nipping at her heels either: Her first day of work, she finds a dead body in the parking lot. But since the deceased wasn't a regular on any TV series, no one seems all that concerned, least of all her cynical coworker, Jack, or her boss DeMassi (appropriately nicknamed Massa). So Sara's got to solve the crime on her own time.

If you're feeling like your job forces you to contribute to the de-evolution of humankind, escape with *Trust Me on This* and remind yourself that somehow, in some way, you're going to make a difference (and nab yourself a great guy in the process).

It's Not Our Cup of Tea, But . . .

■ *The 7 Habits of Highly Effective People* (1989)
by Stephen R. Covey

Paradigms are inseparable from character. Being is seeing in the human dimension. And what we see is highly interrelated to what we are. We can't go very far to change our seeing without simultaneously changing our being, and vice versa.

Okay, we admit it. We have no idea what a paradigm is. We've looked it up in several dictionaries but still can't quite wrap our heads around it. It's one of those big important concept words like *hegemony* and *matrix* that make us have to reread each page of this book over and over until we're ready to pound a couple of Advil. So we're a bit cold on Stephen Covey's famed book, which is full of advice on how to achieve paradigmatic shifts. Oh, he tries to warm it up with anecdotes about raising his sons, but that can't make up for all the business jargon and overly complicated visual aids that bog down his concepts.

Maybe some people find Covey's approach to business very accessible. But if you have any common sense, you'll be able to sum up all of Covey's wisdom in a sentence or two. Probably the point of actually reading *The 7 Habits of*

continued . . .

Highly Effective People is to light a fire under your feet and get you all excited about improving your productivity and communication, and setting goals for yourself. It's Covey who popularized the idea of making a mission statement for yourself, which is also something we'd like to see phased out of our popular vocabulary. Drawing up a mission statement is a noble undertaking, but unless you're in business for yourself, you'll probably have as much success carrying out your mission and as much support from your coworkers as Jerry Maguire had.

Still, creating a formal mission statement is the kind of activity that will help you get focused, and Covey's advice will come in handy when you're job hunting after being forced out due to corporate restructuring despite all your best efforts to be a company woman. If slogging through this tome makes you feel that you're taking control of your career, ah hell, go for it. ▪

▪ The Woman's Dress for Success Book (1977)
by John T. Molloy

If women adopt the uniform, and if they ignore the absurd, profit-motivated pronouncements of the fashion industry when they select their uniform, they will no longer be malleable. They will automatically and irrevocably break the hold that the male-dominated fashion industry has had over them.

Looking back on John Molloy's heavily researched, scientific approach to women's business image, it's easy to write him off as just another man trying to mold women into fake—and inferior—men. Hey, we can understand that corporate culture and glittery tube tops don't mix. But with all the freedom that the work world promises, why should women be shackled into such narrow options for dressing? A suit but no vest (too sexy), gray and navy but no pinstripes (too masculine)—unless, of course, it's a pinstriped dress, and then the hem has to be just above or below the knee. Molloy's strictures seem to call for a franchise of dress-for-success stores that feature rust-colored—but never green!—blouses; dark, unaesthetic glasses for blondes and redheads (since wire frames would draw attention to these "sexy" hair colors), feminine fedoras, and standard-issue double-breasted camel hair winter coats. And you thought *Color Me Beautiful* limited your choices! Couldn't we just swear off blue eyeshadow and dark hose with light shoes?

What we forget is that back in '77, when Molloy wrote this guide, he was simply taking a masculine approach to a very real problem: If men, who had the power and were still uncomfortable with "girls" in the office, could be persuaded by visual trickery to treat women as equals, then women ought to arm themselves with power suits that demanded executive treatment. If we were going to play on the team, we'd better don the uniform, even if we didn't quite know what to do with that support cup.

Molloy scolded us women for refusing to compromise our femininity and individuality to fit into the corporate structure. He insisted that everyone who worked in an office was the man in the gray flannel suit, so we gals might as well set our jaws, get over our need for self-expression, and invest in some power suits.

Maybe we all reacted so violently back then to those restrictive Molloy rules because we truly wanted to believe that the sheer force of our competence would win over men and get us those promotions, without our having to dress like androids. But it took a lot longer to break through the glass ceiling than we thought in those heady Mary Richards days. Molloy was right about the uphill battle for women, about the difficulty of being taken seriously by men when you look feminine or sexy, and about the handicap of dressing according to your working-class tastes. Now that we women have a little more power, we can don pink suits and big jewelry if that's a part of our personal style, without compromising our authority.

Still, for all that Molloy's power suits have been mothballed along with our Danskin wraparound skirts, it's surprising to see how sensible his general advice is. For any woman looking to play it safe, a medium-length haircut, button earrings, and a just-below-the-knee skirt suit still looks right. So if you're feeling that maybe an image makeover is needed, *The Woman's Dress for Success Book* can help.

Can I Get That Printed on a Coffee Mug?

*I have yet to hear a man ask for advice on
how to combine marriage and a career.*

—Gloria Steinem

Cautionary Tales of the Glamorous Life

Feeling bad that you didn't pursue your dream to become a superstar?
Wishing you had a little more glitz in your life? These books will
convince you that the limelight isn't all it's cracked up to be, and that
sometimes, at least, slow and steady *does* win the race.

Call Me Anna (1987)

by Patty Duke

Poor Anna Duke felt compelled to pursue a career as a child. Her father
wasn't around, and her mentally unstable mother wasn't exactly a reliable
breadwinner. So Anna sacrificed her name, her opinions, her privacy, and
even her sanity to a couple of managers who were determined to grind her
into the perfect child star. "Patty" smiled through such indignities as having
to ingest some godawful product called Beanie Weenies on a live TV commercial and frying up Alpo for that insufferable little chihuahua Bambi that
her managers carried everywhere. No wonder she did such a marvelous job
playing an out-of-control child who can't speak, and two "identical cousins."
Talk about fracturing one's personality! Luckily, some good therapy, a couple

continued…

of decent husbands and kids, and a prescription for lithium later, Anna got it all together.

A powerful story about what it's like to drive in the fast lane before you've had a chance to discover yourself.

Little Girl Lost (1990)

by Drew Barrymore

She achieved stardom at 6, sneaked her first cigarette at 9½, was nightclubbing at 10, and in rehab at 13, bloated and burned out, addicted to cocaine and alcohol. And then she relapsed. Sure, she's as peppy as popcorn now, but after reading about Drew Barrymore's harrowing childhood, the fast track isn't quite so enticing, is it?

Neon Angel (1989)

by Cherie Currie

Yes, Cherie Currie was a neon angel on the road to ruin. At 15, she became the lead singer for the influential all-female proto-punk band the Runaways (which also featured Joan Jett and Lita Ford). But just as stardom hit, pulling her away from her identical twin sister at home and her parents (who were splitting up), Cherie Currie found herself burned by the searing spotlight. She had a lead guitarist whose jealousy was acidic, a manager who thought a great marketing ploy was to tell reporters that Cherie was an egomaniac, and a taste for the wide palette of drugs available to up-and-coming rock stars in the glitter era. You know the rest—hospital, rehab, and a cautionary tale that rivals David Crosby's, all before the age of consent. Kind of makes you want to take the scenic route, doesn't it? ▪

Can I Get That Printed on a Coffee Mug?

Meetings are indispensable when you don't want to do anything.

—J. K. Galbraith

■ *Games Mother Never Taught You* (1977)
by Betty Lehan Harragan

Ever been in a sales office that has one of those kindergarteny construction-paper sales rep charts with footballs on a field representing how far along the fellas were on reaching their quotas? And posters exhorting the guys on the team to "go for it" and "never say can't"? In this type of company, unless a gal is versed in sports metaphors, clearly, she is going to be stuck on the bench.

Books like Betty Harragan's are crucial for helping us to make sense of the testosterone mentality that treats it all as a competitive game coached by Vince Lombardi. Harragan, in chapters with titles like "You're in the Ball Game—Fight, Team, Fight!" and sections on "Where You Missed the Ball" and "Recover Your Own Fumbles," teaches women to think and behave like Knute Rockne in a neutral-colored polyester skirt suit. She provides a glossary of sports terms that are often used as business jargon, and she doles out advice on how to deal with male "logic" that stupidly ignores intuition, and how to get paid as if you were a man—everything you need to know to stay in the game and win, win, win.

More than twenty years after Harragan's book was published, much of the locker-room mentality in corporate America has been eradicated, thank goodness. Women have insisted that their own ways of thinking and doing be incorporated into the workplace, much to the benefit of American business. Moreover, many women, coming from post–Title IX sports experiences like playing on soccer teams as girls, are better equipped for acting like the proverbial team player. But *Games Mother Never Taught You* is still surprisingly helpful to a woman who has yet to learn the big boys' rules.

■ *The Tightwad Gazette* (1982)
by **Amy Dacyczyn**

Even Depression-era relatives think that I am too thrifty. One Christmas an aunt gave me two boxes of aluminum foil after learning that I recycled the stuff. (I made it last for years.)

Homemaker and mother of six Amy Dacyczyn admittedly didn't have a great career going. She and her husband had a combined twenty years in the workforce and only about $1,500 in assets, not counting their dilapidated pickup. So she decided if she couldn't make money, she'd cut down on her spending.

We've got to admit that this seems like the pessimist's way out. Cutting corners is a fine way to amass savings, or to whittle down your debt, or to keep your overhead low enough to spend time at home raising your kids. But the stark suggestions in *The Tightwad Gazette* book series (based on Dacyczyn's homey newsletter) make us want to rush out and go on a mad, impulsive shopping spree, and we don't mean at the ninety-nine-cent store. Somehow it's hard to justify knotting old bread wrappers and duct-taping the ends to create a jump rope for your niece when a plastic one at the Toys "R" Us is, what, a buck? And if that's not good enough, couldn't the kid just find a piece of rope? Yeah, all right, it's "green" to recycle bread wrappers, but couldn't we just stick them in the blue bin with the other plastics and cans? And may we never be so broke that we have to resort to the pathetic sight of a coat-hanger toilet-paper-roll holder.

Frankly, it's surprising how many of the suggestions in *The Tightwad Gazette* and its sequels are enormously time consuming and often downright bizarre. Saving money the Dacyczyn way isn't a hobby or an adventure, it's a career. How many of us would have the intestinal fortitude to spend our days mashing broken facial powder cakes with alcohol, then microwaving and molding them into new ones? How about grating the burned part off a cookie, or cutting those wastefully thick broccoli rubber bands into two thinner ones?

Most unsettling about this frightfully frugal lifestyle, however, is Dacyczyn's own priorities. If she's really doing this all so she can be a better parent to her brood (and indeed, she has said she stopped writing and promoting the books to spend more time with her kids), why does her own time-management plan include "reading no more than one book per day to each child"?

Now, if you are trying to watch your budget, you will find some useful nuggets here that normal folks can use, particularly if you're struggling along at the beginning of your career or have been downsized. Buy mismatched wooden chairs at flea markets, and paint them the same cheery color to make them match. Or use a brown paper grocery bag to wrap a package for mailing rather than buying brown wrapping paper. But if you're at the point where you're reusing frozen juice can lids and dryer lint, shouldn't you be considering ways to boost your income instead?

Can I Get That Printed on a Coffee Mug?

Enthusiasm is very wearing.

—Robert Louis Stevenson

Books to Be Thrown with Great Force

■ **The Seven Spiritual Laws of Success (1994) by Deepak Chopra**

We lack nothing because our essential nature is one of pure potentiality and infinite possibilities. Therefore, you must know that you are already inherently affluent, no matter how much or how little money you have, because the source of all wealth is the field of pure potentiality—it is the consciousness that knows how to fulfill every need, including joy, love, laughter, peace, harmony, and knowledge.

continued . . .

We're big believers in trusting the universe to provide, and in the idea that what we put forth will come back to us. As freelancers, we have to be. If we didn't have faith that the phone would ring and we'd get offered a new project, we'd either be climbing the walls or bashing our heads against them.

So we understand the appeal of Deepak Chopra's abundance thinking. To achieve affluence, or the flow of money in your direction, he says, you must open yourself to it and put out positive energy in the form of smiles, love, and consideration. Well, let's add to that blind mailings and networking—but you get the point. And we don't argue with Chopra when he says that *if* you find your true calling, you are more likely to achieve real success—not just a decent salary but deep satisfaction—than if you chase after the almighty dollar.

However, the danger with books like this is that such simplified Eastern philosophy is just too easily interpreted as advocating a waiting-for-my-patron mentality. For example, Chopra says we should stop focusing on working hard to get ahead and instead focus on how our special gifts can benefit the universe. This is great advice if you're the type to put your head down and work like a madwoman only to wake up three years later and realize all the schmoozers who started with the company at the same time you did have been promoted and you're still photocopying and faxing for your boss, rapidly headed nowhere. But far too many people talk themselves into believing their true calling is something along the lines of international rock star or Academy Award–winning actor, believing that a handful of East Village club dates or a résumé chock full of acting classes, combined with lots of positive thinking, is a recipe for achieving one's goals. Not to throw cold water on anyone's dreams, but somehow a little Protestant work ethic could've benefited a few of these romantics who left us with boxfuls of bad demo tapes and videotapes that definitely do not benefit the universe. ■

Thank God It's Friday

People don't choose their careers; they are engulfed by them.
—John Dos Passos

Labor is the curse of the world, and nobody can meddle with it without becoming proportionally brutified.
—Nathaniel Hawthorne

By working faithfully eight hours a day, you may eventually get to be a boss and work twelve hours a day.
—Robert Frost

One of the greatest labor-saving inventions of today is tomorrow.
—Vincent T. Foss

Work is the province of cattle.
—Dorothy Parker

Work is accomplished by those employees who have not yet reached their level of incompetence.
—Laurence J. Peter

■ The Feminine Mystique (1963)
by Betty Friedan

There are aspects of the housewife role that make it almost impossible for a woman of adult intelligence to retain a sense of human identity, the firm core of self or "I" without which a human being, man or woman, is not truly alive.

So you're ready to chuck it all, have a baby, and live happily ever after in a suburban split level, filling your days with PTA meetings, whipping up delicious and nutritious home-cooked meals, decoupaging with the kids on a lazy Saturday afternoon, gardening, decorating, and putting your feet up for an hour while you watch your favorite soap? If you're like a lot of us, such dreams of domestic bliss play better in your head than in reality. Somehow you find your days eaten up by cleaning the crumbs out of the toaster oven, running out to the drugstore yet again because last time you forgot the coupons, sorting endless orphaned socks, and wondering what sadist designed the floor plan at Toys "R" Us as you wander aimlessly in search of just the right Pokémon accessory to get your kid for his birthday tomorrow.

For all that some women bemoan that they have to work outside the home, at least part time, to make ends meet, reading *The Feminine Mystique* will make you realize that being nothing more than Suzy Homemaker is far less fulfilling than the right wing would have you believe. It's downright scary to read about a generation of American women who got married at eighteen, mutated into housewives, and surrendered their identities without so much as a whimper. Rather than living a warm and fuzzy Ozzie and Harriet existence, they experienced what Friedan called "the feminine mystique": a vague ennui, a hollow and lifeless feeling that was hard to describe and even more difficult to medicate (although a pitcher full of late-afternoon martinis and a Valium prescription apparently tempered it for many women). Frankly, when it came to expressions of the inner self, sculpting happy clowns out of upside down ice cream cones just didn't cut it. The happiest homemakers, Friedan found, were the ones who had a job, paying or not, that they could call their own.

Now, Friedan wrote this classic feminist tome in an era in which people had a lot more time to read, so prepare to do some skimming or you'll get bogged down in minutiae about Freudian theory, advertisers' agendas, and postwar sexual behavior. (And beware: Her outdated speculations about the causes of male homosexuality and promiscuity are real groaners.) Still, it's a real chiller to read about melancholy college women who backed off from science majors because they feared that if they went too far down the path toward an exciting career, they'd never get married, and about women who lost all sense of meaning because they'd given up their very selves. Read this when you need to get some perspective on your own domestic/career conflicts.

Books for the Hopelessly Confused

▪ *What Color Is Your Parachute?* (1970)
by Richard Nelson Bolles

There's nothing like a parachute when you've suffered a professional engine failure at cruising altitude. This sensitive guide to the discovery of your hidden talents is a great place to start when you're free-falling and need a way to break your fall. Each new edition is jam-packed with guidance on résumés, finding the hidden jobs, and instructions for "informational interviewing" (yeah, like that one ever worked!). *What Color* makes you realize that job hunting is a full-time pursuit.

▪ *Do What You Love, the Money Will Follow* (1987)
by Marsha Sinetar

▪ *I Could Do Anything If I Only Knew What It Was: How to Discover What You Really Want and How to Get It* (1994)
by Barbara Sher and Barbara Smith

If you're asking yourself, is it me? the department? the job? the industry? the entire capitalistic system? you can benefit from these career guidance classics. Sinetar and Sher don't kid you about the risks you have to take, the financial instability you may face, and the hard work and dedication that a new career will demand. Instead, they help you become one of those people who have followed their bliss instead of remaining miserable slobs who dread Monday mornings. ▪

■ *How to Win Friends and Influence People* (1936)
by Dale Carnegie

If you want to gather honey, don't kick over the beehive.

Dale Carnegie has become a part of American business mythology. It all started back in 1906 in his junior year at State Teachers College in Warrensburg, Missouri. The odds were against Dale, but his struggle to overcome his inferiority complex led him to discover secrets to interpersonal relations that could be applied to business, family, and friendships, and soon he was the author of the first megabestselling self-help book in American publishing history, *How to Win Friends and Influence People*. Dale Carnegie then launched an empire of inspirational minicourses at Ys and paid public appearances all around the country that we can blame for the success of every gimmicky self-help guru with a cuddly sweater, a handful of platitudes, and an 800 number. Yes, the next time PBS is having a fund drive and you catch one of those inspirational speakers going on endlessly about your authentic self, remember, good old Dale is to blame.

But the weird thing is, over two-thirds of a century later, no one seems to have improved on Dale Carnegie's advice. *How to Win Friends and Influence People* is still dead-on accurate about how to bring people around to your point of view. As you read his amusingly archaic anecdotes about Theodore Roosevelt in the White House asking himself, "What would Abe Lincoln do?" or Al Capone and Dutch Schultz not taking personal responsibility for themselves, what'll really surprise you is how this little old book makes half the self-help section of the bookstore redundant.

Feeling the need for a jolt of empowerment? Forget that $250 weekend workshop upstate. Invest a few bucks in Dale Carnegie's 1936 book, and yessir, you'll have them eating out of your hand just like old Bessie, the milkman's bay mare.

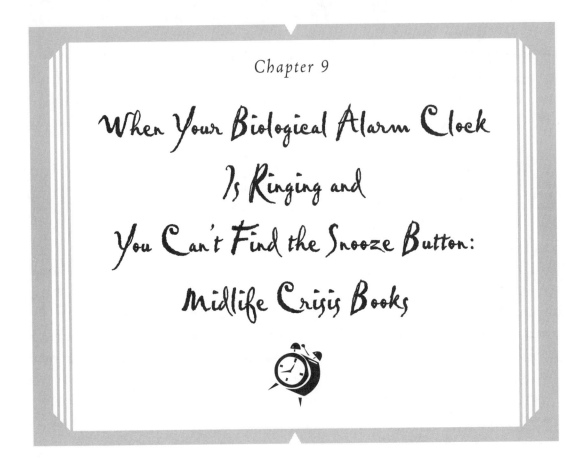

Chapter 9

When Your Biological Alarm Clock Is Ringing and You Can't Find the Snooze Button: Midlife Crisis Books

Guys have it relatively easy. They hit midlife, make a few disastrous fashion statements, call their careers and marriages into question, and then blammo, the Grecian Formula grows out, they enter the distinguished phase, and the crisis is over.

We women have it a little tougher. Things like gravity, menopause, and upper-thigh spread deprive us of our sense of control and remind us that life is short. It seems that from the moment we cross over into womanhood, we're careening toward one time-sensitive goal or another—to go steady, to get married, to find a career direction, to have children, or to give birth to a fully developed vision of ourselves. By the time we hit midlife, we modern gals on the go can be very exhausted from trying to reach all of life's finish lines.

If you're tired of racing against your biological clock to get to your share of the human experience before the alarm goes off, read these midlife crisis books and get ready to relax and appreciate the gifts that each season of your life has to offer.

■ *A Lady's Life in the Rocky Mountains* (1879)
by Isabella Bird

For the benefit of other lady travelers, I wish to explain that my "Hawaiian riding dress" is the "American Lady's Mountain Dress," a half-fitting jacket, a skirt reaching to the ankles, and full Turkish trousers gathered into frills falling over the boots,—a thoroughly serviceable and feminine costume for mountaineering and other rough traveling, as in the Alps or any other part of the world.
   —I. L. B. (author's note to the second edition, November 27, 1879)

Isabella Bird is one of the great plucky middle-aged Victorian ladies of all time. *A Lady's Life in the Rocky Mountains* is the story of her journey to the summit of Longs Peak, which she climbed in a Hawaiian riding dress and a pair of Turkish trousers.

Isabella's guide was an outlaw named Rocky Mountain Jim, a legendary bad boy in a golden age of bad boys, who had long golden curls, smoldering eyes, and an unquenchable thirst for poetry and high country bourbon. Together, Isabella and Mountain Jim ascended the north face of Longs Peak on the brink of winter, creating both a scandal and a legendary love story about the lady and the outlaw, which is still told over buffalo steaks and pints of Flat Tire beer in Estes Park, the tiny Colorado mountain town clinging to the hem of Longs Peak.

Isabella's letters to her sister, Henrietta, in England, collected in *A Lady's Life*, paint a very personal portrait of a revolutionary time and place, and a remarkable woman who at the age of forty-two rode eight hundred miles on horseback by herself across the American frontier to climb a mountain, just because it was there.

Spend a few hours in Isabella's sweeping landscape when you're feeling hemmed in by your horizons and let Isabella remind you that it ain't over until the fat lady climbs to the top of a mountain and yodels.

Points to Ponder

1. If you were going to ascend Longs Peak on the brink of winter guided by a handsome gentleman outlaw, what would you wear on your expedition and why?

2. *How do you think that Isabella's riding costume affected her climb? Do you think those Turkish trousers helped or hindered her? How about that stylish lady's duster? And that oversize hat—with the feather in it?*

It's Never Too Late . . . Over-the-Hill Heroines

Just because you're pushing forty doesn't mean you can't make a splash. Here are a few biographies of our favorite boat-rockers over forty, who prove that it's never *too* late to launch a one-woman revolution and make changes that transcend time.

Eleanor Roosevelt, vol. 1 (1992) and vol. 2 (1999)

by Blanche Wiesen Cook

This definitive two-volume biography details the life of one of America's most celebrated over-the-hill heroines. Eleanor Roosevelt lived in a pre-airbrushed age when character, not cosmetic surgery, and bravery, not youth, were what made a woman admirable to the great masses. She overcame national prejudice, infidelity, and even middle age to become America's most compelling, charismatic, and visionary stateswoman who wasn't afraid to make some noise.

Secrets of the Flesh: A Life of Colette (1999)

by Judith Thurman

Colette was the belle of the Belle Epoque and one of France's most respected and colorful literary treasures who did and wrote as she pleased, regardless of the consequences. How can you not love a woman who

continued . . .

scandalized Paris by wearing a catsuit decades before Emma Peel? Colette was not only a wildly popular novelist but the first real superstar of the twentieth century, whose epic bad behavior throughout her long and colorful life taught the world that women at any age have a few things to say about the secrets of the flesh.

The Life of Elizabeth I (1998)
by Alison Weir

A revealing biography of one of England's most powerful and popular monarchs, Elizabeth I, who made virginity into a philosophy and reigned supreme as queen of the realm for forty-five years. Okay, so she was autocratic, manipulative, and often somewhat less than honest, but it's hard work staying in control of a society populated by a bunch of guys in metal suits with no access to indoor plumbing. Plus, you've got to love a queen who wore her receding hairline like a crown jewel. ■

■ *When I Am an Old Woman I Shall Wear Purple* (1987)
edited by Sandra Haldeman Martz

*When I am an old woman I shall wear purple with a red hat which doesn't go
  and doesn't suit me;
And I shall spend my pension on brandy and summer gloves and satin sandals,
  and say we've no money for butter.
I shall sit down on the pavement when I'm tired;
And gobble up samples in shops and press alarm bells;
And run my stick along the public railings and make up for the sobriety of my
  youth.*

This book is a collection of poems, essays, and photographs that evoke the beauty, humor, and courage of mature women. The title poem, "When I Am an Old Woman I Shall Wear Purple," is a melodic and affirmational ballad about the comforts of aging, which include not having to worry about behaving oneself and not fussing over tasteful color coordination. This is one of those charming literary petits fours: they may not fill you up, but as you get older, you come to appreciate the gentility of cucumber sandwiches and love songs to your liver spots.

Frankly, we see no problem with disregarding these annoying details while we're young, but this literary illustration of the unique gifts that come only with age has been a comfort to many and has become the definitive girlfriend gift for friends in the midst of a midlife crisis.

Morsels of Midlife Wisdom

I refuse to admit that I am more than fifty-two, even if that makes my children illegitimate.

—Lady Nancy Astor

Perhaps one has to be very old before one learns to be amused rather than shocked.

—Pearl S. Buck

It is not all bad, this getting old, ripening. After the fruit has got its growth it should juice up and mellow. God forbid I should live long enough to ferment and rot and fall to the ground in a squash.

—Emily Carr

I'm aiming by the time I'm fifty to stop being an adolescent.

—Wendy Cope

One of the many things nobody ever tells you about middle age is that it's such a nice change from being young.

—Dorothy Canfield Fisher

There are only three ages for women in Hollywood—Babe, District Attorney, and Driving Miss Daisy.

—Goldie Hawn

The great secret that all old people share is that you really haven't changed in seventy or eighty years. Your body changes, but you don't change at all. And that, of course, causes great confusion.

—Doris Lessing

Old age is like flying through a storm. Once you're aboard, there's nothing you can do.

—Golda Meir

■ *Born Free* (1960)
by Joy Adamson

Joy Adamson's saga about raising her orphaned lion cub Elsa and then ultimately returning her to the wild is one of the best-loved "animals as a metaphor for children" books ever written, and it is a good reminder to us all that the price of freedom is having the courage not to hold on to anything too tightly.

Joy Adamson, the wife of a game warden living in Africa, unexpectedly becomes a mom later in life, when a lioness is killed along with her brood, leaving only one cub, Elsa. Elsa isn't old enough to survive by herself in the wild, so Joy adopts her and nurses her from infancy, feeding her with a bottle, protecting her from predators, and teaching her everything she needs to know to be a happy, healthy, and contributing member of lion society.

When Elsa hits adolescence, however, the specter of a life in captivity looms, and Joy must teach her feline charge, and herself, a hard lesson about freedom. Joy realizes that if Elsa, who has grown used to relying on the comforts of human care, isn't forced to face the wild on her own, she will never inherit the life she was born to and will instead live her life in a zoo behind bars. And so she begins the long and painful process of letting go.

When you're feeling that life is passing you by, pick up a copy of *Born Free* and take a deep breath of fresh air straight off the untrammeled savannah of limitless love.

Ch-ch-ch-ch-Changes

When you're sixteen, hormones are the things that convince you that you are the ugliest girl in the whole school and that no one will ever love you as Romeo loved Juliet or Jack loved Rose. When you're in your twenties, they're the force behind your bizarre obsessions with those bad boys with no visible means of support except your paycheck. When you're in your thirties, hormones are what you hope you have enough of to get in a child or two before you reach the next stage: your post-forties. That's when hormones make your PMS symptoms jump up three notches in intensity and force you to give up Mint Milanos and midafternoon lattes because now you're at risk for all sorts of wretched diseases and ailments.

Of course, not all of us follow this chronological path. Sometimes we find ourselves playing a grown-up version of Candyland: We draw a card and are whisked forward, or backward, into a totally different hormonal hell. Which explains Cher and that bagel boy. But if you're at a place in your life where you and your pals are discussing the difference between estradiol and estrogen, be sure to check out the following guides to the wonderful, wacky world of raging hormones.

continued . . .

- *Screaming to Be Heard* (1995)
  by Elizabeth Vliet, M.D.

After having some health problems that left a series of doctors either baffled or dismissive, Dr. Vliet finally verified that her symptoms were not all in
her head, founded a health clinic for women, and wrote this proconsumer,
prowoman book. In it, she lays out just how all those hormones coursing
through various parts of your body can cause everything from premenstrual
migraines and M&M addictions to menopausal fog. Unfortunately, as she
freely admits, the number of studies done on women's health issues is pretty
paltry considering that we're, what, 51 percent of the population? While we wait
for this research gender gap to close up, Vliet recommends combining traditional
Western medicine with alternative (what she calls "complementary") medicine—
and even advocates aromatherapy and massage. Pass the lavender oil!

- *No More Hot Flashes and Other Good News* (1983)
  by Penny Wise Budoff, M.D.

Like Elizabeth Vliet, Dr. Budoff started a women's health clinic because
she recognized that the medical establishment was not offering the best care
to female patients. She too tells you all about all those complicated hormonal
interactions. But unlike Dr. Vliet, Budoff is vehemently proestablishment
and anti–alternative medicine. I mean, do we really need warnings against the
dangers of echinacea and chamomile tea? And could we please just *consider*
estrogen replacement therapy that uses yams instead of horse pee?

- *Dr. Susan Love's Hormone Book* (1997)
  by Susan M. Love, M.D., with Karen Lindsey

Best known as a crusader against the breast cancer epidemic, Dr. Love
rings in with her own opinion on hormone replacement therapy, which is

continued . . .

that you should try to avoid it if at all possible. Black cohosh, bodywork, seaweed—she's got lots of alternatives. But of course they only work if you give up all your dietary vices and exercise regularly. You knew there was a catch, didn't you?

▪ *Women's Bodies, Women's Wisdom* (1994)
by Christiane Northrup

When you come to the point in your life when your and your girlfriends' conversations center not on men, careers, or vacation plans but on cholesterol counts, mammograms, nutrition, osteoporosis, and hormone replacement therapy, it's time for Christiane Northrup. She covers all these topics, but the main reason for the success of *Women's Bodies, Women's Wisdom* is its lesson in listening to your body. Granted, if you're the type who thinks that epidurals are the Cadillac of drugs, Northrup's blissed-out naturalism can be really annoying at times. She claims that the difference in her two pregnancy/birth experiences resulted in one of her daughters being trepidatious while the other, whose birth went more smoothly, is more confident and outgoing. And saying that fibroid tumors are caused by unresolved anger borders on blaming the victim.

Even though we think she takes the mind/body connection a little too far, Northrup raises some interesting questions about our relationship to our bodies. Before you rush to fill your prescriptions, check her out.

▪ *The Premature Menopause Book* (1999)
by Kathryn Petras

Yes, it is possible for menopause to begin in your thirties or even your twenties. If this is your situation, Kathryn Petras's book answers questions about starting hormone replacement therapy and will help you cope with hot flashes, fuzzy-headedness, and the reality that your fertile years have gone the way of the macarena. ▪

▪ *Cutting Loose* (1997)
by Ashton Applewhite

The women in this book came to realize that they had given up something ineffably precious and received little of equal value in return. Strong women, all had nevertheless abdicated a certain central responsibility for themselves, and this bad bargain ate away at them.

We've all heard the foreboding statistics that half of all marriages end in divorce, but plenty of us still buy into the bridal Barbie dream. We cross our fingers and hope that love really will conquer all, that *our* marriage will be different, and that we'll be the ones to win the coin flip. But too many of us find ourselves "dwindling into wives" or losing something of our selves. It can be scary to take a hard look at your marriage, particularly when you've got twenty more years left on the mortgage, a couple of kids, and a lifestyle and routine that have become as comfortable as a pair of broken-in fluffy pink slippers.

So what gives women the courage to leave, and do they regret it afterward? That's what Ashton Applewhite wanted to know, so she interviewed fifty or so women who took charge of their lives and ended their marriages. She was curious about the fact that over two-thirds of divorces are initiated by women, most of whom do try counseling of some sort to save the relationship—so much for the stereotype of the selfish feminist deserting her family because she has hot prospects or hot pants. To her surprise, Applewhite found that not one of the women regretted her decision, not even the ones who ended up in some crummy trailer park eating generic Rice Krispies. At least they weren't eating generic wheat puffs, which he always insisted upon. Hey, breakfast cereal may not seem like an important issue, but when it becomes a metaphor for the loss of self, the difference between cardboard-tasting rice and cardboard-tasting wheat is profound.

Good news too is that Applewhite discovered that divorce is not, on its own, devastating to kids. She makes a strong case that what damages children is fighting, abuse, and bad or neglectful parenting, divorce or no, which makes a lot of sense to us.

Weighing your possibilities as you contemplate the road ahead? Whether you're contemplating separation, divorce, or marriage, *Cutting Loose* will turn on your high beams.

Baby's in the House

The panic sets in as soon as that second blue line magically appears, telling you your life has changed irrevocably. First thing you have to understand is that regardless of how well informed a parent you become, everyone around you will be a self-appointed expert and tell you that you are screwing up your baby. You'll have to duck questions about all the hot topics, like cosleeping ("the family bed"), breast-feeding, and toilet training. Meanwhile, you'll be wondering whether to let the baby cry it out, pick him up immediately, or compromise and Ferberize. Do you shampoo more often, or less often, when cradle cap appears? And if you're supposed to toilet-train them before they get old enough to understand the concept of a power struggle, why do they make those diapers for four-year-olds?

Of course, if you consult a half dozen books, you can figure out what the majority opinion is—but don't be surprised if once you've taken your straw poll, your pediatrician tells you something else entirely. When in doubt, remember what Dr. Spock said two generations ago: You know more than you think you do.

When you face that long wall of parenting advice in your bookstore, you may want to start with these classic guides to bringing up baby.

Dr. Spock's Baby and Child Care (1945)
by Dr. Benjamin Spock

This is the bestselling, best-known parenting book in the history of American culture. It was Spock who first told parents back in the late 1940s to trust their instincts, to stop trying to force the baby into a militaristic feeding schedule, and to relax. Over the years the book was updated again and again, and his advice grew controversial as he became more politicized (to the left, that is). He took time out to rail against nuclear power and got considerably

continued . . .

more whole grain in his dietary suggestions. He started out recommending Karo syrup with evaporated milk for baby formula and, by the end of his life, suggested packing sushi into the kiddies' brown bags. Yet most of what Spock said is remarkably uncontroversial, sensible, and flexible—probably because so much of his advice is about timeless things like stork bites versus birthmarks and when to call the doctor—which makes his book a valuable resource half a century after its first publication.

The Baby Book (1993)
by William and Martha Sears

This touchy-feely guide is pro-baby to a fault. The Searses, both pediatricians, have eight children between them and a decidedly Woodstockian approach to parenting: They advocate cosleeping, carrying baby around in a sling all day—even at work—and responding to baby's every whimper immediately in order to teach her that she can always trust in the world around her (come to think of it, is this really a lesson we want our children to learn?). Reading their book will either justify your need to have your adorable little pumpkin attached at the hip or make you flagellate yourself for having a life.

What to Expect When You're Expecting (1984) / The First Year (1989) / The Toddler Years (1994)
by Arlene Eisenberg, et al.

This conservative parenting trilogy answers every conceivable question about pregnancy and those early years with authoritative and firm advice. Some people find *WTE* too paternalistic toward women and eerily old-fashioned (when you're suffering from morning sickness, the authors say, why not knit a sweater to distract yourself? Uh-huh). Others are alarmed by all the potential problems the authors discuss (although when you're pregnant

continued . . .

and feeling short of breath and weepy, it can be a real relief to discover that it's all hormones). And it's easy to freak out when baby doesn't hit all those milestones at the "right" time that *WTE* outlines.

Moreover, the dietary suggestions are a little extreme for the average American. True, they're very sound, but they're totally intimidating and guilt-inducing if you sneak off to McDonald's once a week for your Big Mac fix and a Happy Meal for the kid. Still, isn't it odd that the authors push wheat germ and tofu, then take a wishy-washy stance on breast-feeding versus formula?

If pregnancy were a book they would cut the last two chapters.
—Nora Ephron

Your Baby and Child from Birth to Age Five (1977)
by Penelope Leach

Leach focuses on baby development, explaining how you can help your baby along toward speaking, crawling, and walking. Unlike *WTE*, *Your Baby and Child* describes these milestones without making you feel that your child is a failure for not meeting them on schedule. She also helps you imagine what it must be like to emerge from the womb into this loud, noisy, cold, and dry world and provides lots of step-by-step illustrations to help you dress a wriggling three-month-old or shampoo a squawking tot (though she doesn't provide one we could really use—how to diaper a baby who insists on rolling onto his stomach).

continued...

Touchpoints (1992)

by T. Berry Brazelton, M.D.

Brazelton's love for babies at all their ages and stages shines through in this gentle guide to the milestones you should watch for and encourage. Controversial for his laid-back attitude on toilet training, he's nevertheless a nice nudger on other stuff. Moreover, he really helps you understand what's going on inside baby's head.

Giving birth is like taking your lower lip and forcing it over your head.

—Elizabeth Adamson

The Girlfriends' Guide to Pregnancy (1995) / to Surviving the First Year of Motherhood (1997) / to Toddlers (1999)

by Vicki Iovine

The hip, witty alternatives to *WTE*, by a former *Playboy* model turned record exec's wife turned mommy, these guides have an attitude. Iovine is definitely into the epidural thing and points out—rather cattily—that formula wins out over breast-feeding in geographical areas where women are most prone to home perming. She also gets gritty about postpartum weight loss (stop holding your breath), sex or lack thereof, and toddler tantrums. In short, these are fun books about *you*, which are great comic relief when you can't bear to read one more sentence about baby's bodily fluids. ■

▪ *Ladder of Years* (1995)
by Anne Tyler

What kind of a life was she leading, if every single one of last week's telephone messages could as easily be this week's?

Your favorite hunk, naked by candlelight and beckoning from a four-poster bed—now *there's* a rich fantasy. But if you're wrestling with lack of personal definition, here's one that ought to appeal to you: starting all over again from scratch, walking out on your unappreciative husband and kids, and constructing a new existence, even a new identity. Imagine being paid, and thanked regularly, for your skills and loyalty. You'd have a room of your own, with only the barest of necessities—no clutter to dust or put away—and your big decision for the day would be what to order for lunch and what book to read before bed. And you'd build a support system of friends as easily as you made the break with your past.

That's the story Anne Tyler has constructed in *Ladder of Years*. One day, while forty-year-old Delia Grinstead is at the beach on vacation with her family, she simply scoops up her bag, heads down along the shore, and just keeps on walking, right into a new life. Hitching a ride from a guy who has absconded with his brother's RV, a gold-shag-carpeted hideaway complete with entertainment center and a sink the size of a salad bowl, Delia finds herself riding along to who-knows-where, mentally calculating how much money she has in her beach bag and formulating a daring plan. She picks a town at random, finds an empty room in a boarding house, buys some underwear at the five-and-dime (it's a little hard to experience the delicious feeling of freedom when your bathing suit's riding up), and finds her first paying job the very next day.

Delia's family is predictably puzzled once her whereabouts are discovered. And to their credit, they do occasionally check in on her over the course of the next year. Mostly, however, they just stand back and allow her to reconstruct her life and her esteem, which had been worn to the bone. Delia had suffered for months before leaving, having been ignored by her kids, dissed by a would-be lover (mental note: Women wearing pink Peter Pan collars are easy prey for rebounders), and taken for granted by her husband, who married this very archetype of the dutiful daughter and wife because she came complete with a demeanor of modesty as well as with home and offices for his budding professional practice.

Read this one when you want to chuck it all but are reluctant to suffer the consequences, and vicariously enjoy Delia's exhilarating albeit improbable journey back to herself. We bet you'll find yourself keeping plenty of cash on hand just in case you get a notion to take a little vacation of your own.

Points to Ponder

1. *If you were to take off one day, with just your determination and your mad money, where would you go? And would your travel plans include an RV?*

2. *How long would it take for anyone to notice you were gone?*

▪ *Taking Charge of Your Fertility* (1995)
by Toni Weschler, M.P.H.

At first, it's party time. Sex without birth control! Boinking like bunnies in pleasurable anticipation, and afterward tossing around baby names. Definitely not that one—that was the name of the boss who made you break out in hives every Monday morning. No, that one sounds too pretentious. And you don't care if it is the hot celebrity girl-name of choice, no daughter of yours is going to be named Fifi Trixiebelle.

And then one day you realize that this conception thing is taking a little longer than you thought. You look back at your cryptic notes on the calendar (you thought that a few clever abbreviations would disguise for the casual observer your copious notes on sex acts and menstrual cycles). And you panic, imagining yourself in some movie-of-the-week plot about a surrogate mother keeping the baby you and your husband paid thousands to conceive and implant. You've entered the Kate Jackson and Judith Light zone, and some *Beverly Hills 90210* starlet is holding your happiness hostage.

If you're afraid your body is not as fertile as your imagination, Toni Weschler's book will reassure you that you're probably just miscalculating. She'll launch you right into a zealous take-charge mode, and you'll find yourself checking mucus consistency, charting basal temperature, and keeping track of something called your luteal phase. You'll feel empowered, trusting your body's signals. Then you can relax, give yourself a little more happy humping time, and feel pride in this newly won wisdom.

Of course, the flip side is, if you try to use this "fertility awareness method" to *prevent* pregnancy, you'd better be aware that the smallest slip-up can make F.A.M. as unreliable as the old "Vatican roulette." But if you're feeling that biological clock ticking, *Taking Charge of Your Fertility* may speed up your production schedule.

▪ *On Our Own* (1997)
by Melissa Ludtke

God doesn't believe there are any illegitimate children. Only white males do.
— Congressman Mike Kopetski (D-Oregon)

If your biological alarm clock is about to ring and Prince Charming has left the building, then *On Our Own* may be just the book you need to stop the clock. That's because Melissa Ludtke paints a happy picture of unmarried women who became moms and—surprise!—did not permanently psychologically damage their children or destroy Western civilization as we know it.

Ludtke interviewed unmarried mothers all over the country to find out what their lives are like, how they feel about their decisions, and whether they became moms accidentally (or accidentally-on-purpose) or adopted or used a sperm donor. Now, it's true that half of this very long book is about teen moms, whose biological clocks haven't even been wound up yet (which is pretty interesting on its own). But if you skip that and read the other half, you'll get the straight dope on everything from how to juggle child care and working to whether your child will ever be able to meet sperm donor number 874 and learn more about him than his SAT scores, hair color, and cuisine preferences.

Reading *On Our Own*, two things become very clear. One is that being a single parent, even if you're educated and have a little money and a mom who is eager to baby-sit, is hard, hard work, which makes this book a great reality check. The other is that until someone decides to do a study on educated, older unmarried moms, we'll probably continue to be bombarded with all sorts of dire judgments about how the sky is falling because of the Murphy Browns of the world.

Listen, as Ludtke admits, a lot of us have our own strong feelings about the differences between carrying through with an unexpected pregnancy at age forty-plus, or going to a sperm bank, or adopting a Chinese baby girl who has been abandoned by her parents because of her gender. But at the same time, once we women get to a certain age, we understand how powerful the need to be a mom can become, and it causes us to consider choices that we might have dismissed before.

If you're thinking about going it alone, *On Our Own* is an invaluable tool for helping you make your decisions.

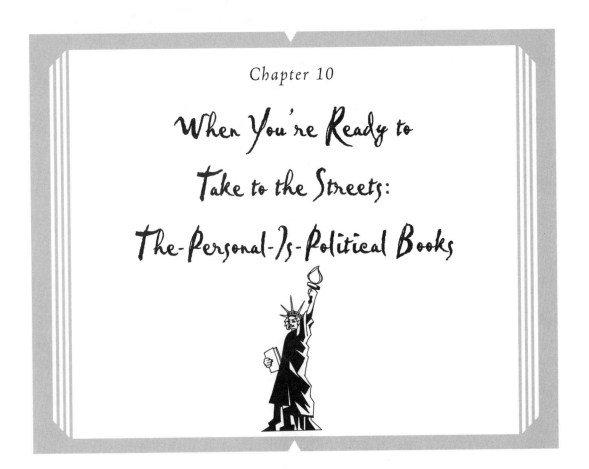

Chapter 10

When You're Ready to Take to the Streets: The-Personal-Is-Political Books

There comes a time in all our lives when we start to realize that we can either give in to misanthropy, disgust, and pessimism and crank up the Marilyn Manson CD, or we can walk out the door, find some other people who are just as fed up, and start the revolution already. True, many of us have grown cynical about the effectiveness of most forms of protest. Yet we all want to believe that we can make a difference.

Now, for some people, the battle is for respect and equality, while for others, it's to save Original Coke. When it comes to political goals that set hearts ablaze, there's no such thing as a trivial issue. Hey, if they ever take the chocolate chunks out of Cherry Garcia, we might very well take up arms.

Anyway, the first step in transforming our world is transforming ourselves. We have to change our perceptions, and this usually means unlearning some of our most readily accepted myths about our history and nature—like that "new" means "improved," or that "low in sugar *and* fat" is a goal to strive for in a dessert. Reading the books in this chapter will, we hope, inspire you to transform your anger into action. Because even if we can't eat a few pints of Ben & Jerry's without changing our thigh measurements, together we can move mountains.

■ *Downsize This!* (1996)
by Michael Moore

New, improved ways to pick the president #6: Cheers. Each candidate will step up to the bar and down twenty shots of tequila (worm optional). First one to recite the Bill of Rights while balancing the shot glass on his nose wins.

Whatever your political bent, it's hard not to love a populist who is willing to go head to head with the big guys who run it all, if only he could get their secretaries to make an appointment.

In *Downsize This!*, Michael Moore, best known for his film *Roger & Me*, in which he tried in vain to meet the CEO of General Motors and ask him why he devastated the Flint, Michigan, economy by sending jobs to Mexico, secures his mantle as the David who fights the corporate and government Goliaths. Moore has created a hall of fame of corporate crooks (and we can credit him with popularizing the term *corporate welfare*—who knew our tax dollars were bailing out so many bumbling CEOs?), pointed out the uncanny resemblance between the Republicans and the Democrats, and tested Pat Buchanan's campaign committee to see if they would accept a financial contribution from the John Wayne Gacy Fan Club (the answer, as we're sure you've guessed, is *hell yeah!*). And who else would call an optometrist at Mount Sinai Hospital to check out the implications of Steve Forbes's ability to go without blinking his eyes for an entire minute-and-a-half interview? We've got to agree: The man's an alien.

It's a good thing Moore is funny, because we'd be hard-pressed to find anyone who agrees with all his politics, which are haphazardly scattered across the board and tend toward an idealistic extreme. After all, anybody with an IRA or 401(k) has an interest in keeping big corporations solvent. But something about Moore's outrageous opinions and guerrilla theater suggestions make you want to go out there and use your buying, and voting, powers to get America back on track. If it seems you have no voice in the democracy, you'll feel empowered after reading this book—even if you end up doing nothing more than refusing to buy Fourth of July decorations that are made in China.

Note: Some of the issues discussed here are a little outdated, but Moore's take on them is still hilarious.

Points to Ponder

1. *Is political correctness an oxymoron?*

2. *What is the role of dignity in the political process? If we replaced elections with a no-holds-barred kick-boxing extravaganza to determine our representatives, would government work any better?*

3. *What if we skipped the middlemen and elected lobbyists instead?*

Us vs. Them

A Conservative is a fellow who is standing athwart history yelling "Stop!"
—William F. Buckley, Jr.

A Liberal is a man too broadminded to take his own side in a quarrel.
—Robert Frost

■ *The Milagro Beanfield War* (1974)
by John Nichols

He was tired, like most of his neighbors were tired, from trying to earn a living off the land in a country where the government systematically gathered up the souls of little ranchers and used them to light its cigars.

One day Joe Mondragón decided to irrigate the beanfield he owned and start up a crop—an impulsive act that, in the New Mexico town of Milagro, was akin to declaring war. Water rights, you see, belonged to the big developers downstate, and little guys like

Joe were supposed to forget about farming their land, hang tight, and wait for those terrific busboy and chambermaid jobs that all the new restaurants and hotels would generate (yeah, right—like the chance to scrape crumbs and scrub bathroom floors is something to hold out for).

But isn't it always that way? One day you just get fed up, tired of having your ass kicked from the corral to next Sunday, and you start your own personal rebellion. Next thing you know, you've stirred up your neighbors (or coworkers, or family), half of whom think you're crazy and half of whom think it's all one big excuse to get tanked at the Frontier Bar and load up on ammo at the local grocery store. Then the big shots who make the rules have to call an emergency meeting to figure out how to buy you out. Meanwhile there are dozens of minor skirmishes and retreats until the community finally wakes up and shakes off the dust of its distractions.

The Milagro Beanfield War is filled with rich, odd characters whose small-town alliances are severely tested. It twists and turns and takes several leisurely detours before reaching its conclusion, but when is real life, or real battle, linear?

Read this when you want to vicariously enjoy the triumph of an underdog and the uniting of a community. Hey, maybe it'll inspire you to irrigate a few fields of your own and see what you can harvest.

Food for Thought

If you're uncomfortable with public protest, you can express your views politically through diet alone with these food-for-thought cookbooks. They take thinking globally and acting locally to new heights, by showing us how to change the world through changing our diet.

Diet for a Small Planet (1971)
by Frances Moore Lappé

This is the book that started a food revolution and changed forever the way many Americans think about the meal on their plate. In *Diet for a Small*

continued . . .

Planet, a vegetarian cookbook, Frances Moore Lappé introduced her theory on the politics of food by asking us to imagine ourselves sitting down to an eight-ounce steak. "Then imagine the room filled with 45 to 50 people with empty bowls in front of them. For the 'feed cost' of your steak, each of their bowls could be filled with a full cup of cooked cereal grains." Pick this one up when you're feeling ineffectual, and say yes to world peace by saying no to a cheeseburger deluxe. (By the way, loooove the peanut soup.)

The Moosewood Cookbook (1977)
by Mollie Katzen

Among the most influential cookbooks of our time, *The Moosewood Cookbook* is based on the Moosewood Collective Restaurant's philosophy of better living through whole foods made with minimal preparation and a complete avoidance of meat. This 1970s classic, complete with hand-drawn illustrations and back-to-nature charm, made vegetarianism groovy and, more important, good tasting. Pick this one up when you want to get back to pure food basics but don't want to bore your dinner guests silly with macrobiotic dinner conversation (and skip the pineapple in the gazpacho unless you want to sear your intestinal tract). ▪

▪ Lies My Teacher Told Me (1995)
by James W. Loewen

You remember your American history textbook, don't you? The one with the eagle and the flag on the cover, the lofty title like *The American Vision,* and the hundreds of pages of turgid prose that no highlighter could make sense of? Yes, books like these were the reason backpacks were invented—you need some major muscle groups to haul around those tomes. So many pages, so little entertainment value.

If you're like most of us, grade school and high school history classes were about as fascinating as diagramming sentences. There were all those dates to memorize, and names and places and wars about God-knows-what, and petty details about things like the Teapot Dome scandal (when was the last time *that* one came up in a conversation?). But of course, it's not history's fault, Loewen explains. Actually, we Americans have led pretty interesting—and inspirational—lives. It's just that talking about all our acts of rebellion and our subversive heroes makes school boards and parents nervous, he explains, so the textbook writers dilute everything into a watery stew.

If you got to discuss what really happened, you'd have some really interesting tidbits for casual conversation. For instance, when white pioneer women who were snatched away by the Indians were recovered, they usually had no interest in going back home, much to the embarrassment of the U.S. government (which says a lot about how much fun it *really* was to be in a little house on the prairie, doesn't it?). Did you know that small, peaceful triracial communities flourished throughout pre–Revolutionary War America? Or that the Pilgrims were grave robbers? Loewen stirs up all sorts of trouble and makes you realize how much you've been missing by zipping past the History Channel on your way to see yet another cheesy disease-of-the-week movie on Lifetime. Who knew?

Read this when you want to understand why everyone's so damned apathetic these days. Because if we Americans realized what we—not our politicians—have accomplished over the last two hundred–odd years, we'd be a lot more optimistic about what we could accomplish in the future.

Power to the People, Right On!

*One revolution is like one cocktail, it just gets you organized
    for the next.*
                                            —Will Rogers

*I hold it, that a little rebellion, now and then, is a good thing, and as
    necessary in the political world as storms in the physical.*
                                            —Thomas Jefferson

The job of a citizen is to keep his mouth open.
—Günter Grass

All issues are political issues.
—George Orwell

If I am not for myself, who will be for me? Yet if I am for myself only,
what am I?
—Hillel

■ *A Shining Thread of Hope* (1998)
by Darlene Clark Hine and Kathleen Thompson

Black women are a prism through which the searing rays of race, class and sex are
first focused, then refracted. The creative among us transform these rays into a spec-
trum of brilliant colors, a rainbow which illuminates the experience of all mankind.
—Margaret B. Wilkerson, from the epigraph to *A Shining Thread of Hope*

Feeling a dearth of personal heroes? Well, this history of black women in America has plenty of them. Even those of us who are white chicks can vicariously enjoy the exploits of these women who helped shape America for four hundred years—especially when they include pipe-smoking cowboys in the Wild West, slaves with the financial savvy of Donald Trump, and schoolteachers who began their jobs by actually building the schools from discarded lumber.

And really, these are great *American* stories—lost stories about perseverance, entrepreneurial vision, ingenuity, and adaptation. Consider that, thanks to a handful of freed blacks and those aforementioned plucky schoolmarms, the literacy of African Americans went from somewhere around nil at the end of the Civil War to 60 percent forty years later. Can you imagine Americans in this era working diligently at resolving a major social problem and keeping the enthusiasm going for *two generations*? In the twenty-first century, once it hits *USA Today*, it's old news and we move on.

Then there are those Charleston slaves who used what little economic clout they had—selling eggs in the marketplace—to fix prices, make a killing, and buy freedom for themselves and their families before the slaveowners figured out what was happening. Think about that the next time you say you don't make enough money to have a savings account. And why aren't there any great old Western movies about Stagecoach Mary Fields, who had a shootout with a cowpuncher, drove a stagecoach, ran a restaurant, and threw birthday parties for the town whenever she felt like celebrating herself?

Iconoclasts aside, *A Shining Thread of Hope* is about everyday heroes as well—regular Jills and Janes who held their heads high and worked their butts off. Reading this book, you have to wonder how America has managed to forget such a rich history.

So when you get tired of hearing celebrity spin and are ready to hear about some genuine American heroines, check out *A Shining Thread of Hope.*

Points to Ponder

Who are your heroines? Are their names listed in the encyclopedia on your hard drive? Then again, do you even know their names?

■ *The Ugly American* (1958)
by William J. Lederer and Eugene Burdick

"You'll have to work among foreigners, but we don't expect you to love 'em just because you work among 'em. I don't care where you go to work for Uncle Sammy, you'll be living with a gang of clean-cut Americans."
—Jovial Joe Bing of the U.S. Foreign Service, in *The Ugly American*

Picture the most obnoxious, smug kids from your junior high school. You know—the ones who threw parties and "accidentally" began discussing them in front of everyone they didn't invite. The ones who mercilessly tormented the boys who grew facial hair early and the girls who grew breasts late. Now imagine those same kids grown up, living in large, airy villas in third world countries, attended to by servants, throwing cocktail parties with plenty of duty-free liquor, and hissing over their Scotch and sodas about the wretched humidity and those awful natives. We think you can imagine what happens next: Communist-backed guerrilla war. And Biff and Buffy? *First to the wall when the revolution comes!*

The Ugly American was written back in 1958 by a couple of fellows who worked in the foreign service and were disgusted by the arrogant Americans who came to Southeast Asia for the cheap booze and "hardship" pay, only to behave like such stereotypical capitalist pigs that Thomas Jefferson himself would have fled to the hills with a copy of Mao's Little Red Book. These stories (which have been fictionalized but are all based on true incidents and real-life dim-witted diplomats) clearly illustrate what happens when people who haven't matured past snickering about the length of someone's pants join America's diplomatic corps.

But *The Ugly American* isn't just a retelling of foreign policy and foreign officer horror stories. Lederer and Burdick also offer a few profiles of regular citizens who did more to enhance America's image in Southeast Asia than a dozen diplomats: a Catholic priest who listened to the needs of the locals and encouraged them to make up their own minds about which form of government would be best for their country, a Wisconsinite who set out to introduce dairy farming into the local economy, and even a harmonica-playing air force colonel nicknamed the Ragtime Kid who charmed everyone he met, making them realize that Americans aren't all rich imperialists out to exploit smaller countries.

This book is a good reminder that the world doesn't revolve around us Americans and that we oughtn't be so quick to assume our superiority. Moreover, *The Ugly American* reminds us why it's so important to make sure that our politicians and diplomats are people we can be proud to have represent us. It's an especially good reality check when you're about to do some traveling outside of the country.

▪ *Bury My Heart at Wounded Knee* (1970) by Dee Brown

Where today are the Pequot? Where are the Narragansett, the Mohican, the Pokanoket, and many other once powerful tribes of our people? They have vanished before the avarice and the oppression of the White man, as snow before a summer sun.

For many years the history of the American West was presented as a sweeping saga about a bunch of well-intentioned white guys who headed across oceans and mountains and plains to manifest their destiny in a brave new world. Their only obstacle, besides the cruel terrain and the biting winters, were the bloodthirsty savages who preyed upon these innocent settlers with bows and arrows and scalping knives, trying to deprive them of their rightful slice of the American dream.

Yeah. Okay. If you're still going for that one, the check is in the mail, the computer's down, and you can cure depression by eating St. John's wort–enhanced potato chips.

Published in 1970, *Bury My Heart at Wounded Knee* was the first major work to debunk the glorious myths about the settling of America. It offered a very different version of how the West was won.

Told from a Native American point of view, *Bury My Heart at Wounded Knee* contends that the Homeric epic about the great expansion westward is at best a biased account, and at worst, an intentional revision of history meant to gloss over the crimes of the white devil as he barged across a land that didn't belong to him, destroying the flora and fauna and slaughtering its local inhabitants.

Beginning with the Long Walk of the Navajos in 1860 and concluding with the massacre of the Sioux Nation at Wounded Knee, South Dakota, this groundbreaking book illustrates how in the space of just thirty years, the American Indians lost their land and their culture to a rapidly expanding white society, which doubled from 31 to 62 million in just three short decades.

This is a great book to read when you're feeling paranoid and antisocial and looking for confirmation that things are not what they seem. *Bury My Heart at Wounded Knee* validates our worst fears: that truth often lies buried beneath the surface, that history is open to interpretation, and that even the most time-honored of national triumphs can disguise a national disgrace.

And So It Goes . . .

If people have to choose between freedom and sandwiches they will take sandwiches.
—Lord John Boyd-Orr

One fifth of the people are against everything all the time.
—Robert Kennedy

Been There, Done That

■ *Steal This Book* (1971)
by Abbie Hoffman

*Our moral dictionary says no heisting from each other. To steal from
a brother or sister is evil. To not steal from the institutions that are
the pillars of the Pig Empire is equally immoral.*

The problem with writing a subversive text for radicals, hippies, Yippies, and
disgruntled youth, Abbie Hoffman found, is that book publishers and bookstores
are not exactly keen on selling books that beg readers to steal them. It's sort of like
naming your band Free Beer; you pose a big dilemma for the bar owner.

But Abbie was out to make a point or two, so in 1970, while in jail in
Chicago, he wrote and later self-published *Steal This Book* (which ended up
being distributed by Grove Press). The resulting guidebook threw everyone
into a tizzy. After all, it's one thing for an author to tell the disillusioned
youth of the country to reject capitalism, forget about getting jobs, and live at
subsistence level, making sandals from old tires and scouring the streets on
garbage day for furniture. (Hmm, do you think Amy Dacyzcyn of *Tightwad
Gazette* fame was an original Yippie? Because we can just see her in Goodyear
Birkenstocks with seatbelt ankle straps.) And we can sort of justify his
providing diagrammed specifics for rigging pay phones to get free calls. But
it's another thing entirely to explain how to build a pipe bomb. To his credit,
Hoffman cautioned fellow revolutionaries to "be careful that you don't injure
a night watchman or guard" when destroying the ROTC building or
whatever. But given Hoffman's half-joking tone and heavy sarcasm, it's hard
to know whether he seriously thought anyone would follow his bomb-
building instructions, or whether he was pretending to advocate violence just
so he could piss off "the Establishment."

continued . . .

For those of us who spent most of 1971 trying to complete our Wacky Pack collection—and those of us who weren't even born yet—it's hard to imagine giving out addresses for underground papers and communes on one page and joking about such sinister matters as bombing buildings, pulling knives on cops, and gathering collections of Saturday night specials "just in case" on another. But that's what makes *Steal This Book* such a fascinating—and disturbing—period piece.

If you missed the dark days at the end of the 1960s, or if you're trying to forget them, there's nothing like Abbie Hoffman's guide for radical living to bring to life that extraordinarily strange and tumultuous chapter in American history and to make you ask just what led so many young people to such explosive anger and cynicism—and just what the hell the punchline was. ■

Points to Ponder

1. Who are today's radicals?

2. Are they any fun at a party?

Let God Sort 'Em Out

Whenever a man has cast a longing eye on office, a rottenness begins in his conduct.
                                            —Thomas Jefferson

If you ever injected truth into politics you would have no politics.
                                            —Will Rogers

Politics is the gizzard of society, full of gut and gravel.
—Henry David Thoreau

Politicians are the same all over. They promise to build a bridge even when there is no river.
—Nikita S. Khrushchev

■ *The Inner Jefferson: Portrait of a Grieving Optimist* (1995) by Andrew Burstein

There are at least two Thomas Jeffersons in the American consciousness. There's the hero who wrote the Declaration of Independence and got his name grafted onto thousands of schools, congested highways, and unimaginative small towns and counties. Then there's the man who wrote lofty pieces about the natural inferiority of the African American and the animalistic passions of the race, only to secretly get down and funky with his slave Sally Hemings and force his own children by her to work, what, fifteen hours a day?

So is Jefferson a hero or a villain? The man Burstein portrays is arguably both, and what's more, he's the quintessential American white guy politician. Think about it: Jefferson was a total hypocrite. He had high ideals but an extremely messy personal life. He wrote beautiful pieces on the nature of love and kept up his image as a chaste widower, but he fathered six children by his slave. He pontificated about honor and self-restraint, then died a debtor, unable to free his slaves because of the economic mess he left behind, all because he went way over budget decorating his house, thereby paving the way for deficit spending by politicians for generations to come. Come to think of it, a lot of us regular Americans have followed his patriotic lead, too, resulting in an economy based on going into hock to buy more stuff for our living rooms.

Moreover, Jefferson was, like most of our elected representatives, a sellout. In the beginning of his career he was antislavery—he even outlawed it in the first draft of the Declaration—but he backed off from his position later in order to make nice with his buddies. He wallowed in the muck, slinging mud at his opponent during his campaign for president, pouting that the other guy started it. He was a renaissance man who exhibited the best of Yankee ingenuity and loved to breed new plants, but he wasn't above smuggling a few seeds in illegally from another country, figuring that a fellow in his position ought to be able to bend the rules when it suited him. Really, you can see why Strom Thurmond, Jesse Helms, and Oliver North love the man.

But as any good biographer should do, Burstein paints a picture of a man who, for all his flaws, had a lot of good points too—qualities that led him to establish the University of Virginia and freedom of (and from) religion. He also educated his daughters, had the vision to expand America through the Louisiana Purchase (which was a great bargain, unless, of course, you were an Indian), introduced many new plants to the country (those smuggled seeds helped a lot), and envisioned a form of government that would grow with his people. He was perpetually on a self-improvement kick and tried his best to be a good father and friend (although apparently not to anyone with African blood in them, which, let's face it, is a pretty big oversight).

But maybe Jefferson himself offered the best excuse for his failings. At the end of his life, he said he figured that this "race business" would tear the country apart but that it was up to the next generation to solve, since he'd already busted his butt trying to create the country. Yeah, our new nation had a fatal flaw, but come on, what do you expect from one guy? And you know, he was probably right.

Reading this book, you'll realize that often the people with the greatest vision, optimism, creativity, and leadership abilities have character flaws that run just as deep. And once we accept that our heroes and icons aren't angels and saints—unless we engage in a little creative historical revisionism—we will be able to open the ranks to a lot more human beings who have something great to offer us. Check it out when you're feeling there are no leaders you can respect.

Points to Ponder

If we hold our presidents to the highest personal standards, is there anyone we can elect?

Back to the Future

It's often said that the best way to learn about our own time is to measure it against the past, but sometimes a glimpse into the future can be just as illuminating. While foresight is not 20/20, as hindsight can be, the horrific futuristic societies suggested by these back-to-the-future books are often chillingly accurate, and they can teach us a lot about the terrifying implications of today's decisions when we project them into the world of tomorrow.

Brave New World (1932)
by Aldous Huxley

Aldous Huxley's *Brave New World* eliminates all difficult human emotion that might interfere with the smooth flow of the body politic. The novel depicts a scientifically balanced, efficiently controlled state that allows for no personal emotions or individual responses; art and beauty are considered disruptive, and *mother* and *father* are terms and concepts that have been entirely eliminated. So the upside is that there is no violence, no anger or depression, no hunger, and no dysfunctional family issues. The downside is that the entire population is sterilized and on antidepressants, babies are born in laboratories, and love and marriage are against the law. The next time you're wishing for world peace at any cost, you might want to pick up a copy of *Brave New World* and remind yourself to be careful what you wish for—because you just might get it.

1984 (1949)
by George Orwell

Well, 1984 has come and gone, and we aren't all living in fear of the thought police, and Big Brother isn't waiting around every corner. Or is he? George Orwell's grim depiction of Oceania, a futuristic police state in which

continued . . .

thoughts, words, and deeds are mandated by the government, is a frightening reminder about the power of the press to create reality and what happens to a society in which history is a lump of clay in the hands of the powers that be. Read this one when you need to be reminded to believe only half of what you read and none of what you hear.

The Handmaid's Tale (1986)
by Margaret Atwood

Margaret Atwood's *The Handmaid's Tale* presents a futuristic society in which women are categorized according to their reproductive capabilities. In the Republic of Gilead, women's activities are determined entirely in terms of their usefulness to men, and in an age of declining births, much of this activity is accomplished from a horizontal position. The next time you get tired of doing it all, read *The Handmaid's Tale* and remember the terrible cost of inertia. ▪

▪ *Random Acts of Kindness* (1993)
by the editors of Conari Press

[E]very hand we extend, every act of kindness we commit, sends a ripple out into the world that is magnified by every life it encounters.

They say the personal is the political, and if you're feeling burned out about changing the world, *Random Acts of Kindness* is the book for you. Its anecdotes teach us that one moment, one person at a time, we can create a revolution and bring back human dignity and respect. Which is definitely good news if you work in a service profession (check out the bit about the couple who left the waitress $100 for a $20 tab).

Actually, although we discovered this book to be uplifting, it's a little disappointing, too. Sure, it's fun to vicariously enjoy, and even more fun to emulate, the person who paid the toll for the car behind her, or who gave her ice cream cone to the little boy who just dropped his. But some of the stories and the suggestions for random acts of kindness seem like they shouldn't be so, well, random. Shouldn't we all reach out with a kind word to a stranger in the mall who is clearly overwhelmed by her kids' demands, or chase after someone who we realize has accidentally dropped something valuable? Coming from the Midwest, we have plenty of stories of strangers who came out of their houses to push a car stuck in the snow or give someone a jump. Shouldn't looking out for your fellow travelers be a given? 'Cause if it's not, there are going to be a lot of cars stuck on the side streets of life.

If you haven't read *Random Acts* yet, check it out when you're feeling that you are too inconsequential to make your mark on the world. We hope it inspires you to go above and beyond, just for the fun of it, and watch the ripples you create.

Chapter 11

When You're Feeling Unnoticed and Unloved: Bad Hair Babe Books

We all go through those bad hair periods where we feel like Georgy Girl before she got up off of the shelf. You know the drill—bad hair, bad skin, bad attitude . . . and then there's that inch you can pinch. Whether it lasts a day, a week, or even longer, we all go through phases where no matter how much we've managed to accomplish, and how much we benefit the lives of others, we feel like the bottom rung on the food chain, just a few steps up from pond scum.

When you're feeling like a creature from the Black Lagoon, venturing outside of the swamp can be a very scary experience. Lights glare, strangers stare, and even your own family members can seem uncaring and unappreciative.

So the next time you're engaged in hand-to-hand combat with your self-image, and losing, pick up one of these bad hair babe books and spend some quiet time alone counting your blessings and making peace with that weird sister in the mirror.

■ *If I'm So Wonderful, Why Am I Still Single?* (1998)
by Susan Page

The biggest problem with going frog kissing in search of a prince (or princess) is that the terrain is swampy. As you go about looking for magic, it is far too easy to get pulled into a quicksand pit and spend a lot of time mucking around with a lot of frogs.

We all want to believe that love is magical, that it will sweep us away into happily-ever-after. As little girls, we're total suckers for flouncing ballgowns, fairy dust, and pumpkins turned into carriages. Then we graduate to romance novels. Soon we find ourselves thinking that if we just let our pluck and pride shine through, the most inscrutable and eligible bachelor in the country will simply go mad for us. And then we go on that blind date our mom set up.

Yes, we know true love is our due, but sometimes it needs a little push. So why not start by forming an action plan? When we're in this zealous mode, we're just ripe for ten strategies, dozens of exercises that involve journaling and asking friends for feedback about our personality flaws, fill-in and multiple-choice questionnaires, and charts that pinpoint exactly what our problems have been in the past.

Susan Page goes into great depth about the dynamics of dating and even draws on Gestalt therapy to create plenty of little exercises to force you into introspection whether you want to go there or not. If you pass her relationship readiness test, you'll be reassured to know that you can just ignore those statistics that say you'll never find someone. Why? Because *you're special.* Hey, Mister Rogers said it way back when, and sweetheart, you can believe it. Best of all, Susan Page promises that Mom is wrong—you are *not* being too picky. Instead, you're refusing to tie yourself up by tolerating a mediocre lover. You're keeping yourself available for your real soul mate, who is just around the corner, ready to sweep you off your feet and carry you away to a land of romantic evenings, financial stability, and an even distribution of housework.

If you're in the mood to analyze all your missteps to the smallest detail and be your own budget therapist, this is the book for you.

Points to Ponder

1. *If I'm so wonderful, why do I want to be married?*

2. *Can you find Mr. Right when you're looking for him?*

Words to Live By

Anxiety is the dizziness of freedom.

—Søren Kierkegaard

■ *Bride of Pendorric* (1963)
by Victoria Holt

I had married a man who had seemed to me all that I wanted in a husband—solicitous, loving, and passionately devoted.

Bride of Pendorric is arranged around a timeless formula: a fair maiden with flowing golden locks, flawless skin, and flashing blue eyes falls in love with an aristocrat far above her station, marries him, and lives happily ever after. In this novel, the maiden is Favel Farington, who is left suddenly vulnerable by the death of both her parents. She meets and quickly marries a debonair but mysterious aristocrat, Roc Pendorric, who is of course tall, dark, and handsome. Trouble ensues.

No sooner do they marry than Favel begins to question Roc's intentions. After all, they married so quickly, and she knows so little about him. He is often given to prolonged periods of brooding silence, and as many of us do when faced with the inscrutable silence of a mysterious male, she begins to get paranoid. Is he actually the good and loving lord of the manor he seems to be, or is he a rapscallion, prone to ravishing whole caravans full of gypsy virgins on the side, and peopling the island with little boys who all bear the telltale

Pendorric ears and patrician nose? And just what is the deal with the dead mother roaming the hallways just outside the dayroom?

Ultimately, of course, the true scoundrel is unearthed, and Favel Farington's Roc Pendorric is proven to be the good husband and would-be father that she thought he was. And thanks to a twist of fate that leaves her a wealthy woman (an inheritance from a heretofore-unknown and recently deceased uncle), Favel is once again a woman of her own means who can proceed forward with full trust in her husband's affections.

The classic romantic formula has changed somewhat throughout the years. For example, these days Favel wouldn't inherit her wealth—she would earn it as, say, the CEO of her own parfumerie, which would probably be called something like Favel's Fragrances. Yet despite the new job description of the romantic heroine, the message of romance novels remains essentially the same: If we're good enough, and pretty enough, and plucky enough, and vulnerable enough, then someday our prince will come.

When you're feeling disappointed by romance, when the flashing has gone out of your eyes and your formerly glowing ringlets are feeling particularly dull, dry, and lifeless, it can be comforting to read a formula romance. Books like *Bride of Pendorric* remind us that while love is real, romance is something of a conceit, a set of manufactured expectations based on the fairytale formulas of childhood, and that while we may not be Favel Farington, neither is anybody else.

Yeah, We Wish

It's a good thing publishers don't offer unconditional guarantees for their books, because we have a feeling we'd demand our money back with these promising-the-moon titles:

Thin Thighs in 30 Days

Cook One Hour, Eat All Week

Seven Days to a Brand New Me

continued . . .

Toilet Training in Less Than a Day

How to Borrow Up to $25,000 in Just One Hour on Your Signature
Alone

Mail Two Letters and Earn $15,000 in One Month

Never Be Lied to Again

Never Be Tired Again

Never Be Nervous Again

Never Be Lonely Again

Never Catch Colds Again

No More Bad Hair Days

The Dating Game: How to Find the Perfect Man and Have Fun While
Searching

Discover Your Perfect Soul Mate

A Perfect Home Wedding

How to Kill Cockroaches and Never Again Be Reinfested

Train Your Dog in One Hour

No More Naughty Cats

and of course, our personal favorite . . .

The One Hour Orgasm

It's Not Our Cup of Tea, But . . .

■ *The Beauty Myth* (1991)
by Naomi Wolf

Men are visually aroused by women's bodies and less sensitive to their arousal by women's personalities because they are trained early into that response, while women are less visually aroused and more emotionally aroused because that is in their training.

Can a woman be a feminist and still wear bright red lipstick? Or must we don Birkenstocks and refuse to shave under our arms?

That's a big question for those of us who had a long awkward phase that entailed wearing big plastic glasses and ill-fitting Treasure Island jeans. We weren't making a political statement so much as holding up a flashing neon sign that shouted "I am fifteen and utterly without self-esteem! Do not ask me to the homecoming dance!" Now that we are full-fledged, self-actualized, confident women, can't we have a little fun with really loud lipsticks with names like Red Zone and Bold Berry?

We think Naomi Wolf understands. Though her bestselling book criticizes the beauty culture we have created, the fashion industry that encourages women to hate their bodies, and the makeup industry that pretends to have found the scientific solution to aging, Naomi—who seems to have a penchant for nice lipsticks herself—doesn't believe that a plain face is a litmus test for sincerity. We know she feels this way because she tells us so in the introduction to the paperback edition of *The Beauty Myth*, and she discusses how her words have been twisted and turned every which way, making it seem as if she is antibeauty.

If Naomi Wolf has been misunderstood, though, she has only herself to

continued . . .

blame. Because for all the provocative questions she raises in her book, for all the fascinating points about American women's near-religious zeal for beauty and our tendency to equate unattractiveness with frigidity, very few readers of *The Beauty Myth* ever figured out what the hell she was talking about. Wolf, who went on to pen far more intelligible books than this one, doesn't exactly write beautifully. The poor reader has to slog through all sorts of confusing references to the Rites of Beauty (don't you hate when writers capitalize all their terms, as if they were trademarking their self-created jargon?) and an argument that is harder to follow than a conservative's defense of homophobia.

Our take on *The Beauty Myth* is that, at its core, it's just another book bitching about those damn supermodels—which makes us all for it. So buy it when you're tired of feeling bad about your looks, support the cause, forget about trying to make heads or tails out of her rhetoric, and feel good about your act of political rebellion. Then go to the mall, get a free makeover, refuse to buy any of the pricey products, and take yourself out for the evening. Because, girlfriend, you are beautiful. ■

■ *Guerrilla Dating Tactics* (1993)
by Sharyn Wolf

Guerrilla soldiers are brave, scrappy troopers who owe their success to spotting unconventional opportunities in out-of-the-way places and making the most of each one. They operate without formal guidelines, flashy uniforms, or a reliance on safety in numbers.

You've been trying to find Mr. Right for years now, and you've finally come to face facts: This is an out-and-out war, and you are a soldier of fortune, a Rambo seeking to beat the odds and rescue the hope of marriage from the sheer hell that is your dating life. Hon, you need Sharyn Wolf's book.

In Wolf's pull-no-punches approach, you've got to be determined, fierce, devious. If you decide to come on to your waiter by asking his boss where his car is parked so you can slip your phone number under his windshield wipers, and you see some competitor has already beaten you to the punch, well, just tear up her note and stick in your own. Honey, there's no glory in being nice. You've got to nail him any way you can. Pick-up lines? They're here. Icebreakers? Spill your drink on him. Need flirting advice? You'll get the play-by-play description of how to do it, with specific details on how long to hold eye contact (at least three seconds), how to wink (once, never twice), and what bar props to use to signal that you're hot tonight (we always thought stroking your long-neck beer bottle was a bit forward, but you'll have to put aside your modesty and go for it). There's even a six-step guide to rising from your bar stool without tripping all over yourself, spilling your drink, and ensuring that you will be plagued by loneliness and embarrassment ever after.

Now, some would say you'll find your mate when you're not looking. If that's true, then these aggressive tactics will serve only to make you feel as if you're making progress. But isn't that what you need to believe when you're going through a long dry spell? There's a time for enjoying yourself and confidently assuming that you will naturally attract wonderful lovers who will approach you, and a time for panic and desperate measures. That's why Sharyn Wolf clues you in to the personal ads that will net the best prospects (hint: Do not place it in the "Anything Goes" column in *The Village Voice*) and how to set up a low-risk first date that won't demoralize you any more than you are already by the seemingly slim pickings.

Laugh as you might at the brashness of her suggestions and the insinuation that the reason you may be single might just possibly be that you're a social moron, the reality is, there will be times when you feel that this is a book you absolutely must have in order to face the dating scene. Go ahead and read, and then take a chill pill already, because if you're this manic about your pursuit, we don't want to think about who you are willing to spend an evening with.

Yet Another Reason We Preferred the Book . . .

Character	Description	Hollywood's Interpretation
Jo March (Little Women)	"very tall, thin, and brown, and reminded one of a colt" . . . "a decided mouth, a comical nose, and sharp gray eyes" . . . "round shoulders had Jo, big hands and feet."	*delicate, gamine Winona Ryder*
Scarlett O'Hara (Gone with the Wind)	"Scarlett O'Hara was not beautiful, but men seldom realized it when caught by her charms . . ."	*ethereal and luminescent Vivien Leigh*
Jane Eyre (Jane Eyre)	"I felt it a misfortune that I was so little, so pale, and had features so irregular and so marked. . . . I am poor, obscure, plain, and little."	*exquisite Joan Fontaine*
Erin (Strip Tease)	"The modest dimensions of Erin's breasts had been an issue for a long time. Erin's mother (who was on her third set of saline implants) believed that surgical enhancement would increase Erin's chances of attracting a good man . . . Erin said she was satisfied with the God-given size of her breasts, and confident that customers would find her sexy."	*silicone-enhanced Demi Moore*

■ *Bridget Jones's Diary* (1996)
by Helen Fielding

Tuesday 3 January
I can actually feel the fat splurging out from my body. Never mind. Sometimes
you have to sink to a nadir of toxic fat envelopment in order to emerge, phoenix-
like, from the chemical wasteland as a purged and beautiful Michelle Pfeiffer fig-
ure. Tomorrow new Spartan health and beauty regimen will begin.

A sure sign of self-confidence is the ability to laugh at oneself. And the surest sign that a movement—like, say, feminism—has taken solid hold is that its followers can laugh at their decidedly un-PC behavior. You see, despite our grandest ambitions, we all sometimes develop a sort of acne of the esteem: Under stress, we break out in eruptions of neurotic, obsessive, self-loathing, desperate-for-a-man behavior. Pathetic? Of course. Agonizing? Definitely. Hilarious in retrospect? Undeniably.

Which is why we never understood why some women dourly dismiss *Bridget Jones's Diary* as an affront to feminism, and Bridget Jones as the literary equivalent of Ally McBeal, another comic character that rankles those too concerned with rulebooks and putting on a public front. If we're going to win the great battle against the patriarchy, the thinking goes, we can't admit our love for short skirts. We're supposed to be incensed by Bridget's addiction to bizarre diets consisting of bananas, pears, potatoes, and Mars bars. We should be embarrassed by her obsession with her boss, whose idea of romance goes no further than a few quickies and some risqué instant messages on the interoffice e-mail. We should frown on Bridget's inability to find meaning in her solidly white-collar publishing job and her neurotic need to tally each day's calorie consumption, alcohol unit intake, cigarettes smoked, and loser lottery tickets bought, along with her body weight and words of self-praise or self-disgust ("130 lbs. terrifying slide into obesity—why? why?").

Oh, lighten up, people! Bridget is hilarious, and all of us have a little of her in us. No, she's not really desperate for the love of her boss Daniel, but obsessing over him is a nice distraction from having to troll among the diamond-patterned-sweater fellows she meets at the parties hosted by her friends, the Smug Marrieds. Bridget can't help being a little too caught up in her defense mechanisms. She is rapidly approaching thirty and just a little worn out from a good ten years of "fuckwittage" from men and from dealing with her certifiable mother who likes to wake her up early on an August morning with a phone call to check what Bridget's Thanksgiving and Christmas plans are. Bridget is often a little strung out, a tad hung over ("11:30 A.M. Badly need water but seems better to keep eyes closed and head stationary on pillow so as not to disturb bits of machinery and pheasants in head"), and trying to maintain her pluck ("Spent the weekend struggling to remain disdainfully buoyant after the Daniel fuckwittage debacle."). How can anyone not love her?

The success of *Bridget Jones's Diary* and its host of imitators is, we think, a good thing for feminism. It's time we stopped feeling the need to put on an act of unflappability and accepted that we all have our Bridget days—well, maybe months—and that this in no way diminishes the fact that we are, deep down, quite confident. If we weren't, we wouldn't be laughing. So read this when you're ready to laugh at yourself.

Words to Live By

Anxiety is fear of one's self.

—Wilhelm Stekel

Any Way You Slice It, You Can't Have Your Cake and Eat It, Too

Most of us have, at one point or another, tried to stick to a diet. But all that willpower doesn't save us from nutritional hell when even the experts don't agree on what the ideal diet is. Are oils bad? Is refined sugar akin to cocaine? And is there any way to justify eggs Benedict and a mimosa on a Sunday morning?

continued . . .

Over the years, these diets seem to have gained the largest number of loyal followers, but until scientists all agree on which one is the healthiest, you're on your own.

Eat More, Weigh Less (1993)

by Dr. Dean Ornish

How can you resist a title like that? And it's true, too—you really can eat more and weigh less. Well, naturally, there's a catch. You cannot eat more Entenmann's coffee cakes—not even the low-fat ones. And you cannot eat more Tostitos and salsa (although you can put the latter on a baked potato—yeah, that's a delicious substitute—*not*). What you can have is lots of vegetables, whole grains, and fruit, and the occasional teaspoonful of ice cream (can anyone stop at just one?). What you have to eliminate is all—that's right, *all*—oils, even olive and canola; all nuts; all dairy fats, meat, olives, and avocados. Then, too, you have to do at least some light exercise—even just walking—and stress reduction, like meditation, to get the full benefits.

Upside: Once you get the hang of it and once you get used to the flavors, or lack thereof, Ornish's is the only diet proven to actually reverse heart disease, which is a real plus considering that that's what most of us women will die of.

Downside: The real trick to making Ornish's system work is cooking without oils and using lots of herbs for flavor, which accounts for the fact that the recipes here are mighty tasty and *extremely* involved (note that Ornish followed up with *Everyday Cooking with Dean Ornish*, which has easier recipes). Also, you may find yourself intensely craving sugars and fats.

In the same vein: *Stop the Insanity!* by Susan Powter, and *The Pritikin Program for Diet and Exercise* by Nathan Pritikin.

continued . . .

Enter the Zone (1995) and Mastering the Zone (1997)
by Barry Sears

If you can't make heads or tails out of Sears's explanations of how various substances are digested by the body, don't worry—following the diet is a lot simpler than making sense of the breakdown of amino acids (and Sears's follow-up, *Mastering the Zone*, clarifies further just how to put the diet into action). Basically, Sears thinks we need to get over our fat fear and make sure we have enough protein to run our engines—eat enough protein and other good stuff, and avoid too many carbs, and your body will flush out the excess fats instead of storing them on the lining of your arteries.

Upside: *The Zone* has helped a lot of people lose weight and gain energy, and it doesn't require vegetarianism or austere nonfat eating.

Downside: If you're concerned about heart disease, there's really no evidence that *The Zone* will help prevent it. Also, if you eat fats (such as the ones found in meat), you'll have to watch how much you eat, or your weight will creep up again.

In the same vein: *Dr. Atkins' Diet Revolution, Protein Power, Carbohydrate Addict's Diet, The Diet Cure, The Complete Scarsdale Medical Diet.*

The Beverly Hills Diet (1981)
by Judy Mazel

This is one of those lose-ten-pounds-for-the-high-school-reunion diets that we now know just lead to yo-yo dieting. But if you're determined to lose quickly, lots of women swear by it.

Upside: You get to eat lots of fruit and yummy pineapple.

Downside: This diet is pretty hard to follow if you don't live in a papaya or mango grove. It's not healthy over the long term. And let's be honest here—the anal fissures are a truly unpleasant side effect. ■

■ *Fat Is a Feminist Issue* (1978)
by Susie Orbach

My fat says "screw you" to all who want me to be the perfect mom, sweetheart, maid and whore. Take me for who I am, not for who I'm supposed to be. If you are really interested in me, you can wade through the layers and find out who I am.

Any biologist will tell you that fat has its function in the body. We can't get our periods or get pregnant without it; nor can we stay warm, or produce all our hormones, or even maintain our mental faculties. Still, wouldn't we give all of that up for Cindy Crawford's body? I mean, what's a little premature senility when you can look great in a thong?

Actually, psychologist Susie Orbach claims, fat has some psychological functions we haven't even thought of. In this culture, fat desexualizes us and allows us to be one of the boys, or one of the girls—it takes us out of the competition for getting the guy. It allows us to occupy space, literally and figuratively, making us a force to be reckoned with. It provides us with an excuse for our failures. And our fat says to Mom, "See, I still do need you, because I can't take care of myself," while simultaneously telling her, "You can't force me to be a good girl and control my appetite." Fat, it seems, can be a very useful item in our psychological toolbox.

Then again, the compulsive eating that brings on the fat serves a lot of useful purposes, too. We can stuff our rage, let ourselves go out of control, be bad girls who inhale chocolate cheesecake instead of good girls who nibble on steamed asparagus. And anorexia has its psychological purpose, too, keeping us desexualized little girls in control of our lives and our food consumption.

Let's face it—for a lot of us, a Twinkie is not just a Twinkie. It is a powerful weapon in our battle against patriarchal expectations, an archnemesis over which we must exercise control, evil incarnate. Rather than jeopardize our health, Orbach suggests, maybe it's time we started stripping our food of its power and rechanneling our willpower in more productive ways. Until then, we'll be no more than the chattel of cheese fries.

Read this when you're ready to dig deeper into the reasons behind your Mint Milano jones.

Doomed But Inspired Heroes

■ *Buried Alive: The Biography of Janis Joplin* (1973)
by **Myra Friedman**

*Maybe my audiences can enjoy my music more if they think
I'm destroying myself.* —Janis Joplin

The image of Janis Joplin that I have burned into my mind is not of her
onstage, giving another electric performance as a raunchy, roaring rock vocal-
ist: feathers woven in her hair, legs twitching, face scrunched and drawn as
she wails with raw emotion. It's from a film of Janis at a press conference
when she returned to her hometown of Port Arthur, Texas, to attend her ten-
year high school reunion. A reporter asked her about going to the prom, and
Janis muttered that she hadn't attended. But surely she'd been asked, the
reporter pressed. Janis replied quietly, "No, I wasn't." Her pain was palpable,
and watching it years after her death (and years after I had put on a face
of bravado and gleefully downed rum and Cokes at my girlfriends' prom
reject party in Cindy Sieber's basement, insisting that I hated formal events
anyway), I winced in sympathy. Janis recovered quickly, pretending to sob and
saying, "And I've been crying ever since." The reporters laughed, but I didn't
because I knew damn well that, in fact, she had been.

Uncontrollable vulnerability beneath a mask of confidence is the eternal
appeal of Janis Joplin. And what woman can't identify with a sweet and beloved
child—beautiful, talented, intelligent, even precocious—who in a matter of a
few months as a teen mutates into a frizzy-haired, acne-scarred young outcast?
Once she entered puberty, Janis found her clever questions were now perceived
by insecure teachers as annoying challenges, her artistic aspirations caused
jealous grumbling among her peers, and her unwillingness to place herself into

continued . . .

the straitjacket of postwar, small-town conformity infuriated the locals. What, she had to wonder, had gone so horribly wrong?

Unfortunately, Janis began to quiet her anxieties and insecurities with every sedative she could get her hands on. Over the course of her career, she tried often to stay away from drugs, knowing that her crutch had the capability of destroying her, but her inability to handle the intensity of her emotions brought her back to drugs again and again. Using drugs also arrested her emotional growth, artificially keeping her in an adolescent state that helped create a public image that an entire generation embraced. Their vicarious enjoyment of her destructive behavior became a prison for her, one she didn't have the confidence to break out of.

Like so many women struggling to define themselves, Janis had so much turbulence on the inside that even the best of external events couldn't pull her out of a blue funk and ameliorate her agony. She OD'd on heroin when she was at a high point in her career and in the midst of planning her wedding; she hoped to stop touring soon, maybe have a baby. Instead of composing a new life for herself, she ended it—accidentally.

We all struggle with self-definition at various times in our lives. We never know when we're going to hit a growth spurt. But we have to go with it— even if we seem a little wobbly or silly at first. And we have to stand up to people who think we should have stayed with Big Brother and the Holding Company, even though they couldn't keep a beat or play a lead guitar riff in tune. We have to move on.

And if we are lucky, we manage to muddle through our journey of self-discovery without falling victim to disaster. If we are really lucky, we discover road maps along the way; we learn from the stories of women like us who took a wrong turn, or who didn't get off the road in time to save themselves, and we wrest control of our own destiny before it's too late. ▪

—N.P.

■ *Persuasion* (1818)
by Jane Austen

Mary had acquired a little artificial importance, by becoming Mrs. Charles Musgrove; but Anne, with an elegance of mind and sweetness of character, which must have placed her high with any people of real understanding, was nobody with either father or sister: her word had no weight; her convenience was always to give way;—she was only Anne.

Every once in a while, singlehood can seem a lonely prison. You dream of escape with a man who is the perfect lid to your pot, who completely fulfills your desires, from his piercing eyes to his patience with your personal neuroses. But probably the worst part of being unattached is that dreadful feeling that Mr. Right already came along and you blew it. You look back at your previous relationships (with rose-colored glasses firmly in place, of course) and start pondering whether you hadn't been too hasty. Maybe you shouldn't have listened to your friends, who convinced you that you could do better. Maybe it could've worked out somehow. After all, they dropped the charges against him, didn't they?

Woulda, coulda, shoulda. This is precisely Anne Elliot's problem in Jane Austen's *Persuasion*. Anne's dancing days are over, and it seems she's doomed to spinsterhood. When her family rents out their estate to a naval officer, Anne comes face-to-face with the consequences of her decision eight years before to turn down a marriage proposal from the man she loved, because of his financial situation. Then, she'd been persuaded by her family and a dear friend not to "settle" for him. Now fortunes are reversed: Captain Wentworth isn't flush, but at least he's not dodging creditors like the Elliots. And Anne is spending her days visiting the sick and the hypochondriacal, trying to stay out of her in-laws' domestic squabbles, and listening silently to her father's pompous pronouncements even though he has nearly led them all to ruin.

Of course, since this is a Jane Austen novel, Captain Wentworth is the kind of prize fellow one should never reject, and Anne gets a second crack at romance. That's why this novel has captured the hearts of so many women, who find inspiration in the story of a woman who finds love again just when she has given up hope.

Unfortunately, in real life, trying to rekindle the flames of a lost love is usually about as successful as reheating a soufflé—you end up with a soggy mess that leaves a bad taste in your mouth. Better to put away those old photos of your weekends together hiking in the mountains and reread your journals instead—the crookedly penned, tear-stained pages filled with all those questions—*Why won't he? Why does he? When will he?*

Do yourself a favor. Scrape out the pan, scour it, and start again from scratch. You'll be glad you did. And then sink into the happily-ever-after world of *Persuasion.*

■ *Breaking Free from Compulsive Eating* (1984) **and**
   When Food Is Love (1991)
   by Geneen Roth

If every time my mother hit me I ate a bag of Milky Ways and felt fat and ugly, I could easily justify her actions: my mom hits me because I am fat and ugly. My mom is not crazy; my mom knows what she is doing; my mom knows what is best for me. Compulsive eating was my way of keeping my love for my smart and beautiful mother intact.

Somewhere in the last quarter of the twentieth century, eating disorders became epidemic among women. There are plenty of theories about how this happened: The media are to blame for showing us images of thinner and thinner female role models; malnutrition from low-calorie dieting causes the obsessive behavior of anorexics and bulimics. Or it's all Barbie's fault: If we'd just played with those healthily proportioned fashion doll knock-offs Tammy and Pepper instead, we wouldn't all be watching Jennifer Aniston and Sarah Jessica Parker and thinking, "Gee, I wish I could achieve that bony look."

Whatever the cause or causes, the fact is that far too many women are obsessed: If only they could lose those extra pounds, that double chin, that tiny glop of fat on the side of their knee, they would find true love, a dream job, and total personal fulfillment. Mm-hmm. Tell that to Karen Carpenter.

While it's true that beautiful people get a lot of breaks and fat people are discriminated against, what Geneen Roth points out in these extremely personal books is that it's really easy to fall into a trap of thinking that losing weight will solve all your problems. It's also easy, she says, to get so caught up in obsessing about what you can and cannot eat that you distract yourself from other thoughts, like, what the hell am I doing with my life? Her controversial recipe is to break free of dieting and eat whatever you want whenever you want it, without guilt. Eventually you'll realize you don't really feel sated and satisfied on a diet of doughnuts, pepperoni pizza, and Hershey's Kisses, and you'll listen to your body, which will tell you it wants real food (although if you ever hear it whispering "Bulghur! Tofu!" you may want to tell it to get a grip).

This all sounds great in theory, and it probably works for some people, but will all compulsive eaters reach the Ding Dongs saturation point? We have to wonder if Roth's program is truly workable in the real world, even though a lot of women swear by it.

Been There, Done That

■ *Color Me Beautiful* (1980)
by Carole Jackson

During my years as a color consultant, I have found that matching people with their colors produces immeasurable happiness.

"The seasonal color theory was inspired by the studies of artist and colorist Johannes Itten of the famous Bauhaus school in Germany," explains Carole Jackson, author of the wildly successful *Color Me Beautiful*, which in the 1980s inspired women everywhere to revamp their wardrobe according to colors most flattering for their skin undertones. There are four types of complexions, she explained, one for each season: Winters look best in pure whites, royal blue, and emerald green; Summers in soft white, periwinkle, and blue-greens; etc. She also inspired hundreds, maybe thousands of women to set themselves up as color consultants—sort of a latter-day Avon lady, only you don't have to order and deliver products. It was the perfect job for homemakers and laid-off autoworkers from Flint, Michigan—somehow, we always picture that infamous nebbish Michael Moore in *Roger & Me* coyly checking himself out in the mirror, a bright scarf draped across his chest,

continued . . .

posing as if there were any color in the rainbow that could possibly make him look less like a doofus. But some people swear by the color consultants' technique, in which they drape solid-color scarves over a client's chest to prove that watermelon and blue-reds bring the face of a Summer to life, while only an Autumn can get away with dark tomato or bittersweet. (Luckily, the book provides color swatches for those baffled by just what color "bittersweet" might be. Is that a J. Crew color or what?) Granted, it's a pretty simple concept, so the book is filled out with other makeup and fashion advice that's oh so Eighties, from floppy bowties to blue eyeshadow and dark blush that cuts a swath up to the temple and ear. Frankly, with that garish Sheena Easton makeup look, it's hard to be attractive in any color, but that didn't stop anyone. Nowadays we've broken away from the rigid color rules, having rebelled in the Nineties with the all-black look, only to settle into that wacky chartreuse jewel tone.

Gee, maybe it's time to get back to the color swatches after all.

▪ *Jane Fonda's Workout Book* (1981)
by Jane Fonda

Exercise won't remove freckles or make your feet smaller or your eyes bigger. But, rosy-cheeked and clear-eyed, you will laugh more, step livelier, and speak out with assertiveness. . . . The color of the leaves will please you more. . . . Best of all, you may rediscover the child in you who was lost along the way.

Post–Hanoi Jane and bulimic Barbarella, pre–Stepford Wife to Ted Turner, in the middle of her Save the Whales phase, Hollywood hatchling Jane Fonda found a cause that not only appealed to women across the board but revamped her own image as a flighty West Coaster with more passion than brains. What's more, what she was selling this time had an undeniably

continued . . .

rosy profit margin, what with books, videotapes, aerobics gear, and gym endorsements. Jane claimed working out was an act of self-empowerment, and women by the millions bought it. But the fatal flaw in her advice was her gleeful proclamation to feel the burn: "No pain, no gain," she insisted. We listened, but the initial novelty of color-coordinated spandex bodysuits wore off, and every model or Hollywood starlet released her own workout video, and after we developed chronic shin splints and permanent cartilage problems, we all began to sober up. Realistically, how often could we make it to the gym? And how long could we maintain our enthusiasm for "step step step touch and again"? Many of us discovered less structured—and more enjoyable— forms of exercise, others gave up altogether, and still others continue to puff away on StairMasters, on steps, and in spinning class. So maybe the leaves don't look any greener, but at least we don't feel quite so wiped out by five P.M. nowadays thanks to Jane, et al. ■

■ *The Ground She Walks Upon* (1994)
by Meagan McKinney

I'm not here to die for her. I'm here to die just for the ground she walks upon.

On our worst flyaway and split-end days, we've found that one of those romance novels about a perky gal from some bygone era who spars with a bad boy only to cure him of his arrogance and live happily ever after provides just the sort of deep conditioning we need. It doesn't matter that Meagan McKinney's romantic novel is totally implausible (and not just because the heroine, Ravenna, ends up balancing homemaking with a career as a novelist in nineteenth-century Ireland). We all understand the attraction to bad boys like Niall—you know, Lord Trevallyan, wearer of the serpent ring, with that gorgeous blond hair and eyes that are green stones awash in deep water, a man whose name keeps ringing in your mind like a druid chant? But in real life, a man who is deeply wounded by his past doesn't find himself miraculously healed by the fiery words of a feisty young woman who teaches him to admit to his vulnerability lest he remain forever alone. And aristocrats or no, men who wish to enslave us and possess our souls should not be considered possible marriage material. In fact, they should be immediately crossed off our cocktail party list.

Hey, we all want to believe that by standing up for ourselves and demanding the best, we won't send him running—that our refusal to submit or to compromise will magically transform him from a boorish frog into a nurturing, supportive, powerfully masculine and yet tender prince with a big old castle to boot.

Yep, if you're in the mood for fairy tales and denial, you'll love this one.

Books to Be Thrown with Great Force

▪ *The Rules* (1995)
by Ellen Fein and Sherrie Schneider

The Rules is a simple set of do's and don'ts guaranteed to produce the golden fleece of a marriage proposal from the man of your dreams. For reluctantly single gals everywhere, this book is like the literary equivalent of *Thin Thighs in 30 Days*, promising a quick fix to the perplexing problem of how to hook a man.

The Rules features helpful hints like "Don't tell a man what to do, let HIM take the lead, don't meet him halfway," and "Fill up your time before the date" with crucial activities like giving yourself a manicure or taking a nap. It also boasts of a philosophy of treating yourself with respect and dignity so that men will do likewise. In actuality, what *The Rules* puts forward is a vision of a woman as some kind of carrot on a stick, which must be dangled in front of a hungry potential mate, then snatched away before he gets a chance to satisfy his appetite and move on to a new delicacy.

Indeed, the entire tone of this book suggests that a woman must trick a

continued . . .

man into wanting to choose her as his life partner, as if there was no such thing as the human propensity toward coupling or the biological urge to perpetuate the species.

More disturbing still is that these time-tested secrets for convincing your man that you're fascinating—even when you aren't—have to be kept up after marriage in order to keep the man of your dreams satisfied. Call us crazy, but we thought the whole idea of marriage was a bond of honesty, trust, and commitment between two best friends, and as most of us who have been married know, there are no time-tested secrets for capturing that treasure. You have to make them up together, as you go along. How, we wonder, is a couple supposed to achieve good channels of communication if you're not allowed to call him ever and only rarely return his phone calls?

This is a good book to read when you want to remind yourself that, in love as in life, when it comes to finding your heart's desire, honesty is usually the best policy. ■

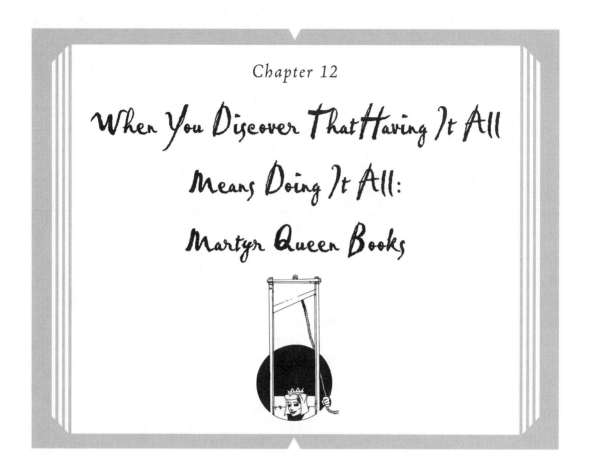

Chapter 12

When You Discover That Having It All Means Doing It All: Martyr Queen Books

Since time began, women have been martyrs to the cause. In Salem we were burned at the stake, in the Old West we were mail-order brides, in Victorian times we were jailed for demanding the right to vote. In the hopeful days of the resurrected women's movement, we welcomed the dawning of new opportunities for ourselves and our daughters and the chance to become independent, autonomous conquerors of the universe, just like our male counterparts. Then the honeymoon ended and it became clear that having it all meant doing it all, and even when we're doing it all, it's still not enough— and nobody appreciates it anyway.

When you're feeling tied to the railroad tracks of your guy's inability to multitask, the books in this chapter will help you to examine the nature of the ties that bind you. These books offer examples of world-class martyrs who have struggled to throw off the sackcloth and rise above or at least redistribute a few of the household chores.

▪ *Codependent No More* (1987)
by Melody Beattie

Much of recovery is finding and maintaining balance in all areas of our lives. We need to watch the scales so they do not tip too far to either side as we measure our responsibilities to ourselves and to others.

The measure of a book's influence? When the term it coins ends up being recognized by your computer's spellcheck ten years later.

But what exactly is a "codependent"? Beattie says it is "someone who has let another person's behavior affect them and who is obsessed with controlling that person's behavior." Others in the recovery field have called it a disease, similar to alcoholism. Still others have called it a dis-ease. We're not sure what that means, but it sure makes for a clever bumper-sticker slogan—and God knows there are a lot of people looking for a clever bumper-sticker kind of way of describing their problems, a catchy label for themselves so they can proudly wear their self-diagnosis on their sleeve.

From what we gather, a codependent is someone who is overly involved with a dysfunctional and self-centered person—or to put it into the vernacular, a schmuck who is hung up on some jerk. And the "jerk" can have any sort of an addiction—to alcohol, drugs, sex, shopping, sports, or to being a jerk. The codependent plays martyr and gets caught up in the psychodrama and can feel sorry for herself for having a bona fide "disease" that's as complex and deserving of empathy as, say, alcoholism. The cure for her "sick" behavior? To "work" a 12-step program, just as an alcoholic would.

Time will tell whether *codependent* makes it into the Oxford English Dictionary or goes the way of *valley girl* and *yuppie*. And you may not feel that a 12-step program is the cure for your tendency to just say yes, no matter what the question. But even if the concept of codependency becomes as outdated as synthesized soundtracks and big hair, when you're feeling like a reactor instead of an actor, reading *Codependent No More* can teach you a lot about finding a balance between your needs and everyone else's.

Notes from Nancy's Reading Journal

Back in 1987, when I first read *Codependent No More*, I didn't buy into this codependency-as-disease stuff. But I did know that I needed to learn how to stop mooning over my ex-boyfriend and get some focus in my life, and the codependent movement, along with my little 12-step group, helped me to kick my own ass, make some real goals, and start establishing a career and a life outside of the bar scene. I suspect a lot of other women took the same message from the movement. But somewhere along the way—perhaps around the time Louie Anderson started writing books about how hard it was to avoid eating cheesecake when he was still mad at his father—the movement mutated into one big whinefest. Suddenly, meetings were filled with would-be actresses performing monologues about their pain, angst-ridden James Dean types inarticulately blathering on for half an hour, and professional 12-steppers moaning like Jacob Marley about how, no matter what we all do, in the end we die alone. No wonder *codependent* became synonymous with *pain in the ass*.

Rereading this classic recovery movement text, I was glad to discover that this wrong turn toward narcissism happened independently of Beattie's book. She advocates behavior modification and a change in attitude and perception, not self-indulgent overanalysis and endless fretting over what Mom and Dad didn't do for us.

Given my own experience, I hope the core of the recovery movement has survived despite all the yahoos who used it as an excuse to be the center of attention and to evoke pity for their victimhood, and who overlook the fact that the recovery movement requires *movement*. ▪

Books to Be Thrown with Great Force

▪ *Ten Stupid Things Women Do to
Mess Up Their Lives* (1994)
by Dr. Laura Schlessinger

*I sincerely believe that if women studied
male lessons in concepts of assertion,
courage, destiny, purpose, honor, dreams, endeavor, perseverance, goal
orientation, etc., they would have a more fulfilling life, pick better
men with whom to be intimate, and have better relationships with
them.*

Let's be honest. Most of us, when throwing a pity party for ourselves,
are well aware that we know exactly what we have to do to change our
situation. And though we may ask our friends for their take on matters, really
we're only asking them to validate what we know deep down: We don't need to
date emotionally frozen men who are ambivalent about their sexuality, or work
for a boss who enjoys verbally abusing us in front of large groups of our
coworkers. But sometimes we go ahead and do "stupid" things anyway. Why?

Well, if you ask Dr. Laura (as she calls herself), the "why" is irrelevant.
That's probably because she comes from southern California, land of "hang
up a surfboard shingle and call yourself a therapist," so she doesn't have the
time to muck about with peripheral issues like accepted psychoanalytic theory.
No, Dr. Laura is a woman of action, and she's here to slap you upside your
head and kick your sorry ass—especially if you're queer. Her answer to every
problem posed by callers to her syndicated radio show is to shape up, quit
sniveling, and change your life already! Next caller!

Now, sometimes when we are caught in an endless spiral of worry, we do

continued...

need a good pep talk: a gentle reminder that things aren't so bad, that we know the answer, and that just as we have in the past, we will once again find the courage to do what we need to do. But do we really need an arrogant drill-sergeant-cum-critical-parent, who stands by "don't ask, don't tell," berating us?

For all that Dr. Laura's books sell and her radio show attracts listeners across the country, we have to ask, who is she really helping? Are the chastened callers hanging up the phone and changing their lives for the better once and for all, now that they've received the earth-shattering news that their married boyfriend will probably never leave his wife and kids? Or is the main audience for the Dr. Lauras of the world people who want to feel smug about how they know the answer to everyone else's problems, and how they would never find themselves in such a pathetic situation?

If you're feeling stuck and sorry for yourself, wouldn't it be better to sit with it for a while, get in touch with your support system, tell yourself you can do what you know you have to do, and if you fail to make a change, start considering therapy if you aren't in it already? Then again, if you're into self-flagellation and verbal abuse, this is the book for you. ■

■ *The Portrait of a Lady* (1881)
by Henry James

Henry James's classic doomed heroine, Isabel Archer, is a beautiful, intelligent, willful woman whose uncle, impressed by her independent spirit, settles sixty thousand dollars on her, thinking it will preserve her autonomy in an age that fostered dependence for women. Unfortunately, her financial independence becomes the very thing that undoes her, and despite her better instincts, she falls for a fortune-hunting bounder who squelches her proud spirit and chains her interminably, like so many women before her, to the yoke of classic codependence.

If you're thinking that money is the answer to all your problems, *The Portrait of a*

Lady is a good reminder that it takes more than cash to resolve your deep-rooted psychological issues and get your life on track.

■ *Saint Joan: A Chronicle Play in Six Scenes and an Epilogue* (1923)
by George Bernard Shaw

Well, well, Peter, I hope men will be the better for remembering me; and they would not remember me so well if you had not burned me.

Joan of Arc is perhaps the world's most famous martyr, one of literature's most cherished symbols of the divinity of the faithful virgin and the eternal endurance of her devotion. Shaw's play brings to life the soul of this prototypically selfless woman who would sacrifice all, even her life, to stand by her man (who is, in this case, the king of France) and God—not necessarily in that order.

Although Joan was ultimately burned at the stake for her beliefs, being a saint did have some perks. She could cause the natural world to reflect her inner feelings, so when the dauphin refused to grant her an audience, she made the cows stop giving milk and the hens stop laying. How's that for passive aggression?

If you'd like to believe they'll all be sorry when they no longer have you to kick around, *Saint Joan* is the read for you.

Courage, Camille!

I'm not afraid of storms, for I'm learning to sail my ship.
—Louisa May Alcott

You don't develop courage by being happy in your relationships every day. You develop it by surviving difficult times and challenging adversity.
—Barbara De Angelis

What I am looking for is a blessing not in disguise.

—Kitty O'Neill Collins

A wounded deer leaps the highest.

—Emily Dickinson

People are like stained-glass windows. They sparkle and shine when the sun is out, but when the darkness sets in, their true beauty is revealed only if there is a light from within.

—Elisabeth Kübler-Ross

■ *The French Lieutenant's Woman* (1969)
by John Fowles

Who can forget the haunting hooded figure of Sarah Woodruff, gazing out to sea with hollow, injured eyes, scanning the horizon for a glimpse of her lost French lover's sails from the wind-worried ramparts of nineteenth-century Cornwall? This doomed heroine has it so rough that the author has even nicknamed her "Tragedy" just in case we missed the point that Sarah is more than a martyred woman—she is a symbol of the martyrdom of all women in an industrial-age society that limited female endeavors to becoming a wife and mother, an indentured servant, or a prostitute.

After reading *The French Lieutenant's Woman*, your own encounter with the glass ceiling won't seem so bad by comparison.

Notes from Bev's Reading Journal

▪ *Meditations for Women Who Do Too Much* (1990)
by Anne Wilson Schaef

The recovery movement was a cultural contraction that cramped the progress of the women's movement late in the Reagan Eighties. This inner child, conceived in the womb of popular dysfunction, gave birth to a self-obsessed literary genre that elevated self-pity to the level of religious devotion.

Suddenly there were support groups and accompanying affirmational volumes and daily minders on everything from chronic fatigue to chronic nail biting. Everything became a disease that needed to be cured or an addiction that needed to be controlled. While the recovery movement had the advantageous effect of prompting a good many of us to take a moment out of every day and reexamine our priorities, it also had a number of disturbing side effects.

First, it glued "ing's" to everything, transforming nouns and adjectives into verbs without giving so much as a single, well-diagrammed thought to its long-term effects upon the health of American syntax. All of a sudden we were "journaling," "lessoning," and "iffing" our way into a talk-show English that haunts us to this day.

Second, it turned women everywhere into martyrs regardless of whether they had ever actually endured an ordeal, seen a vision, or defended the faith of their native France.

Third, there are only so many syndromes and dangerous addictions to go around, and when the movement ran out of pathological fodder, it began turning function into dysfunction. Nowhere is this more clearly illustrated

continued . . .

than in the volume that epitomizes the extremity of self-help mania, *Meditations for Women Who Do Too Much*, an affirmation book for women who are afflicted with an addiction to work and the curse of overachievement.

Now, it is true—women do a lot. We were doing a lot before, and with our introduction into the workplace, we were free to do even more. *Meditations for Women Who Do Too Much* is a daily, verb-crunching reminder of the fact that we are doing more than our share. It reminds us in 365 different ways that our desire to bring home the bacon, fry it up in a pan, and never ever let him forget he's a man is a sickness. And in the dulcet, self-nurturing, tea-with-honey tones of the self-help genre, this book instructs us that it is who we are and not what we do that makes us lovable, and charges us with the task of doing less.

This is clearly a valuable message for all of us harried moms/wives/girlfriends/workers to hear, but it begs a conclusion that the author never quite addresses. It's only logical, after all. If women everywhere are doing too much, then there have to be a whole lot of men, right alongside of them, who are doing nothing at all.

This, anyway, is the message I took away from the book. And in fact, rather than directing my gaze inward, it directed my focus outward toward the fountainhead of my dysfunctional overactivity. Read this book, and you too may begin the long and difficult process of redistributing the labor in your household. And for that, your future serene and well-rested inner self, and your soon-to-be-self-reliant significant other, will be forever grateful. ■

▪ *The Yellow Wallpaper* (1892)
by **Charlotte Perkins Gilman**

John laughs at me, of course, but one expects that in marriage.

At the turn of the last century, there was no such thing as a self-help movement. There were no consciousness-raising or support groups, no books about dancing with anger, or codependency, or nurturing the child within. So when women were feeling depressed or anxious or out of step with society's expectations, they usually had only a few escape routes: get consumption and die, go insane, take an extended "rest" in the country, or all of the above.

Such is the situation for the nameless heroine in Charlotte Perkins Gilman's classic autobiographical novella of marriage as martyrdom, *The Yellow Wallpaper.* Suffering from nervous exhaustion after the birth of her first child, a young woman writer moves to a lavish country estate at the insistence of her doctor husband, whom she refers to appropriately as "dear John." Dear John has prescribed bed rest, fresh air, and a total lack of intellectual stimulation for his "little girl" in an effort to remedy her nervous condition.

Languishing without companionship, books, or outside stimulation of any kind, our heroine, whom we know only as "dear," or "darling," or "little girl," begins writing in secret about the only thing that feeds her eye or her imagination: the decaying yellow wallpaper that lines her marriage bedroom and prison chamber. The wallpaper becomes a metaphor for her own spiritual, intellectual, and emotional imprisonment. Ultimately, she goes stark raving mad and is reduced to a creeping lunatic, tearing at the wallpaper in order to free her shackled spirit.

If you're feeling trapped in a cramped chamber, so starved for outside stimulus that you begin to fall in love with a pair of wallpaper eyes that are a metaphor for your own captivity, read *The Yellow Wallpaper.* It's a good reminder that no matter how bad it gets, at least this is the twenty-first century, when women have a few more options, like divorce, financial independence, and a good refillable prescription for Xanax. Who says there hasn't been progress?

Books to Be Thrown with Great Force

■ *Healing the Shame That Binds You* (1988)
by John Bradshaw

If you have messed-up parents, they'll teach
you to feel lousy about yourself, and your life
will be a wreck, too.

There. We've just saved you the cost of John Bradshaw's book.

Oh, there's a little more to it than that—Bradshaw fills in the details a
bit. But the problem with his book is the problem with far too many self-help
books. Instead of using clear language to make his points, Bradshaw invents
all sorts of jargon. On top of that, instead of using simple anecdotes to illustrate his points, he writes about one family whose dysfunction is so extreme
that he actually has to map it out for you so you can keep straight the alco-
holics and the rage-a-holics. He's also got plenty of illustrations of layers of
defenses (we were sorta hoping he had one for a shame spiral, but he didn't)
that obfuscate his points far more often than they clarify them.

If you can wade through the references to "e-motions," "shame parfaits"
(now there's another one we'd like to see rendered as an illustration—we're
picturing something like one of those Jell-O desserts from the 1960s), "feeling
rackets," and "isolation of affects," you might learn something about overcoming your dysfunction. But if you're like most people, you'll spend less time
analyzing yourself than trying to figure out what on earth Bradshaw is trying
to say. ■

■ *Prozac Nation* (1994)
by Elizabeth Wurtzel

Why hadn't K-Tel long ago released a compilation called something like Depressing Dylan Songs for the Broken-hearted?

Is she brutally honest, or just a whiner? Those who haven't suffered from depression are most likely to see this memoir as just another in a long line of 1990s "let me reveal in exhausting detail the minutiae of my dysfunction" tell-alls. But if Elizabeth Wurtzel was the very picture of narcissism, it wasn't because she was playing at being the misunderstood goddess of despair. Her clinical depression kept her feeling hopeless and miserable for half her life until the nation's now-trendy wonder drug, Prozac, came along. Until she was in her twenties, Wurtzel was in such agony that she simply didn't have the energy to care about how exasperating she was to the people around her. And in her self-absorption, she developed a sense of smugness about her tastes in music and fashion. Normal girls wore makeup and hung Andy Gibb posters on their walls; cool girls read Nietzsche, listened to the Sex Pistols, cut themselves, and posed Fiona Apple–like for ultra-hip author photos.

We can understand if Wurtzel feels she's earned the right to be the Prozac poster girl. These days, as she points out, everybody and their kitty cat is on Prozac and most people have taken a far less harrowing route than she has to America's favorite happy pill. Three minutes of complaining in a therapist's office and there you go, a magic cure. It's enough to make a Patti Smith wannabe downright resentful.

With her moods regulated, Wurtzel is now able to keep her mind off herself long enough to ask bigger questions about a country that is so quick to self-medicate, and a generation (her twentysomething peers) that so readily embraces the dark side of life. Reading *Prozac Nation*, you realize that even the most fascinating, gifted, and witty person can become, in the throes of depression, a royal pain in the ass. Because let's face it: Depression isn't cool, it's, well, depressing. And once she escaped her gray world, Wurtzel was astonished to discover that the pain that she thought defined her was something her friends and family barely tolerated, and that they saw in her other qualities that she was completely oblivious to.

If you're caught up in the glamour of being the Queen of Pain, you may recognize yourself in these pages and realize that no matter what your soundtrack is, psychodrama eventually gets really monotonous.

▪ *Tess of the D'Urbervilles* (1891)
by Thomas Hardy

Yet another pure and virginal nineteenth-century maiden is tossed onto the pyre of industrial age British society, in Thomas Hardy's ode to debauched aristocracy, *Tess of the D'Urbervilles*. Although the image that most of us get when we think of Tess is that poster of Nastassja Kinski with that milkmaid complexion and those pouty Slavic lips puckering up to an extremely red and ripe strawberry, Tess is a classic doomed heroine. The author even names his heroine's child Sorrow, just in case we missed the point that not only Tess but Tess's offspring are marked for sacrifice at the hands of an unfeeling and dysfunctional moral construct (much like Fowles named his doomed French lieutenant's woman "Tragedy"). Tess, who begins as a spirited, intelligent, and fiercely moral daughter of a proud but debased lineage, is offered up like a vestal virgin to the wolves at the door. Sadly, the sacrifice is unappreciated by the gods of an industrial age society, and rather than being able to pull her family out of the mud, Tess is dragged down along with them in a classic Hardy unhappy ending.

This one's an especially satisfying read if you feel yourself the victim of a sexual double standard.

▪ *Madame Bovary* (1856)
by Gustave Flaubert

Emma Bovary, a well-brought-up, virtuous, respectable nineteenth-century woman, is thrown on the pyre of restrictive social mores…do you think a pattern is beginning to suggest itself here? Emma, however, in a revolutionary divergence from the classic nineteenth-century model of the doomed heroine, is not British but French. Emma becomes drunk at an early age with the intoxicating words of the poets and the romantic environs of wealth. Unfortunately, her husband, Monsieur Bovary, is a simple country doctor who affords her no such prosaic luxuries. So Emma looks for love in all the wrong places, taking and discarding a series of lovers and running her family into unsupportable debt in order to feed her shallow appetites. Ultimately, she settles on the amoral pharmacist/gigolo Homais and engages in a torrid affair that ultimately drives her to drink rat poison taken from his shop. She dies with her face twisted into a horrible grimace. The good news is that a little while later, her selfless noble husband, Monsieur Bovary, dies of grief.

Feeling misunderstood and out of sync with your world? You don't need a powerful pesticide—just a copy of *Madame Bovary*.

Courage, Camille!

If you can keep your head about you when all about you are losing theirs, it's just possible you haven't grasped the situation. —Jean Kerr

Trouble is the common denominator of living. It is the great equalizer. —Ann Landers

I personally think we developed language because of our deep inner need to complain. —Jane Wagner

It takes courage to push yourself to places that you have never been before . . . to test your limits . . . to break through barriers. And the day came when the risk it took to remain tight inside the bud was more painful than the risk it took to blossom. —Anaïs Nin

Perhaps catastrophe is the natural human environment, and even though we spend a good deal of energy trying to get away from it, we are programmed for survival amid catastrophe. —Germaine Greer

▪ *Anna Karenina* (1877)
by Leo Tolstoy

Happy families are all alike; every unhappy family is unhappy in its own way.

Leo Tolstoy's symbol of the fallen housewife, Anna Karenina, is perhaps one of the greatest heartbreakers in literary history. Married to a respectable but incredibly boring government middle-management type, supercivilized Anna courts a primal passion for the dashing and wealthy young army officer Count Vronsky. She abandons her family for her paramour and commits the unpardonable sin against the bourgeoisie of refusing to be discreet about her scandal. And like most nineteenth-century tragic heroines, Anna is quickly buried in the profound consequences of her crime against a patriarchal society. Anna ends up living in virtual exile, eaten up with resentment against her lover and plagued by fears that he is unfaithful to her. Where once she saw passion in her lover's eyes, now she sees only a reflection of her sins. In a pre-Prozac world, what's left but a walk on the train tracks?

Chapter 13

When You Desperately Need to Believe That There's a Purpose to It All: Embracing-Your-Inner-Light Books

At a certain point we all pull over into a rest stop on the highway of life and take a breather. We stretch our legs, take a look at the map, calculate how far we've come, and plot out where we're headed. It is at times like these that we can find ourselves in need of a little good advice, from people who know the territory.

Now, if your journey is a Sunday drive in spring through the rich Toulousian countryside, then you're probably in a pretty good place and don't need any directions. In fact, you're probably not in a rest stop at all. You're probably in some charming, rustic roadside café just outside of Provence, eating cassoulet made with haricots blancs and fresh farmer's sausage.

But if you're in the spiritual equivalent of the Hash 'n' Splash truck stop in East Egypt, Arkansas, during rainy season on your way to West Podunk, you're probably not feeling quite as good about the road ahead. And chances are, you don't want to know what's in that casserole you're eating. So you could probably use a little helpful advice—or a sign that says "This Way Out," or at least a number for a nearby poison control center.

When you hit a bump in the road or lose your way, whether you need to rediscover your path or rethink your journey, these embracing-your-inner-light books can help to put the wind back in your sails and light the way to a more scenic journey and a happier destination.

■ *The Little Prince* (1943)
by Antoine de Saint-Exupéry

"All men have the stars," the Little Prince answered, "but they are not the same things for different people. For some, who are travelers, the stars are guides. For others they are no more than little lights in the sky. For others, who are scholars, they are problems. For my businessman they were wealth. But all these stars are silent. You—you alone—will have the stars as no one else has them—In one of the stars I shall be living. In one of them I shall be laughing. And so it will be as if all the stars were laughing, when you look at the sky at night . . . you—only you—will have stars that can laugh!"

One of the fundamental texts in the "children are closer to God" school of spirituality is Antoine de Saint-Exupéry's *The Little Prince*. In a series of simple drawings and lyrical allegories, *The Little Prince* weaves together a parable that elevates the Peter Pan Syndrome to the level of religion.

The story is narrated by a pilot whose plane goes down in a remote desert. With only five days of drinking water left, our narrator struggles against time to fix his engine before he expires in the blazing heat. While tinkering with his propeller, he is approached by a little blond prince, who comes from a planet where everything is tiny. The Little Prince asks the pilot to stop and draw him a picture of a sheep, and as the pilot scribbles, the enchanting little boy tells our narrator stories about all of his adventures traveling to the remotest regions of the universe. In the course of their illuminating conversation, the Little Prince and the pilot both learn a lot about sheep, foxes, elephants, flowers, life, death, immortality, and the ultimate futility of all human endeavor.

Basically the message of *The Little Prince* is this: All adult thoughts, words, and deeds are worthless, and it is the occupations of children—drawing pictures, discovering new worlds, or lovingly tending a special flower—that put one on the road toward truth, happiness, and fulfillment.

In other words, don't grow up.

Despite this book's dubious message to the perennial adolescents among us who are looking for any excuse not to grow up—and the unsettling quality of this narcissistic love affair between a man who grips a joystick for a living and his golden-haired and cherubic inner child—there is something simple and compelling in this book. Saint-Exupéry speaks to the child's sense of wonder in us all, to the inner self who knows that the life of the imagination is forever young.

The next time you crash-land in the middle of an emotional desert, pick up *The Little Prince* and spend a few moments with the golden-locked and cherubic embodiment of your inner child, and see if the stars in your galaxy start to giggle.

Notes from Bev's Reading Journal

The Little Prince has been a very important book in my life because most of the men (read: boys) that I have dated were really into it. In fact, it came up a lot in the course of our more serious disagreements over such issues as employability, future prospects, family planning, and paying the rent on time. I'd say something like "You really need to think down the line about what you are going to do for a living," and my little prince of the moment would say, "What does it matter as long as I water my special flower? Now will you shut up and draw me a picture of a sheep?"

Obviously, I've got some baggage where this book is concerned, yet despite its appeal to the perennially adolescent all-stars of my romantic past, I have a lot in common with the narrator. I, like the pilot, am prone to crash-landing

continued . . .

in the middle of emotional deserts without a drop of nourishment in sight. And I, like the pilot, seem to have an uncanny knack for attracting any little prince in the area.

I begin by innocently sketching pictures of sheep to delight a lost little boy—and inevitably, like our pilot, I wind up on the slope of a lonely and removed hillside, waiting with an ache in my heart for my vanished prince to return, trying to comfort myself with an abstract notion of love's immortality and the precious fragility of a single rose.

■ *Simple Abundance: A Daybook of Comfort and Joy* (1995) by Sarah Ban Breathnach

Book browsing is a meditative art. Every woman should have three well-paved avenues for page-turning adventures: a proper bookstore stocked by bibliophiles, a choice secondhand haunt, and a civilized lending library. Books are as essential as breathing.

Simple Abundance is a collection of essays—one for each day of the year—along with a list of monthly projects, all designed to put us in touch with our Higher Power and our "authentic" self. You know—the self that delights in the first blueberries of the season and yet also appreciates the Zen of a glass of wine and an *Ab Fab* video. The self that dares to start her own business, to set boundaries with the people around her, to be a "bad" girl and wear halter tops, and listen to Billie Holiday. The self, in short, that values herself.

To get in touch with that wonderful woman within, Breathnach asks us to contemplate the empty spaces in our homes and in our lives rather than rushing about to fill them, and to think about whether we are expressing our personal style through clothing or knuckling under to the latest fashion trend. She encourages us to listen to our inner voice and follow our dreams no matter how foolish they may seem to others. And she offers lists of joyful simplicities for us to indulge in, which are often related to the season—like arranging a fall bouquet in a vase made from a pumpkin, which can encourage even the most devoted concrete jungle dweller to slow down and appreciate the natural world around us. To maintain the right perspective, she also recommends keeping a gratitude journal in which you record all the blessings in your life. In addition, she suggests you might want to keep a bitching journal in which you can vent, vent, *vent*—something we feel is a great tool for keeping a gal on an even keel.

If you could use a daily reminder to stop putting your spiritual life on the back burner and stifling the inner you, check out *Simple Abundance*.

The Holy Bible

No chapter on spiritual literature would be complete without a discussion of the Holy Bible. It is unquestionably one of the most influential books ever penned or channeled, and it has had its hand in most of the landmark events in the history of Western civilization. Not to mention that it's also the biggest bestseller in literary history.

The Bible, which means "books" in Greek, has provided one of the few instances in which men and women were willing to kill or be killed for their editorial point of view. Kings and saints, pilgrims and popes, synods and nations have gone to war over the interpretation of particular words and phrases. Even pronouns have been a cause of major schisms in the Christian body.

The consequence of this devotion to ecclesiastical minutiae has been a proliferation of versions of the Bible, each written according to the editorial sensibilities of its particular camp. Given the flammable nature of biblical editorial criticism, and being pacifists at heart, we are not going to draw conclusions about matters over which ecumenical councils have been

continued . . .

convened for centuries. Far be it from us to review the word of God. So reflected below is our bibliotherapeutic summary of some of the versions of the Bible currently in publication. You draw your own conclusions.

- ### The New International Version
  The conservative Protestant Bible, with lots of *thees* and *thous*, and even more *hims* and *hises*.

- ### The New Revised Standard Edition
  The more liberal Protestant Bible, which got rid of the *thees* and *thous* as well as the *hims* and *hises*.

- ### The Good News Bible
  The 1970s-style, feel-good Bible designed to connect with a younger audience, with hipper language and more inclusive pronouns.

- ### The Way: The Living Bible
  Another 1970s translation aimed at the modern generation, complete with pictures and even a few quotes from the Bee-Gees. (Really—we don't make this stuff up.) We've also heard that The Way is the name of one of those mysterious and slightly disturbing Christian communities centered somewhere in the north woods, but we don't want to spread rumors.

- ### The New American Bible
  The first officially sponsored Roman Catholic Bible translated into English. It was published, by the way, in 1970. Not 1670, mind you, but 1970.

- ### The Jerusalem Bible
  An academic Bible translated directly from the original languages into contemporary language, with lots and lots of footnotes.

continued . . .

▪ **The Gospel According to Jesus**
by Stephen Mitchell

A scholar's cobbled-together version of what he thinks Jesus really said and did, tossing out iffy stuff that might've been added later. Purists will be aghast, but at least those poor pigs don't get driven off the cliff just because they're possessed by demons.

▪ **The Gideon Bible**

Those Bibles you find in the drawers of hotel rooms.

▪ **The Book of Mormon**

Those Bibles you find in the drawers of Marriott Hotel rooms. ▪

▪ *Kitchen Table Wisdom* (1996)
by Rachel Naomi Remen

If we fear loss enough, in the end the things we possess will come to possess us.

Dr. Rachel Naomi Remen has a life-threatening chronic illness, has counseled despairing cancer patients and burned-out physicians, and as a doctor herself once worked in a ward where at least one child died every day. Listen, if that's not enough to make you start questioning it all, we don't know what will. Kind of puts your own life into perspective, doesn't it?

And that's what *Kitchen Table Wisdom* is all about—perspective. One of the most moving and resonant stories is of a woman who, after a tough round of chemo, told her doctors she was taking off to San Francisco for the weekend, where, because she was so very weak, she would spend two days in a hotel room. Her doctors thought she was nuts, but when she returned to the hospital, she described the great joy she experienced ordering up room service and eating on the balcony while in a big fluffy robe. She even appreciated the smell of the tiny bars of hotel soap and the little flower-shaped pats of butter. Hmm, when's the last time you really cherished a condiment?

Remen's a keen observer of human nature. Whether her stories are about children who speak mysteriously of going home and then die quietly hours later, or about scrupulously honest and professional health care workers so cut off from their feelings that they heatedly deny having kissed a juvenile patient on the forehead as he slept, they speak of what it means to be human.

Read *Kitchen Table Wisdom* when you need to get a little perspective on your own suffering.

Angels We Have Heard on High

People seem to be running into angels everywhere these days—on highways, in airplanes, on trains, in the thick of cities, and in the middle of deserts. Apparently, there are more angels among us than ever before. There are certainly more angel books. Here are just a few:

Angels Among Us by Don Fearheiley

Angels Among Us by Laura Shin (editor)

Angels in our Midst by the editors of Guideposts Magazine

An Angel a Day: Stories of Angelic Encounters by Ann Spangler

Angel Days: A Journal and Daybook for Everyone Who Walks with Angels by Terry Lynn Taylor

Angelspeake: How to Talk with Your Angels: A Guide by Barbara Mark and Trudy Griswold

Angel Oracle: Working with the Angels for Guidance, Inspiration and Love by Ambika Wauters

continued . . .

Angelic Healing: Working With Your Angels to Heal Your Life by
  Eileen Elias Freeman

and, of course, the definitive . . .

All About Angels by A. S. Joppie

All About Angels by Jill Hartman

All About Angels by L. Miller

All About the Angels by Paul O'Sullivan

■ *Lost Horizon* (1933)
by James Hilton

We all have days when we feel that the only way we'll ever live in harmony with our fellows is if we discover some perfect little utopian community hidden away from the main highway. You know—a place with a nice big library, breathtaking views of the mountains, terrific food, and little narcotic berries that slow the aging process to a crawl. Now, nearly eternal youth is great and all, but why couldn't Hilton have given Shangri-La a Jacuzzi as well? And maybe a buttery chardonnay, and those chocolate-covered coffee beans from Starbucks that give you a major caffeine buzz, and Brad Pitt standing ready with a big fluffy Turkish towel, and . . . okay, okay, enough quibbling.

Written back in the 1930s, before the general population knew much about Tibet and its monasteries (or Jacuzzis, for that matter), *Lost Horizon*, a classic utopian novel, describes the abduction of four people to a magical kingdom—one without multinational corporations that knuckle under to large human-rights-abusing regimes—where anyone would want to live out their days. Of course, there's always a dissenter, someone who just can't do without his daily newspaper and daily grind, who can't bear the serenity of it all for another minute. And one of the party—the only woman—is maybe just a bit too eager to impose her religion on the locals. Even so, read *Lost Horizon* when you feel your life is airless. It will sweep you out of your mundane world and have you imagining just what your own Shangri-La would be like—and what you'd be willing to sacrifice to live there.

Points to Ponder

1. What would your own Shangri-La look like? What would it include, and what would it exclude?

2. Could anything make you want to leave your Shangri-La?

▪ *Talking to Heaven* (1997)
by James Van Praagh

If everything is going right and there seem to be no glitches, you are open to spirit and following your guidance. If, on the other hand, nothing seems to be working out, you are not listening to the guides and will end up on the wrong path.

Oh, you want to believe him, don't you? We know Houdini debunked the whole speaking-with-the-dear-departed thing early in the twentieth century, but the human heart still wants to know that Mom's forgiven you and that Aunt Grace remembers where she hid that cash stash that's been eluding you.

As mediums go, James Van Praagh is pretty convincing. True, he does egg on his clients to reveal that yes, indeed, they do have someone who has passed over who went by the name John or Johnny or Jack or Joseph, whatever—it's a little hard to decipher those fast-talking spirits at times. But just when you're wondering when this guy left the carnival circuit, he comes up with some detail like a necklace chain broken near the clasp in someone's small jewelry box in the third right-hand drawer of the dresser, and you start to wonder. Maybe he's "only" reading minds, but he's got a lot of great stories about people who later discovered that his mysterious messages made total sense—they just didn't realize they'd had an uncle named Robert who died years ago. Really, this postdeath communication system can sometimes be more frustrating than using a cell phone outside of range.

Anyway, maybe it's all bunk (your BS meter will probably ring pretty loud when he talks about the celebrities who've contacted him, and the dog spirit who described his favorite afghan—in color). But Van Praagh's anecdotes are absolutely fascinating, and you may find his message—that spirits choose to suffer in order to grow spiritually, that we can all communicate with those who have "passed over," and that the dead are right beside us looking out for our best interests—is really quite comforting. Hell, why not put your skepticism aside for a while and enjoy reading this reassuring little book?

■ *Book of Shadows* (1998)
by Phyllis Curott

Most people know intuitively that when you fall in love the world is full of magic. What they don't know is that when you discover the universe is full of magic, you fall in love with the world.

For those of us who can't quite grasp the whole crystal/pyramid/white light/chakra thing, *Book of Shadows* is a terrific guide to metaphysical reality, written with enough lyrical prose to make it magical and enough commonsense explanations and plain English to keep it from floating away. Curott, one of those smart New York chicks with a law degree from NYU and a soft spot for bad boy rock 'n' rollers, has written a combination Persephone-like memoir, salute to the goddess, witches' spell book, and guide to Wiccan spiritual practice for the city-bound corporate slave who is seeking the sacred. Here's the deal: Wicca's got nothing to do with Satanism or upside-down crosses or curses on abusive bosses. (But don't worry—there are still a few spells here that you can do to get your nemesis to stop torturing you. Come on, the woman's a New Yorker—she's got to be practical.) Instead, it's all about reconnecting with the great web of life, discovering the play of magic in your world, spending an afternoon riding a carousel again and again, and refusing to compromise your spiritual self just because you want to pay the rent and have a little left over for that darling dress you saw in a shop window.

If you're looking for a book that will give you some ideas on how to incorporate spirituality into your life instead of selling your soul to corporate America (hint: Quit your job), *Book of Shadows* will light up a path.

Points to Ponder

Is there such a thing as a well-paying job that doesn't grind your soul into gravel?

▪ *When God Was a Woman* (1976) by Merlin Stone and
The Chalice and the Blade (1987) by Riane Eisler

When our ancestors began to ask the eternal questions (Where do we come from before we are born? Where do we go after we die?), they must have noted that life emerges from the body of a woman. It would have been natural for them to image the universe as an all-giving Mother.

Remember all those "fertility cults" your college anthro teacher dismissed? Stone and Eisler say that they were full-fledged religions practiced by the majority of people on Earth—yes, even men were bowing to the feminine deity. Then along came worshippers of the male sun god. You know how it is—everything's all groovy and sunny and then those nasty marauders and raiders crash the party, wielding clubs and spears and all manner of phallic symbols, destroying the peaceful matrilineal cultures and laying the ground for a world in which women are denied the priesthood, the right to vote, and comfortable yet stylish footwear. Don't you just *hate* when that happens?

Evidence that the feminist golden era existed, Stone and Eisler say, can be found in the myths that were rewritten again and again by the invaders. It's no coincidence that serpents, symbolic of the goddess, were chased from Ireland by Saint Patrick or demonized by the author of Genesis, or that the cow, sacred to Isis, was used as a symbol of debauched religious idolatry back in the Old Testament. I mean, you start casting golden cows from goblets and bangles, next thing you know, women are shakin' their groove thang, cackling wildly, and knockin' back more than a few goblets of wine while poor Charlton Heston has to hang out on the mountain for forty days waiting for those tablets to cool so he can bring them down to the Children of Israel.

So what difference does it make if back then people prayed to Her instead of Him? Well, say Eisler and Stone, in the good old days, thousands of years ago, the worship of a female deity resulted in a respect for the power of flesh-and-blood women. Women weren't chattel to be coveted along with the neighbor's cow and superior home entertainment system—they were priestesses, whose sexual expression was a form of worship. And Eisler points out, early Goddess worshippers realized you can organize people without using a hierarchical pyramid structure of self-important men lording it over the poor slobs at the bottom.

Now, it's true that in this "golden era," things could still occasionally get ugly. After all, for a while there, the Queen, earthly symbol of the goddess, annually chose one handsome young man to copulate with her, then had him chopped up and spread across the fields as a sort of fertilizer for the crops. See what happens when you take metaphors literally?

But the question now is, if we reconceived God as a feminine force today, could we return to the peaceful days of art, music, poetry, mutual respect between the genders, and ecstatic sex in the temple? Could we change our destructive course, replenish the planet, and get rid of war, strip mining, and the NRA once and for all?

Read these books when you feel yourself distanced from patriarchal religions and thinking about the feminine aspect of the divine.

Morsels to Mull Over

Reality leaves a lot to the imagination.　　　—John Lennon

The finding of God is the coming to one's own self.
　　　　　　　　　　　　　　　　—Meher Baba

God requires no synagogue—except in the heart.
　　　　　　　　　　　　　　　　—Hasidic saying

▪ *Jonathan Livingston Seagull* (1970)
by Richard Bach

"Your whole body, from wingtip to wingtip," Jonathan would say, "is nothing more than your thought itself, in a form you can see. Break the chains of your thought, and you break the chains of your body, too."

Every period has its own pet philosophies, a handful of cherished ideas and images that capture the imagination of the age and help people to put a finger on the unique pressures and aspirations of their time.

In the early 1970s, we had, to name a few, the flower, which represented the power of love; the rainbow, which symbolized equality; the Man from Glad, who represented perpetual youth through miracles of modern technology; and the seagull, which represented the unlimited freedom of the human spirit.

The 1970s were obviously a hopeful, feel-good era that gobbled up secular humanism like Lay's potato chips and believed absolutely in the power of life, love, dreams, and Ziploc sandwich bags to stave off the ravages of time and the inevitability of death.

The seagull, with its wings outstretched, soaring into the heavens, heedless of the physical laws of the universe, was introduced into the popular culture by Richard Bach in his book *Jonathan Livingston Seagull*. Jonathan is a rare bird indeed, who becomes exiled from the flock of workaday gulls through his pure love of flight. Jonathan lives to fly and pushes the envelope of the possible, ultimately transcending death itself and becoming a prophet and savior for his flock.

With the egalitarian spiritual sensibility of the time, *Jonathan Livingston Seagull* was a flexible metaphor. One can see, at its heart, the central death-and-rebirth myth of the Judeo-Christian tradition, as well as the less linear, circular mysteries of Zen Buddhism, like karma and reincarnation, and even a few of the seeds of Freudian and Jungian psychoanalytic theory. People expected a lot out of their metaphors in those days.

The next time you are feeling that your wings have been clipped, soar into a limitless horizon at breakneck speeds with Jonathan Livingston, and remember the ecstasy of free flight.

Morsels to Mull Over

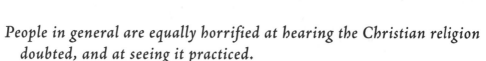

If Jesus Christ were to come today, people would not even crucify him. They would ask him to dinner, and hear what he had to say, and make fun of him.

—Thomas Carlyle

People in general are equally horrified at hearing the Christian religion doubted, and at seeing it practiced.

—Samuel Butler

▪ *Mutant Message Down Under* (1991)
by Marlo Morgan

The time has come to listen to the frightened moans of our fellow brothers and sisters and indeed the earth itself in pain. Perhaps the future of the world would be in better hands if we forgot about discovering something new and concentrated on recovering our past.

In 1991 American author Marlo Morgan borrowed the old "noble savage" idea when she wrote the fiction-based-on-fact bestseller *Mutant Message Down Under*. We "mutants," she explains, are too hung up on gravy and frosting to appreciate the meat and the cake (admit it—if you were eating lizard and kangaroo meat, as she was, you'd probably want to whip up a little roux and drippings to doctor it up a bit, too). We in the industrialized world have lost the ability to appreciate the beautiful and delicate interplay between God's creatures that occurs when swarms of flies go up our noses and into our ears to clean them. We are addicted to the extras, like water and possessions, and we live by the clock instead of by the seasons of nature. We have forgotten how to respect the Earth and use our resources wisely. (Take the aborigines—in war, they killed only as many people as they could eat. Very Earth-friendly.)

Now, many have discredited Morgan for blurring the lines between truth and storytelling. Her story of being kidnapped and taken on a three-month walkabout by a tribe of Aborigines who dubbed themselves the "Real People" sounds awfully fishy to those who have respectfully studied the ways of the Aborigines. Come on—a hidden garden where the secrets of the ages are kept? Isn't that a little too Indiana Jones to ring true?

But *Mutant Message Down Under* isn't supposed to be an ethnography. Instead, it samples a bit of this and a bit of that from an obscure (to Americans) culture to tell a simple (albeit poorly written) story about a journey of discovery. In essence, what Morgan says is that the indigenous peoples of the world have a corner on the truth and that the rest of us had better listen up if we want to save ourselves from destruction. And when you've had your fill of Day-Timers, insurance forms, bottom lines, fat gram counting, and concrete jungles, *Mutant Message* is a nice little trip to take—from a distance.

Even God Has a Sense of Humor

If only God would give me some clear sign! Like making a large deposit in my name at a Swiss bank.

—Woody Allen

God is a comedian whose audience is afraid to laugh.

—H. L. Mencken

God is coming. Quick—look busy.

—Anonymous

Christ—an anarchist who succeeded.

—Axel Munthe

■ *The Celestine Prophecy* (1993)
by James Redfield

Think of James Redfield as the Oliver Stone of the New Age world. In *The Celestine Prophecy*, he's created an adventure story about suppressed wisdom of the ages that has priests leaving the church under cover of night, armed thugs shooting Uzis, and a race amongst soul seekers to discover contraband texts or "insights." And just like Oliver Stone, Redfield has a penchant for the overwrought, the ridiculous, and the far-fetched. And yes, the CIA is involved. But at least there isn't some 16-millimeter film you have to watch over and over again.

Well, there's an ingenious explanation for all those miraculous coincidences in Redfield's book that make for such an implausible plot. The first of the nine "secret insights" that the narrator learns is that all coincidences are to be taken seriously. This means that all the insights from a mysterious manuscript that contains the secrets of human destiny are neatly dropped in our hero's lap, then explained in depth by the latest stranger who conveniently crosses his path. In addition to the government conspiracy to suppress the nine insights, there's also an exotic foreign locale (Peru) for color and a threatened power structure (the Catholic Church) for portent, which are meant to give the book all the urgency of a Harrison Ford action/adventure vehicle.

But hey, the dopey plotting isn't the point of *The Celestine Prophecy*; it's the underlying spiritual ideas that made it a sensation. If you can get past the badly rendered fiction overlay and the conspiracy nonsense and focus on the insights, you too might actually be interested in what Redfield has to say: The physical universe is pure energy, which is affected by how we think; we need to wake up to who we really are; the universe will provide; do unto others as you would have them do unto you; think positive; and so on.

Since the insights are presented in an order that makes it seem as if you're delving deeper and deeper into ancient wisdom, it manages to suck you in. Moreover, the whole prophecy has to do with the millennium, which gives it a sort of immediacy. See, it's all about the inevitable post-twentieth-century shift in human consciousness to a more spiritual existence. This shift, the insights reveal, will eventually allow us to disappear *à la* the ancient Mayans.

And can we just discuss that ancient Mayan thing for a moment? Why are we supposed to *want* to disappear like the ancient Mayans? Where did they go, anyway? Are they really all that much happier in the other dimension or wherever they ended up? Do they have a better quality of life there—is there universal health care and plenty of beach-front property to go around? Have they at least gotten a respite from all that sacrificing of virgins to please the gods?

And while we're at it, why should human beings want to vibrate at a higher frequency (as in subatomic particle movement, not the Magic Fingers bed)? Is this how you get to visit the Mayans? Does it allow you to carry on conversations with animals, vegetables, and minerals? Or does it just make you feel really good, kind of like a shiatsu massage?

Whatever the case, the idea that human beings are on the brink of a huge evolutionary step toward a kinder, gentler existence sure is an attractive one, particularly when you're feeling alienated. *The Celestine Prophecy* suggests ways you can connect with your fellow human beings and feel at one with the universe, even if it doesn't provide a road map for astral travel. Guess you'll have to call the Mayans to get directions. Moreover, Redfield teaches us that no matter how humble our lives are, all the events in our daily existence are part of a grand and meaningful design, and that we are all on an evolutionary journey—a journey that must include not only self-examination and ruminations on the fruits of human endeavor but also pure enjoyment of the moment. Of course, you can achieve the same effect by boogie boarding, but if you're up for a wacky ride to some spiritual insights that will help you make sense of the synchronicity in your own life, this is the book for you.

Morsels to Mull Over

In mutual service we forget the little self and glimpse the one measureless self, the spirit that unifies all men.

—Paramahansa Yogananda

When it is dark enough, you can see the stars.

—Charles A. Beard

- ## *Embraced by the Light* (1992)
  by Betty J. Eadie

Each drop from the waterfall had its own intelligence and purpose. A melody of majestic beauty carried from the waterfall and filled the garden, eventually merging with other melodies that I was now only faintly aware of. The music came from the water itself, from its intelligence, and each drop produced its own tone and melody which mingled and interacted with every other sound and strain around it. The water was praising God for its life and joy.

Fear can be a catalyst for the most profound spiritual journeys. When we become hyperaware of our own mortality—like when we realize the famous actor we had a crush on when we were a teenager is now barrel-shaped, gray-haired, and doing infomercials—life-after-death tales are especially engaging.

And as life-after-death tales go, *Embraced by the Light* is a doozy. That's because lucky Betty J. Eadie didn't just whoosh through a birth canal–like tunnel toward a white light, say hello to God and a favored deceased aunt, then pop back into her body. No, Betty was out of touch with the material world long enough to gather an entire book's worth of otherworldly wisdom. "No knowledge was kept from me," she claims, "and it was impossible not to understand correctly every thought, every statement, every particle of knowledge. There was absolutely no misunderstanding here. History was pure. Understanding was complete." So here's the Cliff's Notes version: Miscarriages happen because the babies' souls mean to make only a short visit to Earth; in the afterlife you'll have to relive all your bad behavior, this time feeling all the pain you caused others; and the fashion in the great beyond is hand-loomed gossamer gowns made of threads that are opaque on one side and translucent on the other.

Now, in this world, Eadie's experience with brutal boarding school nuns made her fear God as a youth, but her later Methodist upbringing, which was less fire-and-brimstone but still traditional, certainly colored her after-death experience. While she says that all religions have a corner on the truth in their own way, "heaven" looks suspiciously like a Christian fantasy and most definitely like a patriarchal one. She learns from the nine men who put us on trial for our sins that the legacy of Eve's behavior in the Garden of Eden is that women are more tempted by sexual sin than men are. The result is a breakdown in family, which greatly displeases God. Hmm, wasn't this the thinking behind all those witches being sexually tortured in the Middle Ages? Wonder if those poor souls would agree with those nine men at the kidney-shaped table in the boardroom of judgment. Or are they stuck hand-weaving all those celestial garments in that great sweatshop in the sky? Frankly, we don't care if there's a library with all the wisdom of the universe contained within, celestial music that makes Bach sound like industrial machinery, and gardens of unearthly beauty. Send us to the place where women aren't answering to men and carrying the weight of original sin, and we'll really be in heaven.

Still, if you can get past Eadie's limited perceptions of gender relations in the great beyond, which we're guessing are a shadow cast by her limited earthly beliefs, the afterlife seems like a really beautiful vacation spot. Moreover, her explanations for why bad things happen to good people and why the worst sins are forgivable can be deeply comforting. Whether you buy her story or not, one thing's for sure: You can't argue with the edict she brought back: Be kind to one another, for it is in giving that we receive.

Read this when you're hyperaware of your own mortality and in need of some reassurance.

Points to Ponder

1. What would it take for you to stay on in heaven rather than pop back into your body on earth for a few more years?

2. If you were your own fashion designer in heaven, what delicious number would you be decked out in?

Even God Has a Sense of Humor

I care not for a man's religion whose dog or cat are not the better for it.
—Abraham Lincoln

Every day people are straying away from the church and going back to
 God.

> —Lenny Bruce

If triangles had a god, he would have three sides.

> —Charles de Montesquieu

God is coming, and boy, is she pissed.

> —Anonymous

It's Not Our Cup of Tea, But . . .

- ▪ *Chicken Soup for the Soul* series (1993 and later)
 by Jack Canfield and Mark Victor Hansen

*"I am trying to bring love back to New York," he said.
"I believe it's the only thing that can save the city."*

Originally a self-published book, now a let's-milk-it-once-again series
with titles like *Chicken Soup for the Pet Lover's Soul* and *Chicken Soup for the
Golfer's Soul*, the *Chicken Soup* series serves up short anecdotes about how love
works in our lives. For example, in the original there's the little boy who
volunteers to give blood to his sick sister even though, the doctors later
realize, he mistakenly believes it means he will have to give up all his blood
and die. And there's that story about the fellow who is throwing beached
starfish back into the sea because even though thousands of the creatures will
die, each starfish he saves will matter. All great little stories, just right for
weaving into a sermon or an inspirational talk by a keynote speaker at some
conference somewhere.

continued . . .

Therein lies the problem with *Chicken Soup for the Soul*. Stories like this need to be told well to really pack a punch, and the authors aren't exactly Hemingway. Let's hope it's just amateurishness and not arrogance that accounts for the self-serving stories about the power of the authors' own seminars and speeches. Then too, the further you get into each book, the weaker the stories are.

But this hasn't stopped the *Chicken Soup* series from going and going and going like the Energizer Bunny, or from spawning lots of imitators. Now we have anecdotes about angels, stories of amazing coincidences or miracles, and tales of female empowerment for a female audience. It's too bad that the *Chicken Soup* authors couldn't have gathered better collections without so many clunkers. Really, *Chicken Soup for the Soul* is kind of like a pack of powder stirred into boiled water. But who can argue with *Chicken Soup*'s sales figures?

Anyway, if you're looking for a spiritual snack, go ahead and indulge. It might be your cup of soup. ▪

▪ *Illuminata* (1994)
by Marianne Williamson

Prayer is the pilgrim's walking stick. We pray for the capacity to forgive, to see the innocence in people and to surrender all things to God. We pray to enter the mystery, to remember now, to no longer forget.

A lot of us are a little intimidated by the prayer thing. Most of us have memorized a few traditional prayers that give us a certain comfort with their familiarity, even if we forget a line or two now and again, but they don't always fit our situation satisfactorily. Then we have our own prayers—the please-let-me-find-a-parking-space prayer and the bargaining-with-the-big-guy prayer ("I swear I'll never say a nasty word again if only

You . . ."). Sports-minded women have their bottom-of-the-ninth-one-run-behind prayers, gardeners have their modified rain dances and please-no-frost-until-I-cover-the-tomatoes prayers, and even if we're big enough not to curse our enemies we all have been tempted to say a prayer for instant karma to smote them but good.

But somehow, we know that prayer ought to be a little meaningful, maybe a little more eloquent, and certainly a little more uplifting (though of course, when they actually do come true, prayers are not just uplifting, they're positively magical). In *Illuminata*, Marianne Williamson puts into beautiful and simple words what we want to say, really, if only we could stop thinking about our immediate needs and be in touch with our larger ones. She offers sample prayers for occasions many of us haven't thought much about as prayer fodder, such as healing the pain of prejudice that hurts so many of our sisters, or healing the pain of divorce—not just our pain, but his. There are prayers asking forgiveness, and forgiving those who've trespassed against us. There are prayers for work and creativity, which focus on growth and abundance rather than a specific dollar amount and job title, prayers that address our fear of aging and our hopes for a newborn baby, our concern for our families and for the earth itself, all of which will help dissolve your illusions of powerlessness.

Looking for some inspiration for your talks with you-know-who? *Illuminata* will get you started.

It's Not Our Cup of Tea, But . . .

We can understand the need to connect with the larger human experience and create meaning in one's life by identifying with archetypal myths. But we've always been less likely to identify with Persephone than with Jan Brady. The archetypes that resonate for us always seem to come from Seventies sitcoms—you know, yearning to be either a perfect and beautiful Marcia or a self-possessed and precocious Cindy, looking for wisdom in the words of pontificating and bossy building

continued . . .

supers while ignoring our own boundaries, *à la* Ann Romano. And we've always felt that the ideal man has the looks of Keith Partridge and the drive, brains, and charisma of little Danny. But if you never had a thing for bad Seventies television, you might want to check out the following.

■ ***Women Who Run With the Wolves*** (1992)
by Clarissa Pinkola Estés

We are all, deep down inside, wild women, says Estés, given to fits of bacchanalia in which we dash freely across the fields, our spirits soaring as we howl with the pack. If it weren't for the chains of civilization binding us, we'd all be out there running with wolves. When we read the myths of many civilizations, we can connect with this wild woman, indeed, with all the archetypal women hidden beneath the shell of our outer existence. Once enlightened, we find the power to say no to patriarchal authority figures who want to hem us in, and we are able to heal our wounds.

If you believe that calling on your inner Athena will give you the gumption to stand up to your boss, go for it. We prefer to connect with the inner Mary Richards and turn the world on with our smiles.

■ ***The Power of Myth*** (1988)
by Joseph Campbell

Like Estés, the late Joseph Campbell believed that when we understand our mythology, we begin to understand ourselves. Across cultures, across time, even in Hollywood movies like *Star Wars*, we find stories that tell us the great truths about human experience.

Some of *The Power of Myth* (a transcription of Campbell's conversations with PBS's Bill Moyers) makes enormous sense even if you don't agree with

continued . . .

him—for example, when he says, "Every religion is true one way or another. It is true when understood metaphorically. But when it gets stuck to its own metaphors, interpreting them as facts, then you are in trouble." And who could argue that all societies need heroes? But we have a problem with the idea that the world is "great just the way it is. And you are not going to fix it up. Nobody has ever made it any better. It is never going to be any better." Or that there are no sacred places. Hey, tell it to the Pueblo Indians. Tell it to anyone who has stood atop a mountain or swum in the ocean.

Campbell is always provocative, but he's definitely an acquired taste.

■ *Care of the Soul* (1992)
by Thomas Moore

Our chief problem in modern society, says Moore, is that we've lost our souls, and we don't have leaders who can advise us on nurturing them (we imagine a lot of clergy would object to that generalization). But we can draw on the wisdom of the past, he claims, and so Moore has written this non-self-help book. He says he's more interested in accepting human foibles than in trying to transcend the human condition and that *Care of the Soul* is a "fiction of self-help."

All right, we admit it. We have no idea what "fiction of self-help" means. A friend of ours suggested that the reason Moore's writing is so frustratingly obtuse is because he is discussing matters of the heart and spirit, which can only be captured through metaphor. All very fine and well, but then why didn't Moore write a poem or a song about the importance of ritual, confronting one's dark side, or using one's imagination, any of which would've made the point more clearly than this baffling book does? Look, we're all for soul work, but slogging through this book made us less than spiritual. Still, if you're on a mythology kick, this is key reading. ■

▪ *Awakening to the Sacred* (1999)
by Lama Surya Das

Enlightenment is as enlightenment does. It's where and how you live, not just what you believe in. It's who you are and can be, not just who you imagine you are. In the meantime, stay awake to what you are experiencing right now. It's the best show in town.

While some of us come from a single spiritual tradition, one we've always been comfortable with, a lot of us are spiritual mutts. You know, a little bit Episcopalian, a smattering of Buddhism, a hint of Quaker—or like Lama Das, we could be "Jewish on my parents' side." In *Awakening to the Sacred*, Lama Das teaches us how to stay in touch with our spiritual selves no matter what our pedigree. And the book is far more fun and engaging than you'd expect a spiritual guide to be, perhaps because the Lama spent months meditating in an uninsulated wooden horse stall on a freezing mountaintop somewhere in the Alps, which must have given him an even greater appreciation for the absurd and a good one-liner.

Luckily, Lama Das's prescription doesn't require us to mentally ward off frostbite—it's a lot easier than that. And his humor and dual-tradition background make this, his guide to "creating a spiritual life from scratch," remarkably accessible to us Heinz 57-ers. How can you not love a guy who struggles with an ice cream addiction? and who pens haiku-esque poems like "work accidentally deleted/lost yet again/a new beginning"? Remember, the next time your hard drive crashes, that it's an opportunity for growth and fresh starts. Honest.

Basically, Lama Das explains how to apply the basic Buddhist principles to our lives and to enhance our own spiritual traditions. For example, isn't Christian forgiveness about letting go of your attachment to rage and renouncing your need for revenge? And in a world where we're regularly smacked upside the head with overstimulation and slammed against the wall by yet another injustice, we could all use a little mindfulness and meditation, whether it means staring at a candle or into your own eyes in the mirror.

Read *Awakening to the Sacred* when you need a little help detaching from your anger and frustrations and from the distractions of the material world.

Index

Ugly American, The (Lederer and Burdick), 173–174

Ulysses (Joyce), 120–121

Van Praagh, James, 230–231

Venus in Furs (Sacher-Masoch), 36

Vidal, Gore, 50

Vliet, Elizabeth, 155

Voluntary Simplicity (Elgin), 134

von Sacher-Masoch, Leopold, 36

Wagner, Jane, 219

Waiting to Exhale (McMillan), 57–58

Walsh, Joe, 45

Wauters, Ambika, 228

Way, The: The Living Bible, 226

Wechsler, Toni, 163–164

Weir, Alison, 151

Wells, H. G., 23

Wells, Rebecca, 101

Westlake, Donald E., 134–135

What Color Is Your Parachute? (Bolles), 146

What to Expect When You're Expecting (Eisenberg), 159–160

When Food Is Love (Roth), 200–201

When God Was a Woman (Stone), 232–233

When I Am an Old Woman I Shall Wear Purple (ed. Martz), 151–152

White Palace (Savan), 66

Who's Afraid of Virginia Woolf? (Albee), 2–3

Why Men Are the Way They Are (Farrell), 127–128

"Wife of Bath," 3

Wilde, Oscar, 103

Williams, Tennessee, 103–104

Williamson, Marianne, 242–243

Wolf, Naomi, 188–189

Wolf, Sharyn, 189–190

"Woman: A Hate Song" (Parker), 7–8

Women's Bodies, Women's Wisdom (Northrup), 156

Woman's Dress for Success Book, The (Molloy), 136–137

Women's Room, The (French), 122, 125

Women Who Love Too Much (Norwood), 48

Women Who Run With the Wolves (Estés), 244

Woolf, Virginia, 78

Wurtzel, Elizabeth, 217–218

Wuthering Heights (E. Brontë), 44–45

Yellow Raft in Blue Water, A (Dorris), 105–106

Yellow Wallpaper, The (Gilman), 215

Yogananda, Paramahansa, 238

Your Baby and Child from Birth to Age Five (Leach), 160

Zen and the Art of Motorcycle Maintenance (Pirsig), 94–96